BUILDII
TRUST
IN
IRELAND

THE
BLACKSTAFF
PRESS

The papers contained in this book were commissioned by the Forum for Peace and Reconciliation. The views expressed are the views of the authors and are not necessarily those of the Forum or its members.

Published in 1996 by the Blackstaff Press Limited,
3 Galway Park, Dundonald, Belfast BT16 0AN, Northern Ireland,
in association with the Forum for Peace and Reconciliation, Dublin.

Cover Design by Wendy Dunbar
incorporating the logo of the Forum for Peace and Reconciliation,
created by Ed Miliano.

Printed by Brunswick Press Ltd.

ISBN 0-85640-577-9

CONTENTS

PREFACE

THE FORUM FOR PEACE AND RECONCILIATION was established through an undertaking of the Joint Declaration of 1993 and commenced work following the ceasefires announced by the IRA and loyalist paramilitaries in autumn 1994.

The Forum's terms of reference include a statement of intent to consult on and examine ways in which lasting peace, stability and reconciliation can be established by agreement among all the people of Ireland, *and on the steps required to remove barriers of distrust, on the basis of promoting respect for the equal rights and validity of both traditions and identities.* One of the Forum's four Sub-Committees, the Committee on *Obstacles in the South to Reconciliation*, commissioned the five papers collected here to help address those perceptions or misconceptions in the North about life in the South which would make reconciliation difficult to achieve. Trust and reconciliation are themes which have been fundamental to the work of the Forum since its inception.

We have been fortunate in being able to draw on the expertise of six leading experts, North and South: Professor Brice Dickson (University of Ulster, Jordanstown), Dr Arthur Aughey (University of Ulster, Jordanstown), Professor Dermot Keogh (University College Cork), Professor Terence Brown (Trinity College Dublin), Professor J. J. Sexton (ESRI) and Mr Richard O'Leary (Nuffield College, Oxford).

All five studies provide new research and important insights into areas which are central to the Forum's work and to the wider peace process.

I wish to take this opportunity to record our thanks to the authors of the papers. I hope that the papers will receive the widest possible readership and I am confident that they will make a very constructive contribution to a better understanding between the different traditions on this island.

JUDGE CATHERINE MCGUINNESS SC
Chairperson of the Forum for Peace and Reconciliation

OBSTACLES
TO RECONCILIATION
IN THE SOUTH

ARTHUR AUGHEY

UNIVERSITY OF ULSTER
AT JORDANSTOWN

INTRODUCTION

THE DOWNING STREET DECLARATION speaks of a future and hoped for 'meeting of hearts and minds' which would enable a bringing together of all the people of Ireland. The Irish Government promises that there would be no violence nor would there be any coercion of unionists. There would be only persuasion. The Forum for Peace and Reconciliation was specifically dedicated to the task of making 'recommendations on ways in which agreement and trust between both traditions in Ireland can be promoted and established'. This was advanced as an 'opportunity for a fresh start and a new beginning'. To some extent that is true and is to be welcomed. Yet the hearts and minds proposition has its own history within Irish nationalism. It has quite a distinguished pedigree.

For instance, in 1924 Stephen Gwynn argued that:

> Nothing that is not Irish stands in the way of its accomplishment [Tone's ambition of cementing the separate traditions of Ireland]: and if it cannot be accomplished by Irishmen no outside power can convert our national aspirations into a reality. [1]

That was an early recognition that the British Government had no selfish strategic interest in Northern Ireland. Gwynn also argued that 'complete nationhood can only be achieved by reconcilement of the divergent ideals'. The Free State, he went on, 'may persuade' Northern unionists to 'secure their position in Ireland as a whole'.[2] Gwynn was a

Redmondite and as one of the authorities on modern Irish history, Paul Bew, has noted it 'is easy to pick up the Redmondite echoes' in the Downing Street Declaration. This 'moving back to the world of Redmond' and a 'more relaxed, less charged version of Irish political destiny', argues Professor Bew, has come to characterize the practical attitude of the Irish State since the late 1950s.[3]

Whether more relaxed and less charged or not, most unionists still consider with suspicion, if not hostility, the disposition of the Republic of Ireland towards them. Unionist politicians fear that experience obliges them to believe that when the Irish Government speaks of 'reconciliation' it is still reconciliation within a framework set by exclusively nationalist assumptions. Their response to the Framework Documents in February 1995 reveals that belief in action. And national-ist political destiny, of whatever version and however expressed, still remains the unionist apocalypse. In such rigid and highly charged circumstances, profoundly affected by twenty five years of terrorist violence, it is difficult to get a sense of proportion about political possibilities. This is a truth which applies as much to nationalist as it does to unionist expectations. That the Downing Street Declaration achieved some measure of tentative support amongst Ulster unionists is an indication that elements of it — especially the commitment to consent — did approach a sympathetic understanding of their position.

This paper approaches the question of obstacles to reconciliation in the South by examining the implications of the Declaration in terms of a number of recurring distinctions. These distinctions include nationalism and nationality, people and State, integrity and diversity. They may help to focus attention on the boundaries of the politically attainable while also indicating possible avenues along which peace and reconciliation might be pursued. The paper tries to do this by abstracting from unionist argument what appear to be consistent criticisms of the Republic of Ireland and its disposition towards the North. These criticisms are presented in the light of how the Republic has come to understand itself today.

THE POSITION IN THE DECLARATION

In the Downing Street Declaration the Taoiseach makes a number of references to the 'fears', 'uncertainties', 'misgivings' and 'lack of trust' which inform 'Northern unionist attitudes *towards the rest of Ireland*' [our emphasis]. This phrase could be understood in two ways. On the one hand, the 'rest of Ireland' could mean all other people living in Ireland, North and South. On the other hand, it could mean more specifically the Republic of Ireland as a State.

Often nationalists in the South and usually nationalists in the North (for obvious reasons) understand the phrase in the first sense. They assume that the 'problem' lies in unionist inability to come to terms with the majority on the island. Unionists are cast in the role of a 'national minority' amongst the people of Ireland, a people which has the right of self-determination (albeit North *and* South). In their different ways, that is the message of the leader of the Social Democratic and Labour Party and of the President of Sinn Féin. The Tánaiste, Dick Spring, introduced a new formulation in a recent speech to the United Nations when he proposed that in future talks unionists would need to confront the nationalist case which would be represented 'in its integrity'.

Often nationalists in the South and less often nationalists in the North mean it in the second sense. They assume — and this is deeply embedded in the political culture of the South — that the problem lies in unionist inability to come to terms with the new social and political realities of the Republic of Ireland. This is a more formal attitude which takes as its starting point the existence of distinct political structures and jurisdictions, though nationalists would seek ultimately to erase these distinctions through mutual understanding. In 1965 this meant dealing directly with a unionist government at Stormont in the mode of the Lemass-O'Neill talks. To a degree, it implied an engagement between equals, even though the Republic was a sovereign State and Northern Ireland was only a regional authority within another State. Since 1972, the Irish State has reverted to an older tradition. The procedure once more is to deal with unionists via the authority of the British Government and via the influence of British public opinion. Some unionists suspect that the purpose of the Forum for Peace and Reconciliation itself is to give the impression of a reforming impulse in the South in order to foster a British willingness to 'persuade' unionists towards major political concessions. That suspicion is bound up with a calculation of the objectives of 'pan-nationalism' which are referred to below.

The Irish Government's passages in the Declaration move back and forth between both of these understandings. If this creates ambiguity, that is because Irish nationalism itself is ambiguous. It is most clearly displayed in the attitude of the Republic's Government towards Northern Ireland. There are two key passages in the Declaration which illustrate this ambiguity and which also set the parameters for this study. The first passage states:

> In recognition of the fears of the Unionist community...the Taoiseach will examine with his colleagues any elements in the democratic life and organisation of the Irish State that can be represented to the Irish Government in the course of political dialogue as a real and substantial threat to their way of life and ethos, or that can be represented as not being fully consistent with a modern democratic and pluralist society, and undertakes to examine any possible ways of removing such obstacles. Such an examination would of course have due regard to the desire to preserve those inherited values that are largely shared throughout the island or that belong to the cultural and historical roots of the people of the island in all their diversity.

The second passage states:

> He [the Taoiseach] asks the people of Northern Ireland to look on the people of the Republic as friends, who share their grief and shame over all the suffering of the last quarter of a century, and who want to develop the best possible relationship with them, a relationship in which trust and new understanding can flourish and grow. The Taoiseach also acknowledges the presence in the Constitution of the Republic of elements which are deeply resented by Northern Unionists, but which at the same time reflect hopes and ideals which lie deep in the hearts of many Irish men and women North and South.

Both passages illustrate inconsistency in the use of language and therefore ambivalence in meaning (which may not be the same thing as confusion of purpose). There are six expressions here — the unionist community, the people of the island, the people of Northern Ireland, the people of the Republic, Northern unionists, Irish men and women North and South. Elsewhere the Declaration speaks of the 'peoples of Britain and Ireland' and 'the people of Ireland, North and South'. In sum, and to avoid labouring the point, it can be argued that it is unclear with what precise authority the Irish State addresses unionists. There are two possible claims which are being made. Does it speak with the authority and legitimacy of a properly constituted *government* representing the people of the Republic? Or does it speak with the authority and legitimacy of an *ideal* which lies deep in the hearts of all Irish people (except, of course, the unionist community)?

In truth, the Irish State claims to speak with the authority of both and therein lies the initial problem for unionists with the Downing Street Declaration. This was also the problem faced by John Bruton when recently he refused a meeting with John Hume and Gerry Adams. The Taoiseach was challenged for not being a leader of the 'nationalist people', a role which his critics clearly felt was more important than his role as head of an Irish Government, a Government intent on seeking a 'balanced political settlement'. There may be an irresolvable contradiction here and politicians in the Republic need to confront this issue seriously. Tribal posturing may be insufficient when reconciliation with Northern unionists is at stake. If it is not taken seriously then unionists will continue to question the seriousness of the will to reconciliation on the part of Irish nationalism and for the term 'reconciliation' read 'pressure for unity'. For an example of such questioning, one can point to the dismay which was felt when unionists discovered the reasons for cancelling the scheduled British-Irish summit in September 1995.

This double claim — or 'double talk' as the Reverend Ian Paisley would put it — is also the historic difficulty unionists have had with the South. If the Irish Government were speaking on the basis of the first claim, unionists can happily contemplate the value of what they have called 'good neighbourly relations' between Northern Ireland and the Republic. They might even acknowledge that at some unspecified time in the future such relations might mean that the border would become a practical irrelevance. Lord Craigavon at one time considered that if the circumstances were right it was possible that there could be a restoration of political unity in his lifetime (he died in November 1940). If, however, the Irish Government speaks on the basis of the second claim, unionists understand this to be the language of 'take-over', albeit the language of take-over articulated in a new liberal grammar. Articles 2 and 3 of the Constitution are beyond the remit of this study yet they cast their shadow over unionist trust in the good faith of the Republic. It is the suspicion of pan-nationalism, a suspicion which has actually grown since the Downing Street Declaration and not diminished. It is a suspicion which Dick Spring's speech to the UN in September 1995 about the importance of approaching all-party talks on the basis of 'nationalist integrity' appears to have confirmed. As the distinguished historian of Irish nationalism D. George Boyce put it recently, 'Irish nationalism has so often confounded itself through its mixture of pluralist rhetoric and sectarian activity that it may yet stumble over its past, and lose sight of Unionist fears yet again.'[4] This stumbling over the past is something which the Declaration seeks to avoid by overcoming 'the legacy of history'. It may be useful to remind ourselves, therefore, of what that legacy in part has been.

ZONES OF MAJORITARIANISM

In 1933 Craigavon famously or infamously remarked that he was glad to preside over a Protestant parliament and a Protestant State in Northern Ireland. That remark was made in response to the claim by Éamon de Valera that Ireland of the twenty six counties and later, if Articles 2 and 3 of the 1937 Constitution were to be fulfilled, Ireland of the thirty two counties, was a Catholic State. Craigavon explained his position in the Northern Ireland House of Commons some years afterwards. He argued that while he accepted that the government of Southern Ireland should be carried on along lines which were appropriate to its Catholic majority it was surely right that the government of Northern Ireland should be conducted in a manner appropriate to the wishes and desires of its Protestant majority. For unionists like Craigavon and in practice for most Irish nationalists, the settlement of the 1920s had divided Ireland effectively into zones of majoritarian democracy. The Southern Parliament embodied Catholic majoritarianism (which it defined as Irish) and the Northern Parliament embodied Protestant majoritarianism (which it defined as British). These were the realities. Despite all of the massive changes which have taken place in Ireland, North and South, in the sixty years since the enunciation of what we might call the Craigavon/de Valera doctrine the great divide on the island is still understandable in these *terms* if not in that *form*. As Ernest Gellner has argued, without a 'sacralized religious differentiation, there is no real cultural boundary in Ireland'.[5] Nor would the playing or not-playing of 'God Save the Queen' at a Queen's University graduation cause such a fuss.

Of course, in the last twenty five years there have been changes in the character of policy in Northern Ireland such that unionists would laugh at the proposition that it is today a Protestant State for a Protestant people. Indeed, they are concerned that legal changes, especially in fair employment legislation, mean that Protestants are now the ones discriminated against. On the other hand, there is something of an irony about the claims of greater pluralism in the Republic. As the Republic has apparently become more pluralist it has also become more (nominally) Catholic. The numbers of Protestants have diminished further into political insignificance. Whereas pluralism in Northern Ireland has come to mean greater *inter*-community tolerance, pluralism in the Republic means almost entirely *intra*-community tolerance. The argument that there is little or no discrimination against or hostility to Protestants in the modern Republic is a fair argument. However, one reason may be that Protestants have little or no political significance as a community. They tend to be encountered purely and simply as individuals. As such they disappear more easily into the body of the nation.

In other words, the debate in the Republic takes place within a set of assumptions which is often invisible to the public in the South both Protestant and Catholic but is all too visible to people in the North, both Catholic and Protestant. As Arthur Balfour once said about the parties in the House of Commons, they can safely afford to shout and bicker because on fundamentals they tend to share so much. That may well be the case in the Republic and it invites a preliminary consideration of the spectrum of opinion there about Southern society and its relationship to the North.

SOUTHERN APPROACHES

There are two questions which have been central to political debate in the Republic in recent years. They are, first, which aspects of life and the State in the South, from a Northern unionist or Protestant perspective, might constitute barriers to better relations on the island of

Ireland and, second, which aspects of life and the State might inhibit the development, for its own sake, of a more pluralist society in the South?

For constitutional nationalists, at least since the publication of the Forum Report in 1984 if not before, the assumption has been that these two areas are *related*. There has been an expectation that better relations on the island of Ireland between unionists and nationalists will emerge from the development of a more 'pluralist' Republic; and that a more pluralist Republic will be the condition for the transformation of political relationships between North and South towards a settlement which would be, ideally, Irish unity. Or, if not unity, then a settlement in the North which would be substantially Irish and only residually British. There exist, of course, different views about what is meant by the term 'pluralism' in the Republic (see also Church and State p. 20). These understandings range from a radical liberal and secular agenda, which would involve considerable change in Southern society, to a limited conservative one, which would involve very little change at all. It is notable that the formula in the Downing Street Declaration which addresses this issue is carefully drawn to balance both understandings. It invites critical comment on the practices of State and society in the Republic while reserving the right to dismiss such criticism in the light of 'inherited values' and of the 'cultural and historical roots' of these practices. Article 6 of the Declaration is an example of that creative ambiguity which reflects accurately the traditional ambivalence of politicians and public in the Republic about the North.

Three general and reasonably consistent approaches to the question of unionist attitudes and Southern reform may be abstracted from the general debate in the Republic. These three approaches are not the only imaginable abstractions from the diversity of Southern opinion. (There may even be many people in the South who do not want to think about Northern Ireland at all.) Distinctive contributions have come from many quarters. For instance Professor Joe Lee, throughout his *Ireland 1912-1985*, describes the unionist condition as one of a '*Herrenvolk* democracy' only to finish by describing them as 'no petty people'. It should be remembered, of course, that the fate of Yeats and his 'no petty people' is hardly an enticing prospect for Northern unionists. Lee was fairminded enough, however, to define Southern Catholics as being covetous tempered only by sloth. This disappointment with the Irish as they were and as they are is a recurring theme of much intellectual opinion in the Republic and will be addressed below. President Mary Robinson has also made her own distinctive and imaginative contribution to thinking about peace and reconciliation in Ireland. One could go on. However, the three approaches discussed below have a scope which, at a pinch and at an obvious risk of oversimplification, can accommodate a wide range of particular or even idiosyncratic viewpoints.

The first approach is that of latter-day *social republicanism*. Its most articulate and interesting exponent has probably been Tim Pat Coogan, in whose writings one can detect clearly the main outlines of the case. There are three propositions which sustain the social republican argument. These comprise two related negatives which together become transformed into a final shining, unified, positive. First, Ulster unionists, it is claimed, inhabit a political and cultural wasteland into which they have been led by 'political witchdoctors such as Ian Paisley'. Paisleyism is taken to represent the essential character of this deformed communalism. 'A society which exalts that type of political culture is a disaster society; the stone of history rests on it and nothing wholesome flourishes under it.'[6] This is part of a broader triumphalist assertion frequently found in the North and sometimes in the South that unionist Ulster is in terminal decay, entrapped as it is within a decadent constitutional form — a 'failed political entity' according to first Charles Haughey and latterly to Gerry Adams, an 'unnatural political entity' according to John Hume. Because all of the virile elements in contemporary Irish life are held to be nationalist the future belongs to them. The dull, uncultured Protestants need the 'alien, external power' of 'Britain' to spell it out for them in a clear and persuasive fashion.

Second, the attitude towards Southern society is one of promise unfulfilled, an attitude often conveyed in tones of undisguised loathing for current practices — a loathing for the confessional influence, a loathing for the gombeen politics, a loathing for the business culture of the poor mouth, a loathing for the failure to address the problem of emigration. What is interesting about such an attitude to the Republic is not so much its particular criticisms. What is interesting is the totality of the criticism which implies that the Republic is itself a 'failed political entity' and that its political culture is 'unnatural'. The irony here is that unionist demagoguery propounds much the same view of the Republic.

Third, these negatives of unionist backwardness and republican social frustration become miraculously transformed in the positive of Irish unity. The roadblocks to social and economic modernization will be pushed aside as the energies of the black North invigorate the new Ireland. Coogan noted a conversation he had with an Irish cabinet minister in 1987. The minister argued that they (the unionists):

> ... talk about us trying to subjugate them, wanting to take them over.
> The truth is that when the border goes, and go of course it must some
> day, Leinster House will not be big enough to contain them all — they'll
> be running us, and why not? We could do with their energy. [7]

Social republicanism shows an astonishing lack of confidence in the Irish State; and that lack of confidence is married to a set of astonishing illusions about the qualities, negative or positive, of Northern unionists.

The second approach shares some of the elements of the first but is very different in tone. If the first is old testament republicanism, the second is new testament republicanism. It is liberal in its breadth of vision and is possibly best represented in the writing and in the disposition of Garret FitzGerald. The most appropriate label is possibly *liberal constitutionalism*. In this view, unionists are not the one dimensional Paisleyite loyalists, that 'essential' character to which social republicanism so consistently reduces Protestant society in Northern Ireland. The approach which FitzGerald epitomizes claims to be sensitive to the nuances of unionist opinion and recognizes the diversity of views within Northern Protestantism. However, such sensitivity need not mean that this approach will properly gauge the depth of unionist feeling or recognize its potency. As his autobiography candidly reveals, FitzGerald miscalculated the unionist response to Sunningdale in 1973-74 and also to the Anglo-Irish Agreement in 1985. Today, he cannot understand their obvious hostility to the Framework Documents. Irrespective of the possibility that FitzGerald might have been correct in his judgements and unionists misguided, that is not a very good track record.

Liberal constitutionalism is also severely critical of the reality of the republican State. Nevertheless, that criticism is not comprehensive. It is a limited criticism, confined to certain practices and assumptions of the State. It assumes that reform of provisions in the Irish Constitution and changes in the workings of public institutions are sufficient to transform the nature of Southern society. That transformation will be the key which can open the door to Irish unity. FitzGerald's 'constitutional crusade' of the early 1980s revealed its premises. He believed that 'the thrust of the legislative changes introduced in our State since 1922' had 'tended to encourage the perpetuation of partition' and the political challenge for politicians like himself was to see if 'our people actually *wanted* a non-sectarian State' [emphasis in the original].[8] As he suggested, if constitutional reform were to take place then there might be a basis for Protestants in Northern Ireland to engage constructively with the Republic. However, FitzGerald famously admitted that if:

> I were a Protestant today, I cannot see how I could be attracted to get-
> ting involved with a State that is itself sectarian...the fact is our laws and
> our Constitution, our practices, our attitudes reflect those of a majority
> ethos and are not acceptable to Protestants in Northern Ireland. [9]

An assumption about Northern unionist opinion — that it would be attracted towards involvement with a non-sectarian Irish State — was to be the reason for reform in the Republic. Like the first approach, this liberal constitutionalism is also informed by the politics of 'unfinished business'. It still believes that the formal task of Irish statesmanship is to bring closer the day of unity. Bringing that day closer often remains one of the key justifications for reform of Southern society. Perhaps it is also one of the key excuses to reform Southern society (a rather different interpretation of the same style of argument).

The third approach believes that it is this very politics of unfinished business, in its social republican or in its liberal constitutional guises, which is destabilizing for Irish democracy as well as for democratic politics in Northern Ireland. This approach might be called *critical realism* (for want of a better expression). This politics of unfinished business, it is held, fosters a romanticism which is sharply focused on a mythical, idealized Ireland yet poorly focused on the real Ireland, North and South. It is destabilizing because siren 'ancestral voices' may lead politicians away from the limits and conditions of constitutional politics towards the mirage of 'a nation once again'. It is also critical of the fundamental lack of self-confidence in the achievements of the Irish State which the other two approaches show (ideological variations on a theme of cultural cringe). It is not, however, an approach which is smugly self-satisfied. Indeed it also targets many of those elements in Irish life challenged by both social republicans and liberal constitutionalists. It believes that such challenges must come from within the life of the Irish State and must be convincing on their merits alone and not on a spurious cause of forcing the Protestants to be free or on an equally spurious cause of showing the Protestants how nice the Republic really is. There is also a willingness to accept Ulster unionists on their own terms and not as nationalist ideology would have them be.

Of course, the most prominent exponent of this approach has been Conor Cruise O'Brien who, in the eyes of many in the Republic, has committed the ultimate sin of being sympathetic to the unionists (not so much a case of 'going native' as of 'going colonial'). Yet O'Brien's only sin is that of being politically incorrect, of challenging nationalist convention (which *is* often confused with being a unionist). It is what Eoghan Harris has called 'acting with good authority', challenging the comforting illusions of one's own tribe. O'Brien has argued that:

> There has always been a good deal of ambivalence around, and Northern Ireland has been a kind of joker in the pack of Catholic-nationalist ambivalence. On the one hand, one wants peace with it; on the other hand, one wants to destroy it. And there is an underlying synthesis, in many minds; peace will be achieved, eventually, through the destruction of Northern Ireland.[10]

That may appear shocking only because it is true, albeit in very different ways, of both the social republican and liberal constitutional approaches. There are many ways to destroy Northern Ireland. Even killing it with kindness, as some in the Forum for Peace and Reconciliation might prefer to do, is only another variant. O'Brien's might be a unique voice but his is not the only voice of critical realism to be found in the Republic. Nor is it without sympathy amongst a wider public.

At this point it might be worth briefly considering, by way of introduction, what is the general unionist perspective on these matters. For most Ulster unionists these two questions which have been prominent in Southern debate in recent years — which aspects of life and the State in the South might constitute barriers to better relations on the island and which aspects of life and the State might inhibit the development of a more pluralist society in the South — are *unrelated*. While unionists might applaud the emergence of a more pluralist society in the Republic they do not see any *necessary* connection between such developments and better relationships on the island of Ireland. Certainly, they see no connection at all between such changes and the claims of Irish political unity. Unionist politicians have made and continue to make unfavourable comment about the Catholic and Gaelic ethos of the South and it is possible to examine the nature of their criticisms. However, this does not mean that they or those whom they represent are prepared to discuss the conditions for the removal of these elements in the life of the Southern State. To do so, as they see it, would implicate themselves in negotiating their place in a united Ireland. That is the reason why no official representatives of traditional unionism have involved themselves so far in the work of the Forum for Peace and Reconciliation. Ulster unionists of whatever variety have been concerned to prevent a redefinition of unionism from a definitive constitutional status — British citizenship for the people of Northern Ireland — to a cultural identity — one of the 'two main traditions which inhabit the island of Ireland' as the Downing Street Declaration so felicitously puts it. The terms of reference for the Forum — rightly or wrongly — have been interpreted by most unionists to involve precisely such a redefinition of their position. That is a reality, the implications of which will be brought out in the course of this study. What have been the specific unionist perceptions of the Irish Free State/Irish Republic and to what extent do they correspond to contemporary reality?

ALTERNATIVE IDEAS
OF POLITICAL SOCIETY

The most complete theories of separation between the Republic and Northern Ireland would be based on the assumption that the two jurisdictions in Ireland express competing principles of political and cultural life. It is from these complete theories that one should start. Unionist formulations of such distinctive principles have, not unexpectedly, been reactions to, altered images of, those developed by Irish nationalists. As F. E. Smith put it at the time of the third Home Rule crisis, the fundamental choice in Ireland was between 'parochialism and Imperialism; between ultramontanism and religious liberty; it is between stagnation and economic progress' (Irish nationalists had their own sets of negative/positive alternatives). Ever since then there has been a tradition of presenting the choice between Union and separation in stark terms. For instance, Robert McCartney's *Liberty and Authority in Ireland* of 1985, possibly one of the most intelligent restatements of the unionist case, advances the Idealist proposition that the division between North and South represents the working out of two antagonistic ideas of the nature of the individual and society.

In the first of these ideas 'man is seen as a free spirit, naturally good, but stunted, limited and frustrated by archaic and restrictive institutions whether of Church or State.' According to the second idea man is a 'creature of limited freedom, only partly good and whose only salvation is within the great authoritarian frameworks of States, Churches or parties.' For McCartney, the Union expresses the idea of liberty whereas it is Irish nationalism and the Irish State which has been the modern carrier of authoritarianism. The confessional character of Irish nationalism meant that individual freedom and liberty of conscience were 'to be sacrificed for values which were regarded as being higher and which were determined by no subjective standard but by the objective requirements of Church doctrine and dogma.' The political choice in Ireland, according to McCartney, has been posed in the following manner: either one remains within a liberal, tolerant United Kingdom 'with all its faults' or one owes allegiance to an Irish State constructed on the principles of homogeneity and religious authority. If, argues McCartney, the nationalist claims 'no man has a right to fix the boundary to the march of a nation' then the answer of a unionist must be that 'no nation has the right to set limits upon the development of the individual liberty and the unique nature of man.'[11]

Nationalists would, of course, repudiate such a stark contrast between liberty and authority, especially if it is suggested that liberty is the dominant principle informing life in Northern Ireland whereas authority is the dominant principle informing life in the Republic. They would be correct to do so, of course. But having done so, they might miss the substance of McCartney's argument and what it reveals of widespread and deep-seated unionist opinion about the South. For the argument is not really about freedom versus authority as distinct political concepts. It is really about opposing views of what is and what is not politically *authoritative*. That is a rather different point and concerns historical and collective notions of legitimacy. This is the part of McCartney's argument which is held generally by Ulster unionists, even those who would not go so far as to make the absolute distinction to which his logic leads.

The Protestant idea of liberty does not necessarily mean, despite McCartney's eloquent statement of it, that a Protestant society is liberal in the contemporary, idiomatic sense of that word. In so far as it is Protestant at all, this liberty is not the liberty to do as one likes. It is the liberty to do what is right. It is an ordered liberty disciplined by biblical truth. And if it is a liberty informed by Democratic Unionist biblical truth, many unionists themselves would not only feel uncomfortable with it, but also positively hostile to it. McCartney's distinction between libertarianism and authoritarianism, therefore, may not be visible in the ways of life led by Protestants and Catholics in Ireland. On many moral issues attitudes might be almost indistinguishable. Indeed, the outside observer might well think that Catholics are more free in their ways than Northern Protestants (and of course, many Southerners tend to be convinced that Protestants are either 'sourfaced' or 'hard-headed', i.e. terribly dull).

Therefore, the Protestant idea of liberty which McCartney celebrates is an invisible freedom, freedom of conscience. This is a spiritual freedom which may not be embodied in social practice, for example tolerance of difference. What Protestants would reject are not (necessarily) Catholic *views* on abortion or divorce and so on found in the Republic (and it should be noted that homosexuality is formally treated more liberally in the South than in the North). What they would reject is the *source* of authority for those views. They would reject the constitutional provisions — divorce is a long-standing illustration — which reflect that source of authority. Catholic doctrine is not an authoritative source of belief. It cannot be an authoritative source of law. And this has obvious consequences for the Protestant — but not only the Protestant — view of the legitimacy of many of the established practices of Southern society and of the Irish State itself.

This is not the only reason for unionist antipathy to the project of Irish political separatism, as we shall see. But it is a profound one. It is this absence of legitimacy for political separatism which enables

McCartney, in all good conscience, to make the claims that he does, claims which might strike Southerners as substantially untrue. What might otherwise present itself as a *theoretical* issue concerning ideas about freedom or of conflicts about authority is in effect a *political* statement about the character of the Irish State. This is a point which will be considered again in the discussion of Church and State (p. 20) and Symbols (p. 33).

McCartney's distinctions based on the political embodiment of ideas of liberty and authority have their counterparts in distinctions made about the culture of the Union and the culture of Irish separatism. They continue one of F. E. Smith's themes of parochialism versus, if not imperialism, then internationalism. In a recent contribution to this cultural debate, Arthur Green summed up generations of unionist sentiment when he wrote that the impulse of Irish separatism was carried forward by those:

> ... who narrowed their vision to Ireland, who were petit bourgeois to the marrow, and who left a legacy to Ireland of anti-intellectualism, puritanism, and xenophobia, as well as unquestioned Catholic mores and Gaelic cultural tyranny. It is not surprising that their state was disowned by Yeats, Joyce and AE, not to mention Beckett, nor that a large proportion of Protestants there left, or were forced to leave. [12]

For Green, Irish cultural separatism belongs in the dustbin of history. At the same time he believes that this is impossible for the Irish State to do because (as he cites Denis Donoghue) 'Ireland without its story is merely a member of the EC, the begging bowl our symbol.' The story, whatever its deficiencies, must continue to be adhered to, whatever its consequences for better relations with unionists.

Of course, Green is correct in his view that it is masochistic to suppose that 'our intelligences and our imaginations are uniquely fed by people with Irish birth certificates; and even more self-destructive to treat the rest of the British Isles as alien.' [13] But it would be incorrect to judge the entire cultural life in the Republic in terms of the ideal of cultural nationalism; and it would be equally wrong to assume that Northern Ireland has represented a beacon of light in this world of cultural darkness. That is the sort of provocation which would strike nationalists as a variant of the 'blue skies of Ulster' school declaiming the 'misty Celtic twilight'. That is (partly) why it is done, of course. It is also an attempt to draw clear lines between ideologies where, in practical life, the connections are much messier. Just as one might be no less of a nationalist because one can appreciate the genius of Shakespeare one can be no less of a unionist because one can appreciate the genius of Joyce. They are not alternatives.

Professor Edna Longley has possibly approached closest to the truth of the matter in her view that Northern Ireland or, for that matter, the island of Ireland, is a 'cultural corridor'. Unionists, she has argued, 'want to block the corridor at one end, Republicans at the other'. However, culture 'like common sense, insists it can't be done'.[14] That may be true. Yet once again, the complexity of intellectual and cultural experience is not the political issue. Nor does it depend on a fully accurate representation of cultural life in the Republic. To dismiss Green's arguments as a *jeu d'esprit* would be to miss the point again. The point he is making is that for unionists the *story* of political and cultural nationalism is not authoritative and its legitimacy not compelling. Since unionists do not understand themselves to be part of that story to which the Republic needs to cling they still suspect that nationalists are intent on writing them and their culture out of existence.

The story of the nation, the story of colonialism, the story of post-colonialism, the story of cultural independence, even the story of a post-national Ireland in Europe, these are all inventive tales the authority of which few Protestants and no unionist can accept. They are tales which signify little for them except the moral that nationalists are the goodies and that unionists are the baddies or the dupes of time. Unionist stories are, therefore, designed to reverse these roles and to secure for themselves a different ending. No one has come up with a convincing story which appeals adequately to the sentiments of both — yet. The social republican tale of Catholic, Protestant and Dissenter united in the common name of Irishman or the liberal nationalist tale of the New Ireland Forum — neither of these strikes a positive enough chord with Northern unionists to encourage them to change their own story. Similarly, the unionist tale of civil and religious liberty within a pluralist Union does not convince enough nationalists that they should give up hoping that their story will have a happy ending.

Unionist and nationalist stories have encouraged two opposing dogmas of denial within Northern Ireland. They are: no first step *unless* it is a step towards Irish unity. No first step *because* it is a step towards Irish unity. The predictability of political discourse lies in the grammar of those two dogmas. And each side comes to understand 'peace and reconciliation' within the codes of their respective languages. The unionist conviction that the Forum for Peace and Reconciliation is another chapter in the nationalist story and that its plot is a plot against them is plain in their response to it. Indeed, the more members of the Forum tried to encourage their representatives to attend the more convinced unionists became of its irrelevance. That might seem unfair to the Forum but it is true, nevertheless. The authority of these conflicting stories of identity, their origin and their emotive force, will be considered again under Symbols (p. 33).

CHURCH AND STATE

Possibly the key unionist slogan which comprised their deepest fear of an Irish State was 'Home Rule is Rome Rule'. The history of the Irish Free State and then of the Republic tended to confirm rather than repudiate that slogan. The visible empire of the Catholic Church's influence in Southern politics — which was vast enough — combined with a Northern Protestant sense that its invisible empire of control was all-pervasive. The reason for having a separate Irish State, unionists believed, was in order that it would be a Catholic State. As Stanley Gebler Davies once explained to an English readership, 'Éire is not a foreign country, but it is a Catholic country.' That is what many middle class unionists still feel about the South: it is not foreign but Catholic. For many working class unionists it is both foreign and Catholic. The reason for having an administration in Northern Ireland, unionists were determined, was that it would *not* be a Catholic State. The historical logic of this attitude we noted under Zones of Majoritanianism (p. 8). This view of the Republic as confessional and theocratic remains an article of faith for many unionists, even those who recognize that 'things are changing'.

For instance, despite the removal of the Catholic Church's special constitutional position in 1973, many non-Catholics remain convinced that this merely confirmed the fact that the 'invisible' power of the Church no longer needed 'visible' acknowledgement. Unshakeable convictions like that exasperate liberal politicians in the Republic. They may make them think that nothing that they do to reform the Irish State will make their society attractive to unionists. That is a fact which indicates the gap between how Southern society often perceives itself today — pluralist, open and tolerant — and how it is perceived by unionists — if not dominated by the power of the Catholic Church then deferential towards it. Those who wish to find historical evidence to confirm their view of this power do not have to look far.

An insightful, if often provocative, study of the relationship between the Church and the Irish Constitution is to be found in Angela Clifford's *The Constitutional History of Éire/Ireland,* a study which states intellectually what many unionists feel viscerally. In that study it is proposed that 'there was general consent to the arrangement whereby the Church supervised the State, but along with this went a general insistence that supervision of the State by the Church must not be described.' The compulsory manner of living which the Church demanded was, in other words, the Irish 'philosophy of life', a philosophy which distinguished Ireland from Britain and which gave substance to national separatism.

> The Church has been the guiding influence on the politics of the nation since the fall of Parnell. It determined the inner life of the nation, and later it determined the inner life of the State. All parties and all Governments have functioned within its ambience. When the Church was a sphere of eternal certainty, the nation and the State had a sense of purpose. And when the Church internationally went into crisis, nationalist Ireland became confused. [15]

What seems to be suggested here, first, is that the Republic was an example of the working out of Pope Gelasius I's distinction in the fifth century between the *auctoritas* of the Church and the *potestas* of the State, a distinction which placed the authority of the Church *above* the power of the State. Second, that the crisis and the confusion inspired by the Second Vatican Council have represented interruptions to the normal business inspired by the distinction. It has always seemed clear to unionists from the statements of the Catholic clergy what they assumed (and perhaps still assume) normal business to be.

For instance, Professor John Whyte observed that in their submission to the New Ireland Forum the Catholic bishops argued that 'Catholic influence in a country like Ireland was natural.' He went on to note that if that were indeed the case then Northern Protestants:

... might agree with the bishops that it is natural that a majority ethos should prevail. But they might conclude that, in that case, they would prefer to remain in their own State with its Protestant majority than join a State which would have a Catholic majority.[16]

There is no 'might' about it. It is a certainty. Robert McCartney responded at the time by stating that the hierarchy was 'telling the politicians of the Forum in no uncertain manner that it was not prepared to underwrite any offer that would obstruct or prevent a Catholic majority from imposing the dictates of its conscience or theology upon a unionist minority' in a 'new Ireland'. [17] That was that, straight and simple. And why should unionists think otherwise if Garret FitzGerald was saying much the same thing about the reality of life in the Republic? This returns us to the point made under Alternative Ideas of Political Society (p. 15) about the authoritative source of public morality. The manner of living prescribed for citizens in the Irish State — in the Constitution and in its laws — was a compulsory manner of living appropriate only for those who subscribed to the authority of the Catholic Church. The historical presumption of Irish nationalism in its irredentist form was that the whole of Ireland would ultimately conform to this manner of living, a presumption which, for all its other faults, is not to be found in Ulster unionism. The overwhelming 'majority ethos' in the twenty six counties would be extended into a sufficiently dominant 'majority ethos' in the thirty two counties. As Professor William Magennis put it in 1925, for example: 'You cannot be a good Catholic if you allow divorce even between Protestants.' [18] In the twenty six counties that was still the case seventy years later. The history of Rome rule in nationalist Ireland remains a live issue even for moderate unionists, despite the belief of many in the Republic that things have changed irrevocably. How did unionists view that history?

As the Conservative leader Bonar Law once confided to the Liberal Prime Minister Asquith in 1913, Southern unionists would be 'thrown to the wolves' in any conceivable Irish settlement. The settlement which emerged in the 1920s *did* throw the Southern unionists to the (metaphorical) wolves. The old Anglo-Irish ascendancy was left to fend for itself within the new Catholic democracy of the twenty six county Free State. And abandoned by Northern unionists, one of the ironies of history, as Dennis Kennedy has shown in his excellent study of partition,

The Widening Gulf, is that the sufferings of Southern Protestants as recounted in Northern Ireland's newspapers — their intimidation, their murder, their flight, their falling numbers — enabled the Ulster Unionist Party to consolidate its own regime in the difficult years before the second world war.[19] The memory of the decline in Protestant numbers and the knowledge of their cultural subordination is still a powerful one in unionist Ulster. To many — and not just the extremists — the prospect of Irish unity still suggests a form of 'race death'. Any 'dynamic' form of cooperation with the Republic would represent co-operation in your own undoing. This is a powerful folk memory which the Irish Government needs to be aware of constantly, however irrational it may seem to them.

That even such a gentle and tolerant man as Victor Griffin should voice his concern for the survival of Southern Protestantism and feel shame about the treatment of Hubert Butler by arrogant Catholicism in 1952 indicates the depth of apprehension which Protestants still have about the Republic. Butler was accused of having insulted the Papal Nuncio during a lecture in which he had mentioned the forced conversion of 240,000 Orthodox Serbs to Catholicism in Croatia during the second world war. As a result, Butler experienced petty and narrow-minded persecution. As Griffin notes:

> There was no upsurge of Protestant support for Hubert Butler.
> Protestants were scared. Which tells us something about Protestants but
> also something about the Roman Catholic community at that time. Had
> Protestants good reason to be scared? Looking at what happened to
> Hubert Butler, perhaps they had. I can hear my mother's warning: 'For
> goodness sake, keep quiet, Victor, or you'll get us all burnt out'.[20]

For Griffin, intolerance in Ireland, North and South, comes from religion masquerading as Christianity. To those who follow the Reverend Ian Paisley (and to many more besides) intolerance *only* comes from Catholicism masquerading as Christianity. To Southerners this might appear to be intolerable self-righteousness. They would be correct. But then self-righteousness about wrongs inflicted by others, real or imagined, characterizes much of Irish political debate, North and South. And in its manifold forms, this self-righteousness is not confined to Ulster unionists. It is generally the case, therefore, that Ulster unionists tend to take an uncomplicated view of the role of the Catholic

Church in Irish society. In short, they tend to believe that the interests of the Catholic Church are inseparable from the political project of Irish nationalism which is ultimately inseparable from the designs of militant republicanism. All of them have designs on Protestant Ulster.

Once Protestants in the Irish State were forced to accept the new dispensation after 1921 there was no possible resistance to Catholicism transforming itself from the *de facto* Irish nation into the *de jure* Irish nation. Irish solutions to Irish problems, as Charles Haughey once famously put it, became and remain Catholic solutions to Catholic problems. The confessional homogeneity of the Irish State allowed that State to entrench its legitimacy. And the confessional assumptions about social and political practice became so woven into the fabric of the State that they became almost invisible (except, of course, to Ulster unionists). The Catholic Church became an institutional pillar of the State. It also remained a buffer between its flock and the ambitions of politicians, for good and ill.

An intelligent unionist, for instance, could recognize that if being a good Catholic was tantamount to being a good son or daughter of Ireland then it allowed the Church to provide some challenge and qualification to the claims of radical republican politics. While the grand narrative of Irish national destiny was retailed by the Christian Brothers at school, the effective policy of the hierarchy was concerned with consolidating its own position, using the political opportunities available to entrench the Catholic manner of living. This represented the Catholic Church's own interpretation of Matthew, 22: 21: 'render therefore unto Caesar the things which are Caesar's; and unto God the things that are God's.' And it worked well. Social republicanism — the form of nationalism which unionists wrongly believe to be its essence (just as nationalists wrongly assume that Paisleyism is the essence of unionism) — was a potential enemy of that ecclesiatical project.

The rivalry between the Church and social republicanism has been a rivalry for the soul of the Irish nation. That nation is not the inhabitants of the island but the Catholic inhabitants of the island. Ulster unionists know that. Unionists also know that they are ultimately peripheral to this struggle. On the one hand, social republicans frequently make the mistake of assuming that their hostility to the conservatism of the Catholic Church and its power in Ireland, North and South, will find a positive response amongst unionists. It won't. Unionists will take their criticisms of the Church as insider confirmation of the horrible fate which would befall civil and religious liberty in an Irish State. At the same time unionists will be no more persuaded of the republican cause because that cause is understood to be the exclusive cause of the Catholic people in another guise. On the other hand, the Church is more realistic about Ulster Protestant opinion but has been often cynical in using that realism for its own purposes.

On the linkage between unification and the legalization of contraception, for instance, Cardinal Conway argued in 1973 that 'I think it would be utterly unrealistic to think that the attitudes of the average Unionist towards a united Ireland would be changed in the slightest degree if the law in the Republic were changed.'[21] Conway would have been correct in that precise assumption. Over twenty years later, as if by way of belated confirmation, the Reverend Martin Smyth stated that supporters of the Abortion Information Bill, who suggested that its failure would send a negative message to the unionist community about society in the Republic, were wrong. He went on:

> Let me state clearly and unequivocally that the greater number of people, of all traditions, in Northern Ireland are totally opposed to abortion and would view with dismay any further promotion of the deadly abortion culture. [22]

Those unionists who would be opposed to abortion, like Smyth, as well as those who would be in favour of legalized abortion would not understand it as an issue which implicated them in a statement for or against better relations with the Republic. Once again, the question would not be the authority of the moral case but the *source* of that authority in the practice of the government and of the courts.

Nevertheless, it was not true and it is not true to assume that the attitude exhibited by Conway has had or does have no effect at all. For the Church to show such cavalier indifference to Protestant opinion *in the Republic* is bad for Protestant-Catholic relations *in Northern Ireland*. It is equally bad for relations *between* Northern Ireland and the Republic. For it convinces Ulster unionists in their view that confessional nationalism is not interested in reconciliation but only in domination (see McCartney). To think the worst is always best, be it republicans about Northern Ireland or unionists about the Republic. Those who are sincerely seeking reconciliation need to be aware of such insensitivity regardless of its impact on 'average unionist attitudes towards a united Ireland'. It is not average unionist attitudes towards a united Ireland which matter. It is average unionist attitudes towards peace and reconciliation which really matter. If it is held to be a fault of unionist thinking that it cannot see the difference between these two things then those in positions of authority in the Republic ought not to commit the same error.

There has been a traditional clerical assumption in Ireland that the activity of the State should be formally influenced by the Catholic Church. That is another way of saying that the Church has a firmer understanding of a law which is higher than 'mere' positive law and on points of difference legislators ought to defer to the judgement of Church authority. If legislators themselves accept that understanding then the likelihood of conflict is immeasurably reduced. That higher law is the natural law. For Ulster unionists those rare conflicts between the Church and the Irish State have been exceptions which prove the rules of the political game. The Mother and Child case of 1951 illustrated this clearly for them (and the Dáil debates were published by the unionist government to show to the world the nature of the Southern regime). The Irish Government of the day, when it abandoned Noel Browne's proposed legislation argued that it conflicted with Catholic 'social teaching'. And it was stressed in the Dáil that no government ought to challenge the authority of Catholic 'moral teaching' either.

Yet the simple unionist view that nothing has changed in the South nor will it ever change is insensitive to the modifications in the life of the Irish State, especially since the Second Vatican Council. As Duncan Morrow has argued:

> Although inter-communion remained impossible, Protestant Churches were declared to be 'separated brethren' and Church unity to be a desirable goal. The resultant increase in ecumenical contact with Protestant Churches and Church-people in Ireland caused serious difficulties for Protestants, who remain split about the nature of the Catholic Church between those who regard it as fundamentally evil and unchristian and those who seek meeting and ongoing interchange. [23]

The abortion referendum of 1983 and especially the divorce referendum of 1986 shocked liberal Protestant opinion in Northern Ireland by revealing not only the extent of clerical influence but also the lengths to which that clerical influence seemed willing to go to attain its ends. But these dramatic interventions of the 1980s may ultimately be seen by historians as pyrrhic victories. The extremism of some advocates of the clerical line in both referendums appears to have encouraged a more assertive secular pluralism. Even if Rome today has less sympathy for the agenda of the Second Vatican Council, secular changes are forcing the pace in social matters much more so than clerical reformulations of traditional attitudes.

The recent Supreme Court judgement on the Abortion Information Bill presents an interesting question about the law and popular opinion. Does a legal judgement represent an acknowledgement of reality or does it represent the beginning of a new trend? Thus the Supreme Court in the Abortion Information case restated a judicial argument against the claims of natural law. This judgement could be taken to mean either: that the Supreme Court has acknowledged what is already a fact of life; or that the Supreme Court has opened up a new era of politics in the Republic. It either confirmed a new legal and political culture reflecting the changed society of the Republic or it intimated the emergence of such a changing society. The answer to that question is uncertain for the judgement was an old one. (As old, perhaps, as the judgement of David Hume who wrote that no word was more ambiguous and equivocal than 'nature'.)

The following argument, developed by Mr Justice Walsh *in 1974*, was stressed twice by Mr Justice Hamilton in the Abortion Information case:

> In a pluralist society such as ours, the Courts cannot as a matter of
> constitutional law be asked to choose between the differing views, where
> they exist, of experts on the interpretation by the different religious
> denominations of either the nature or the extent of these natural rights as
> they are to be found in natural law.

His conclusion was that:

> The Courts, as they were and are bound to, recognised the Constitution
> as the fundamental law of the State to which the organs of the State were
> subject and at no stage recognised the provisions of the natural law as
> superior to the Constitution.

The chief political correspondent of *The Irish Times* reflected the ambiguity of opinion about the state of Southern society when he commented that the closure of the constitutional door on the natural law 'with its inherent threat of Catholic control and of a paternalistic/theocratic society, represents the most important step forward' towards a truly pluralist society in the Republic.[24] In other words, according to the Supreme Court the claims of natural law are inappropriate because the Republic *is* a pluralist society and, according to *The Irish Times*, the rejection of an appeal to natural law represents a step *towards* a pluralist society. The Republic both is and isn't a pluralist society.

Perhaps the difficulty lies in the definition of pluralism. For, depending on how one uses the term, it *can* be argued that the Republic both is and isn't a pluralist society. For liberals seeking secular changes in Irish society, the Republic is not pluralist enough. For conservatives seeking to defend the honour of Irish society, the Republic is more than pluralist enough. Pluralism is a codeword for a continuing debate about the character of the Irish State and about the relationship between Church and State. In sum, there are two major alternative possibilities. First, pluralism as understood by contemporary liberals means that the State should be 'neutral' in relation to competing visions of what is the good life. Second, pluralism as understood by conservatives and by the Catholic Church means that, while the State may acknowledge difference, it still has a duty to recognize and to uphold the ethical life of the majority.

Often these alternatives are misunderstood by commentators and leader writers who confuse the realities of life in the Republic with the theories of North American multiculturalism. The Republic is not multicultural in the way in which North America is. It is absurd to pretend that it is. The substance of the pluralist debate in the Irish State is really only intelligible in terms of the second alternative. It best describes the practical limits — an overwhelming Catholic majority and a conservative political system — within which reform would take place. These attributes of Catholicism and conservatism are nothing for which the Irish State needs to apologize. Both have contributed to its social and political stability. Of course, there *would* have to be a radical shift towards the first alternative if Irish unity were ever to be a possibility. A united Ireland would still not be multicultural in the North American sense. But everything that is solid in the Republic would have to melt into air and a new, more ethically neutral order be established. There could be no apology then for the State behaving in a conservative and a Catholic manner. To describe Irish unity in this way reveals the unlikelihood of its attainment. The achievement of unity and its consequences would most likely introduce a general instability into one of the most stable regions of the European Union.

One can say with reasonable certainty what constitutes the change in the relationship between the Church and the Irish State since the 1960s. One can say that the Church's role has changed from that of ecclesiastical magisterium to that of ecclesiastical persuasion. The Church cannot rely any longer on the authoritative majesty of its pronouncements. It must increasingly compete with other opinions in the marketplace of democratic politics. That was probably the real lesson of 1983 and 1986. The Catholic Church was successful on both those occasions. It may not be so successful in the future. Indeed, one can predict with reasonable certainty that it will not be so successful in the future. Given its assumption of natural authority, this has clear dangers for the Church. Competition to persuade the people displaces that authority and opens up the Church to perpetual challenge and criticism. And it is challenge and criticism according to the conventions of social science and not according to the conventions of religious disputation. The exchange of statistics recently over the effects of divorce on society is a case in point. In the long run, that change may significantly alter the character of life in the Republic.

Yet as the Reverend Martin Smyth's comment should make abundantly clear, such alternatives are not always received with great joy in certain unionist or Protestant circles. Most unionists would welcome such steps for their own sake but such steps in themselves would not tend to encourage the thought that the Irish State was becoming better disposed towards *them*. That thought would be encouraged by the deletion of Articles 2 and 3. Indeed, the alien character of the Irish Constitution for unionists is not affected by particular modifications to it. Quoting from the same judgement by Walsh, Mr Justice Hamilton reaffirmed that the people gave themselves the Constitution to 'promote the common good with due observance of prudence, justice and charity'. The substitution of the 'common good' for 'natural law' may be important theoretically and politically. For unionists the common good so defined still lacks relevance. It has no authority for them. It is not their common good for they do not accept the legitimacy of the idea of the people to which it applies (see Symbols, p. 33). This is a point of fundamental importance. Ignoring its importance may lead to false conclusions about the character of unionism and the attitude of unionists towards the South.

For instance, in his essay 'Reviewing the Constitution', Gerard Hogan is correct on both counts for nationalists but equally wrong on both counts for Ulster unionists when he argues that:

> ... even if certain clauses do reflect Catholic social teaching, this should neither surprise us nor persuade us to reject it on that ground alone. It is the content of the Constitution which matters, not its inspirational source.[25]

That passage sums up the imaginative distance between the intelligentsia of the Republic and unionist thinking. The source of Catholic social teaching *is* sufficient grounds for unionists to reject the Constitution; and the content of the Constitution does *not* matter (except for Articles 2 and 3) because the common good it seeks may be admirable in itself but it is estranged from unionists. These may appear to be harsh judgements but they are closer to the truth *today* than the expectations assumed by either social republicanism or liberal constitutionalism that reform of society in the South will alter unionist views about political unity. It must remain an act of faith on the part of politicians in the Republic that changes in the relationship between Church and State will *in the longer term* have a positive impact on unionist attitudes. But the only sound democratic reasons upon which such change should be entered into by the Irish State are the reasons, first, of responsibility to the Southern electorate and, second, of responsiveness to its demands. Concern for that constituency should be paramount for politicians in the Republic.

The two poles of debate about Church and State are secular fundamentalism and religious fundamentalism. In its own way, secular fundamentalism is as dogmatic as religious fundamentalism. In so far as there is little popular pressure to remove clerical influence in education and health, for instance, then Joe Lee's prescription — 'if it ain't broke don't fix it' — does remain 'one of the wiser management injunctions'. It seems sensible to heed his concern that the stability which the Republic has come to take so much for granted this century, with 'an impressive degree of coherence' in social and political life, could be damaged by a form of secular political correctness which assumes a consensus which has not yet emerged to replace the old. [26] It is difficult to imagine the Catholic Church being without great influence in the Irish State since that influence remains a popular one. Very simply, what we have today are intimations that that influence is becoming a strong one within a more pluralist social order rather than an unquestioned one within a confessional State. (The present scandals affecting the Church may help to push this process forward.) That ought to be seen as a sign of self-confidence in democratic politics rather than as a sign of religious decline (see discussion on pluralism, above). The possibility exists to balance arrangements anew formally and legally in Southern society. First, there is the need to balance Catholic morality with the claims of rights of citizenship. Second, there is the need to balance the rights of the majority with its duties to minorities.

The first balance would help to avoid in the future cases like that of Eileen Flynn. She was dismissed from her post in a school in New Ross because she was unmarried and pregnant and lost her appeal in the High Court in March 1985. As Fintan O'Toole reported in *The Irish Times*:

> The Eileen Flynn case made explicit and official what had long been an implicit assumption — that anyone who worked in a Catholic institution had better measure up to official Catholic standards in their private lives, or else. [27]

Such a threat, he argued, still hung over every teacher in a Catholic school and every nurse in a Catholic hospital. *Every* teacher and nurse, not just every *Catholic* teacher and nurse. That sort of moral standard is simply incompatible with the idea of a truly pluralist society which has regard for the secular rights of citizenship. It fails to recognize that such moral standards depend upon their authority being acknowledged by individuals. The tyranny of the (moral) majority can take many forms. The most intolerable form is the practice of making windows into the souls of men and women. That this is publicly recognized to be a problem today is a step forward for citizens in the Republic and an encouraging sign of change.

The second balance would address the concern of Southern Protestants in particular and other minorities in general about the dominant 'ethos' in the provision of health and education. The recent White Paper on Education seems to have gone some way towards addressing Protestant concerns about schooling, though it certainly does not go far enough to address the concerns of those who do think that denominational education is not at all 'constitutionally sound'. There can be little doubt that the proposals reveal a concern to introduce greater flexibility and adaptability into the educational system.

In health provision, concern about the future of the Adelaide Hospital, for example, is a concern about the seriousness of the Irish State when it speaks of 'equality, partnership and pluralism' (the very words of the White Paper on Education). It does seem rather strange that at a time when the issue of 'parity of esteem' is held to be an indispensable part of any settlement in Northern Ireland, there should have been any question mark at all over continuing to accord parity of esteem to the distinctive 'ethos' of the Adelaide in the reorganization of hospital services in the Republic. Thus, in an address to the Culture in Ireland conference Regions: Identity and Power in November 1992, the chairman of the Adelaide, David McConnell posed the crucial question:

> ... will the Adelaide struggle on because it cannot or will not be destroyed, or will it prosper through a wholehearted belief by society that it must be sustained and enhanced precisely because it is an honourable exception?[28]

In other words, would it be possible for an independent Protestant institution to survive in an overwhelmingly Catholic State? Would it be possible to imagine and to sustain medical ethics which do not depend on Catholic teaching? These are real 'pluralist' questions. In 1992 McConnell concluded that, apart 'from the fact that we still exist', the Adelaide had 'quite frankly got nowhere' with the Department of Health. Indeed, he went so far as to suggest that some members of the Catholic hierarchy were less than keen to see the ethos of the Adelaide survive at all. To their immense credit the supporters of the Adelaide have not attempted to make this into a sectarian issue and have successfully isolated it from the passions of Northern Ireland politics, despite one intervention by John Taylor MP. This is certainly an issue of rights for the politicians of the Republic to address in their own terms and according to the appropriate 'plural' needs of the Republic's health service.

Recent evidence by the Board of the Adelaide Hospital, which was submitted to the Forum in October 1995, suggests that an arrangement acceptable to all has now emerged and which only awaits approval in the Oireachtas. The draft charter for the new hospital at Tallaght specifies that it will have a 'multidenominational and pluralist character' and that the new hospital will be 'a focus for Protestant participation in the health services'. The conclusion by the Adelaide Board in their submission to the Forum was:

> The principles enshrined in the Charter and the details agreed by the three Hospitals (Adelaide, Meath and National Children's) who are integrating have happily received cross party support and have been endorsed by successive Governments. This represents a significant commitment to pluralism by our political parties. [29]

Action, the Board argues, must not be delayed.

The importance of such issues in the delivery of services, especially in the field of health care, has to do with matters which go beyond mere consideration of unionist attitudes to peace and reconciliation. They have also to do with more practical matters, for instance the prospect of functional cooperation between government departments in Northern Ireland and government departments in the Republic. If cross-border cooperation of even a limited kind in this or analogous fields is to be a balanced exercise, then some consideration must be given, for example, to the character of medical provision. This does not imply that health care is necessarily better in Northern Ireland. But if there are to be procedures which would involve some patients 'going South' for certain treatments then the 'ethos' of medical provision and the image of the service would need to be looked at.

SYMBOLS

The consideration of symbols and national symbolism played a large part in the discussions of the session of the Forum for Peace and Reconciliation on 24 February 1995. Some interesting contributions were made though the origin of the particular division over symbols in Ireland, North and South, was not properly identified. For it is from that identification that a clearer understanding of the problem will emerge. It is the proposition of this paper that the contemporary division over symbols derives from the distinction between *nationality* and *nationalism*. From that distinction flows the following interpretation.

A sense of Irish nationality based on geographical location was commonly and tenaciously held by Protestants throughout the nineteenth century and for most of this century. Before the second decade of this century, indeed, unionism was Irish unionism. Its leaders argued with some intensity that it was vital for the well-being of the whole island that politicians should make the distinction between nationality and nationalism. In short, unionism asserted that it was possible to be Irish by nationality and yet British by citizenship. As Ronald MacNeill put it clearly and forcefully in the House of Commons on 10 June 1913 during a debate on Home Rule:

> I am sincerely and passionately attached to Ireland as the honourable
> member for Galway or any of his friends. I share their love for Ireland's
> soil, for her scenery, her people, her history, her poetry, her
> romance...but this is a matter of citizenship. [30]

This particular mix of Irish patriotism and political unionism has been severely diminished by events. After partition, it was diminished by the practices of the Irish State. It was diminished by nationalist propagandists who attempted, rather successfully, to appropriate exclusively to themselves the name of Ireland and all that that signifies. The reason why unionists like to call the Republic 'Éire' is not just because it identifies it as a foreign state but because it reserves for themselves the dignity of using the name 'Ireland'. Ireland, their Ireland, is not Ireland, our Ireland. However, the greatest diminishing factor has been the campaign of terror conducted in the name of Ireland by militant republicans and their sympathizers. This has been only one of the historic achievements of IRA violence in the last twenty five years.

For instance, when he conducted his survey of opinion on the eve of the troubles for his ground-breaking study *Governing Without Consensus*, Richard Rose discovered that over 25 per cent of Ulster Protestants still volunteered the answer 'Irish' to a question about their national identity. Today the figure is less than 5 per cent. Since the late sixties, the democratic base of Ulster unionism has increasingly come to make a clear distinction between being Irish and being British. Again, the IRA campaign has helped to turn this tendency into a self-defining unionist dogma, where Britishness has become a spiritual substance as deadly in its destructive potential when taken up by gunmen as the

metaphysics of Irish nationalism. This development has been noted with
some regret by the Fermanagh unionist councillor, Raymond Ferguson:

> The terrorist campaign of the last twenty years and the political instability
> which has accompanied it have caused unionists yet again to seek security
> as a first priority. The effect has been to drive Protestant people in the
> North into a position where they fear to identify themselves in any way
> with things Irish. [31]

The present Ulster Unionist Party deputy leader, John Taylor, was not
being mischievous but entirely serious when he flatly rejected the
notion that he was in any way 'Irish'. And his rejection of an Irish
identity would be in tune with the deepest sentiments of most of his
electorate. The change this century in the use of Irish and Irishness was
experienced not only by Northern unionists but also by Southern
Protestants. As Stephen Gwynn noted: 'I was brought up to think of
myself Irish without question or qualification but the new nationalism
prefers to describe me and the like of me as Anglo Irish.'[32] If it means
suffering the fate of the Anglo-Irish, unionists would prefer not to think
of themselves as Irish at all.

The transformation of the symbols of nationality into the symbols of
nationalism has possibly been — if one were to exclude the Provisional
IRA campaign — one of the most corrupting enterprises of modern
Irish history. As the separatist ideologue Fr Gaynor put it: 'The sacred
word Nation had been "corrupted" because British hirelings had
profaned our symbols — the shamrock, the harp and the green flag —
to destroy their old time significance.'[33] Once this sort of attitude had
taken hold it was extremely difficult to retain any sense of commonality
about symbols and symbolism. As Mary Douglas has argued, in such
circumstances symbols become significant by virtue of their lack of
meaning for others; or, in the Irish case, by their hostile meaning for
others. [34]

What is remarkable in the relationship between nationalist and
unionist in Ireland, then, is not the hostility shown by unionists to the
symbols of Irishness. What is rather remarkable is the fact that unionists
have remained comfortable with so much Irish iconography for so long.
That would indicate a tolerance and open-mindedness rarely associated
with Ulster Protestants. One of the reasons for this may be the fact that
many of the institutions of which unionists are members, sporting,

cultural and religious, are island-wide. From the Church of Ireland to the Irish Association, from the Baptist Union to the Irish Rugby Football Union, political division can exist along with civic and religious communion across the island, a communion not just with those 'of one's own kind' .

The harp and the shamrock and the green are symbols which have been frequently retained in Northern Ireland in State and non-State bodies. The harp — with its crown — remains a symbolic representation of the claim that one could be Irish by nationality (harp) and yet be British by citizenship (crown). The Royal Ulster Constabulary and the Royal Irish Regiment both wear that most expressive of symbols. Their members can also happily wear the shamrock on St Patrick's Day and the poppy on Remembrance Day. The Northern Ireland football team wears green and its strip is probably more symbolically Irish than that of the Republic. The Northern Ireland shirts carry a badge with the representation of a Celtic cross. It has been frequently noted, and it is periodically repeated in the letter columns of *The Irish Times* for reasons best known to the correspondents, that the Unionist Convention of 1895 had the motto 'Erin Go Bragh' emblazoned above the platform. Irish unionism originally presented itself in the symbols of shamrocks, harps and the Irish language. This began to transform itself into the present red, white and blue form of Ulster unionism in the first decades of the twentieth century as Irish unionism transformed itself into Ulster unionism. Nevertheless, these symbols of an Irish nationality were not lost to Ulster Protestants, especially those middle class Ulster Protestants who tend to be rugby supporters. And, reproduced on a mass scale as trinkets and ornaments like round towers, leprechauns or thatched cabins, these symbols can still exert a kitsch attraction amongst all classes. That is because they have been sentimentalized and depoliticized. It is the politicization of national sentiment in the Irish situation which is ultimately corrupting.

Nationalism, as Gaynor's position makes clear, is about drawing those symbolic distinctions which say because this is mine it can't be yours and because that is yours it can't be mine. What is then elevated into national significance takes on a certain magical quality for insiders. It then may take on an evil quality for outsiders. Consider John Wilson

Foster's experience. Foster thinks of himself as Irish because he was born and reared on the island and has an affection for it which reads very much like that of Ronald MacNeill's at the beginning of this century. However, Foster is repelled by what has become the (voodoo) symbolism of political Irishness:

> It is therefore an occasion for genuine regret, even pain, that I do not
> wish to be a citizen of an Ireland resembling the present Republic.
> When I lived there, I found it wanting in essentials of ethos, civil
> liberties, and the consensual pantheon of heroes, in its story of itself. One
> of the most sacred spots in the South of Ireland is the Easter Rising room
> in the National Museum: I stand in it and feel utterly estranged, as I do if
> I stand in a Roman Catholic church: both are mighty formidable spaces,
> but they exclude me and moreover wish to exclude me. [35]

The symbolism of the Easter Rising room is the symbolism of nationality become nationalism. For Foster, at any rate, it is the symbolism of an Irishness become divisive.

Take another instance of the same sort of transformation, the fate of the Irish language. Gerry Adams in his book *Free Ireland: Towards a Lasting Peace* makes much of the fact that Protestants in Belfast were in the vanguard of the revival of Irish and that An Cuideach Gaedhilge Uladh was founded in 1830 by two Protestants, Robert MacAdam and Lord Devonshire. [36] For some reason (unspecified by Adams, of course) this Protestant 'liberal ethos' of the late eighteenth and early nineteenth centuries declines into sectarianism by the end of the nineteenth century. The present leader of the Ulster Unionist Party, David Trimble, provided an explanation of why this should have happened. Speaking at the Varieties of Irishness conference sponsored by the Cultural Traditions Group, Trimble argued that in early nineteenth century Belfast :

> ... there were no antagonistic policies and the hostility displayed in some
> quarters towards Gaelic today stems from the time when the Gaelic
> movement was largely taken over by people with a particular set of
> policies. It will be a very hopeful thing if that ceases to be the case. [37]

In other words, there is all the difference in the world between Irish as a symbol of nationality and Irish as an instrument of nationalist separatism. Protestants who could feel relatively comfortable with the first could not feel comfortable with the second.

There is indeed evidence in the South (if not in the North) that this *particular* form of politicizing the language might be changing. Because of the obvious failure which resulted from using the language as an instrument of nationalist policy (which, it should be stressed, is a rationalistic enterprise completely at odds with the cultural significance of language) the emphasis has now changed. Irish is currently being promoted as a functional educational tool. The new prospectus proposes: 'Become bilingual (English-Irish) because bilingualism has been shown to improve educational attainment.' This utilitarian philosophy of self-improvement sounds like sweet revenge on Daniel O'Connell. However, utility is always a fairweather friend to cultural enthusiasts. For real utilitarians can justifiably respond: why not become bilingual (English-German) not only to improve your emigration prospects in the new Europe but to make the most of your investment in satellite television?

As Trimble suggests, there ought to be nothing which would prevent Protestants confronting the language issue in a positive way. No cultured person in Ireland, North or South, should be ignorant of the linguistic influences — in place-names, in figures of speech for instance — of their own land. This will mean some familiarity with the Irish language, not as a badge of separatism, not as a denial of their British citizenship, but as a means to cultural enrichment. There is no reason why Protestants should deprive themselves of that cultural resource. There is nothing in their political commitment to the Union which ought to deny it.

Flags are the most public symbolic statements of identity. Hayes-McCoy has tried to show that the fate of the Irish tricolour was the fate of a hypothetically inclusive nationality falling victim to an actually exclusive nationalism. After the Easter Rebellion, the tricolour emerged 'not as the flag of an Irish Union in the vision of Meagher [and others] but as the flag of an Irish republic, the flag of an actual revolt'.[38] Maybe so. But then no separatist flag would have been acceptable to unionists since it would have denied their British citizenship. The idea that the 'Orange' in the tricolour symbolically represents Ulster Protestants has never been accepted by those symbolically represented by it. It should be remembered that the majority of Ulster Protestants are *not* 'Orange' and may find the symbol an insult. And anyway, the 'Orange' is seen as (papal) 'Gold'. If the inclusion of the Orange is a symbol of Irish nationalist aspiration (Articles 2 and 3 made cloth) then the Ulster unionist ignoring of it is equally symbolic of their position.

This very brief consideration of the symbols leads to the following proposition. There would appear to be two distinct issues confronting the Forum for Peace and Reconciliation when it considers the significance of symbols. Unfortunately, these two distinct issues are rather confused by the terminology of the Downing Street Declaration. The first concerns the symbols of the *Irish State*. These are the symbols which the Declaration ought to describe as those aspects of Irish life 'which...reflect hopes and ideals which lie deep in the hearts of many Irish men and women'. They are the expressions of Irish nationalism and have a political value because they contribute to the stability of the Irish State. The second concerns the symbols of *Irish nationality*. These are the symbols which the Declaration sought to describe as 'those inherited values...that are largely shared throughout the island or that belong to the cultural and historical roots of the people of the island in all their diversity.' They are the expressions of a non-political sense of Irishness and have a value precisely because they are part of the affective identity of everyone who lives in the island of Ireland. These two distinct issues are confused in the Declaration. They are confused because Irish nationalism itself is confused. It has great difficulty in making the required distinction between nationalism and nationality because historically it has refused to acknowledge that there could possibly be a distinction. Such an acknowledgement might concede some ground to the claims of unionism and that would challenge Dick Spring's political 'nationalism in its integrity'. This intimation of an official mobilization of nationalist interests by the Irish State to seek advantage in future political talks may be at odds with the concern to foster reconciliation on the island of Ireland.

There is no simple conclusion which flows from this distinction between nationalism and nationality. On the one hand, the Irish State probably ought not to agonize so much about its symbols — from green letter boxes to the Angelus — which, one assumes, remain popular amongst its own citizens. There appears to be no constituency of opinion within the Republic which is readily mobilizable to promote such change. The reasonable approach, as suggested by Sean Farren of the SDLP at the Forum on 24 February 1995, might be to extend recognition to other symbolic events and occasions (though, again, there was some unfortunate confusion by the Forum between political nationalism and nationality). This has been done already, for instance, in the belated acknowledgement of Remembrance Day.

On the other hand, there ought to be a greater sensitivity to the fact that things symbolic of a sense of Irish nationality ought not to be corrupted by their appropriation for narrow political ends. That would include those things 'that are largely shared throughout the island or that belong to the cultural and historical roots of the people of the island in all their diversity.' At least a start has been made in one regard by not playing 'The Soldier's Song' before rugby matches during the recent World Cup in South Africa. The Irish rugby team, though it must play its home games in Dublin, is not a side representative of the Republic. It is an all-Ireland side, the distinctiveness of which is discussed in the next section. Perhaps the playing of 'The Soldier's Song' is not appropriate recognition of that distinctive status. The Taoiseach, John Bruton, seems to have gone one step further by recommending a review of the Irish national anthem itself. If the anthem were to be changed it would not of itself change unionist attitudes towards Irish unity. But it would be an interesting symbolic statement about how the Republic seeks to represent itself today. It might contribute to a more positive 'mood music' which in turn might contribute to a more relaxed political atmosphere throughout the island.

Many of these points have been made eloquently and consistently by public figures like Sam McAughtry and Matt O'Dowd. The concern to make a proper distinction between statehood and nationality could be reflected in changing vocabularies of politics. The idea that you can foster a common sense of Irish nationality *in all its diversity* without changing the reality of different jurisdictions on the island could possibly be the idea which squares that famous circle identified by Dick Spring before the signing of the Downing Street Declaration.

SPORT

Sport in Ireland is yet another example of this encounter of nationality and nationalism. To say that is to say that the question of identity is both simplified and complicated by the role of sport in Ireland, North and South. The contemporary position of sport owes much to its origins.

Modern *organized* sports in Ireland were of British origin. These sports such as cricket, rugby union, boxing, athletics and golf remain popular. At international level, many of these sports, for instance rugby and cricket, retain their pre-partition character as sports of Irish nationality rather than as sports of Irish nationalism. The sports of Irish nationalism have traditionally been those organized by the Gaelic Athletic Association. These games were organized and played precisely in order to challenge the influence of things British (including sports) in Ireland. Sport was to be one means to make Ireland a nation once again. As Archbishop Croke responded to Michael Cusack's invitation to become a patron of the GAA:

> We are daily importing from England...her games also, and her pastimes, to the utter discredit of our grand national sports, and to the sore humiliation I believe of every genuine son and daughter of the old land.[39]

In Northern Ireland, on the other hand, association football has emerged during the troubles to become the symbol of Ulster loyalist identity (to the chagrin of many supporters). As Alan Bairner has written recently:

> The impression created...is of a Protestant community seeking to maintain control over a sport in a manner which could be said to reflect Unionist political efforts to maintain the Union in the face of growing encroachment by Irish Nationalists. It should be stated, however, that this is not simply an example of Protestant intransigence. In the case of identification with the national team for example, it is no coincidence that Catholic support for Northern Ireland began to dwindle at precisely the time when the Republic of Ireland's national side started to enjoy international success for the first time ever, thereby providing an Irish alternative for football-loving Northern Catholics. [40]

Football in Northern Ireland, therefore, has become a key signifier of identity. Support for the Republic's team has joined Gaelic sports as a way in which Catholics can assert their distinctiveness from Protestants. Indeed, support for the Republic may be a more appropriate way to show opposition to your communal opponents because it involves real sporting competition (an extension to the international stage of familiar encounters such as Linfield against Cliftonville, Rangers against Celtic). It may give intense pleasure to some Catholics to see Northern Ireland get beaten by 'their' national side. This darker aspect to support for the

Republic's football team is something of which fans in the South are mainly unaware. Equally, it gives intense pleasure to some Protestants to know that 'their' national side could, as in 1993 and in 1995, deny to the Republic qualification in a major sporting championship. This is something of which football fans in the South are all too aware. It confirms for them prejudices about the bigotry of all Northern Protestants. This is unfair. For the sake of their sense of Irish nationality (as defined above) some Protestants were prepared to give passive support to the Republic's footballers in the World Cup finals. They did this despite the sectarian overtones of some Northern Catholic behaviour. This point is made in order to remind a Southern readership of two things. First, that their image of the positive character of the Republic's football team is not universally accepted throughout the island. Second, that the focus of interest on sport and identity in the Republic is rather different from the focus in Northern Ireland.

Sport in the Republic has been identified by some academics as involving a struggle between modernity and traditionalism. In this struggle, the GAA has been accorded the role of the defender of a national identity rooted in the past and the Football Association of Ireland as the promoter of a national identity in tune with the new, modern (or postmodern) Irish society. For example, in an article in *Irish Studies Review*, which to some extent corresponds to the deliberations of the Forum for Peace and Reconciliation, Mike Cronin argued that:

> The future of Irish sport, as with the future of Irishness and Irish
> nationalism, lies with those who can move away from history and accept
> the ever-changing definition of Irishness in a wider world. It does not lie
> with those who still believe in an insular 'one nation' vision, or those
> who believe that Irishness is under threat if pastimes are not drawn from
> the time of Cuchulainn.[41]

For 'the future' read football and for 'insular "one nation" vision' read the GAA. The only dispensation for the GAA which Cronin allows is its contribution to the 'nationalist struggle' in Northern Ireland. That is hardly an inviting conclusion for Ulster unionists and possibly a dangerous one for GAA members in the North.

This sort of ideological embrace of football is really the ideological embrace of *international* football. There are two aspects to this. First, it fits in with a disposition towards the celebration of that 'globalization' which projects Ireland and the Irish onto a world market of imagery. The Republic's football team becomes the sporting equivalent of Johnny Logan in the Eurovision Song Contest. This is a world market in which everything is at one and the same time intensely different (Jack's army, the Italians, the Brazilians and so on) and yet intensely the same (the professionalism and the style). The emotions which are felt in the pubs and on the couches at home are very immediate and very real. The source of those emotions transmitted via satellite is distant and very abstract.

Second, the embrace of football is also international in another sense of being outside the League of Ireland. The interest in football has a habit of being focused on teams such as Celtic, Manchester United, Liverpool or Arsenal. These are vibrant British-Irish links. And now, with coverage of European leagues interest is being shown in teams like Juventus, Inter Milan or Barcelona. This ideological enthusiasm for the future has not yet translated into mass support for Cork City or Shamrock Rovers. Even Derry City, one of the best supported teams in the League of Ireland, is suffering from the effects of competition from football on satellite TV. There is a suspicion that it is partially ideological support for victory rather than for the thing itself. In conformity with the postmodern sensibilities of the Republic's intelligentsia there may be a touch of *fantasy football* about all of this recent sporting enthusiasm. On the other hand, there is evidence of young people voting with their feet in terms of the sort of football they wish to play. Those playing association football have doubled in recent years, a trend which is a source of worry for the GAA.

It could even be argued that there is something of the revenge of the emigrant, especially those exiles in England, in the elevation of football against Gaelic games. The reasoning might be this: the old Ireland did not want us and remained smug in its sporting identity; we have returned to reclaim our inheritance and to show that we are the real Irish. None of this has much of a resonance for unionists, however. As with the old struggle between the Catholic Church and social republicanism, they are peripheral to these arguments about identity. These arguments are really about what sort of nationalism is politically correct rather than about what sort of nationality is most inclusive. That the success of international football in the Republic broadens the sense of *Catholic nationalism* is ultimately irrelevant to most Ulster Protestants.

It might be a different form of nationalist expression — 'There's only one team in Ireland', they sang when Northern Ireland played at Lansdowne Road — but it is nationalism nonetheless. At least one commentator has suggested that it may be peripheral even to Northern Catholics despite how those Northern Catholics may feel about it.

In a recent thoughtful article, Michael Holmes has argued that the football team 'represents and mirrors a change to a more pluralist, heterogeneous and accommodatory society in the Republic and has consequent implications for a sense of national identity'. But this pluralism, heterogeneity and accommodation has a particular focus. It is a Southern national identity.

> The Irish team is made up from a multi-cultural background, and most of the players live and work in a more liberal, pluralist society than Ireland's [i.e. the United Kingdom]. Thus, to some extent the success of the Irish football team mirrors the advance of pluralism and liberalism in Irish society in general. But it is also an expression of national identity that, at least potentially, excludes Northern nationalists and asserts a difference between the republic and Northern Ireland. [42]

All of these observations may be contested. It may be doubted if the plain people of Ireland would be so happy to admit that the United Kingdom is the model for a liberal and pluralistic society. If it is, what was the point of Irish independence in the first place (see, for example, some of the arguments under Alternative Ideas of Political Society, p.15). That these views should be widely held in intellectual circles, however, reveals an interesting tendency in Southern attitudes which might at least give pause for thought to those who believe, as the Department of Foreign Affairs seems to do, in Irish nationalism *in its integrity*.

In these contemporary discussions about national identity, it is interesting to note how rugby, formally the jewel in the crown of those nationalists who wished to see the Irish people at ease with themselves, has lost its major significance. In Ireland, rugby has been extremely successful in retaining its character as a sport of nationality. The game has a large following worldwide. Ireland is reasonably good at it. The rugby team even beats the English (sometimes). The sport now has a powerful media presence and has gone professional. Yet it does not seem to satisfy the need for sporting nationalism in the way that football does. Why? It could be that it is a minority sport, though that ought not to affect its symbolic importance. It could also be that it is too closely identified as a British or imperial sport. Football has lost that connotation and become truly globalized. Football is also a 'people's sport' in the way that rugby has never been. Nevertheless, other possibilities spring to mind. Could it be that there are too many Ulster players on the team and that they complicate the demand for a simple affective, nationalist identity? Could it be that thirty two counties no longer have the same power to excite the plain people of Ireland as twenty six counties — in the South, because they are 'ours' and amongst Catholics in the North, because they are 'not theirs'? If the answer to either of these questions is yes, then it tends to confirm the observations of Holmes. If so, then the Forum really has some hard and honest thinking still to do about the nature of reconciliation in Ireland.

It does seem rather premature of those who would wish to see the modernization of the Republic reflected in its sporting pastimes, to dismiss the GAA. Domestically at least, the flourishing of the GAA is there for all to see, especially for those who travel by train from Belfast to Dublin. The new stadium being built at Croke Park dominates the skyline and represents a £35 million vote of confidence in Gaelic games. A membership of 800,000 is a large vote of confidence in the pastimes drawn from the age of Cuchulain. It may be true that the GAA's strength lies in rural Ireland but it was Dublin which won the All-Ireland football final this year. Gaelic games are insulated from the vagaries of international fortune and it will be interesting to see what happens to the relative importance of football and Irish identity when the Republic's team begins to lose again — as it will. The great strength of the GAA, which even some Protestants can admire, is its local patriotism. If Edmund Burke's notion of the 'little platoons' being the basis of national affection has any meaning at all, then the GAA has had and continues to have a vital importance in the structure of Irish life. The GAA's organization can engage an intense county-based involve-ment which has no real sporting equivalent elsewhere. The major challenge to the integrity of Gaelic sports comes from professionaliza-tion as much as from the competition with football. Once sport in Ireland is universally understood in terms of making a living instead of a way of life then all sorts of career permutations and shifts of allegiance become possible. Money has a habit of bringing change, if not always for the better.

The GAA would still represent for Northern unionists a world from which they are excluded and a world from which they wish to exclude themselves — irrespective of the GAA's attitude to members of the British security forces. The GAA is a metaphor for the Irish State itself, an association given to rituals, practices, symbolism and allegiance, and with constitutional provisions, which are alien to unionist purpose. Like the GAA, the Irish State will be loathed by some unionists, ignored by most (if they can) and its intentions suspected by nearly all. It may not be very helpful of unionists to feel this way about the GAA or the Irish State or for that matter, the Republic's football team. But it is a fact of life. And a fact is simply something which is, for the moment, impossible to get around. It must be treated seriously by all those in the Republic who are seeking peace and reconciliation, even if it is the hope of those attending the Forum that it will be possible *one day* to get around it.

CONCLUSION

This brief paper has examined how certain aspects of life in the Republic are viewed by unionists in Northern Ireland. It has tried to provide an honest estimate of how unionists understand the character of Southern society and how they understand their own relationship to it. Many of the judgements delivered on the basis of that estimate may appear harsh to most members of the Forum. However, that probably indicates the gap between the aspiration to accommodation and the reality of present opinion. The key word here is *present*. The optimistic perspective of the Forum must be that it is possible to change that opinion by changing the atmosphere of public discussion. It must share with the English philosopher Michael Oakeshott the view that a tradition of behaviour is not a groove within which we are destined to grind out our helpless and unsatisfying lives. The Forum, for its own sense of political perspective, however, should keep in mind the pessimistic possibility that things in the world might not necessarily change for the better. If its sessions have meant nothing more than an exercise in nationalist psychotherapy, then the Forum would have only served a limited and transient function.

The position we are in at the moment may be best described in the words of Richard Rorty. We are probably 'between an entrenched vocabulary which has become a nuisance and a half-formed new vocabulary which vaguely promises great things.'[43] The language of traditional Irish nationalism and the language of traditional Ulster unionism have both become a nuisance. Everyone today is struggling to express themselves in a half-formed vocabulary which vaguely promises great things. The Forum for Peace and Reconciliation — as its grandiose title suggests — is only one example of an attempt to transform the vaguely promising new vocabulary of the Downing Street Declaration into a viable political grammar. The problem for unionists is that the new vocabulary of Irish nationalism always sounds very much like the entrenched one to which they have become so used. This is not because they have tin ears but because they are acutely sensitive to meaning and not to sound. Unionist politicians believe that the Irish Government have been selling the same horse for twenty five years and it still has Articles 2 and 3 secure in its constitutional stable.

One problem for peace and reconciliation in Ireland has been the views of the South about itself, views which have implicated Northern unionists in their various understandings. As we have noted, Southern opinion has often swung between moods of self-loathing and moods of self-congratulation. This suggests a State which is not entirely at ease with itself, a State with a tendency to look elsewhere for the cause of its own dissatisfactions. The roles which Northern unionists have been allocated in these emotional mood swings have been equally contradictory. They are destined either to save the Republic from its (worst) self or they are destined to realize how wonderful life already is south of the border. These are political fantasies which make it difficult to get a sense of proportion about reconciliation in Ireland. They sometimes oscillate between ill-disguised hostility to all things unionist or Protestant and ill-informed praise for the supposed sterling qualities of the 'unionist people' in Northern Ireland. Both are dangerous perspectives because they deal in self-willed images and not realities. At its worst, as twenty five years of IRA violence have proved, these illusions can lead to a destructive fervour which can dispense death 'with no more significance than cleaving a head of cabbage or swallowing a draught of water'. [44]

If peace and reconciliation really does mean that pushing for Irish unity irrespective of the active consent of unionists is now off the political agenda then the Forum might wish to consider in its final report how the oneness of the island in many mutually beneficial ways can become a practical reality. A sense of common nationality, which we noted under Symbols (p. 33), might possibly reassert itself if the language *and* the practice are right. This would not entail a necessary move towards Irish political unity. It would mean, rather, a move towards an island at ease with its diversity, a diversity which would include, amongst other things, two separate jurisdictions on the island. This would enable people in Northern Ireland to live their lives — business, cultural, social — if they so wished, partly or even mainly in the context of the whole island without in any way weakening the position of Northern Ireland as part of the United Kingdom, which is what really matters to unionists. Nationalists might find a nationality broader in its sympathies than residual anti-Britishness (the South) and prominent anti-Britishness (the North). As the European Union develops a common citizenship, residents of Northern Ireland could be in the happy position of being British, Irish, or European as the mood takes them while remaining, constitutionally, citizens of the United Kingdom.

Similarly, there could be recognition of the broader oneness of 'these islands' — of the United Kingdom and the Republic of Ireland — where political division has neither impinged upon a shared cultural heritage nor on a vast network of economic, social and other ties. Only the lingering idea of absolute Irish separatism prevents these things happening while at the same time fostering unionist suspicion of mutually beneficial cooperation between the jurisdictions on the island. As the Cadogan Group argued in its pamphlet *Northern Limits*:

> Progress in Northern Ireland surely requires a greater recognition that we share a common cultural heritage which, while it is largely Western and English speaking, from Shakespeare to Shaw to Coronation Street, has also a strong regional element that embraces not just Irish writers in English, but Irish language, art and folk music. This Irish cultural heritage is, and should be, shared by everyone in Northern Ireland regardless of politics.[45]

Unfortunately, the stress of Irish nationalism, especially in its post-New Ireland Forum formulation, defines cultural life in strictly political terms, the 'Irish' one 'directly associated with the government in Dublin and therefore with the idea of unity with an Irish political entity'. This is something which the Forum might wish to consider seriously (see also Sport). As the Cadogan Group went on:

> In approaching a solution, all parties should appreciate the reality of Northern Ireland's position as part of the United Kingdom, and of the fact that the lives of many are lived entirely within that context. Unionists are not reluctant nationalists, waiting to be enticed or persuaded into a united Ireland by the generosity of Dublin. [46]

If one thing should be acknowledged by the Forum in its discussions on the specific aspects of 'obstacles to peace and reconciliation in the South', that is certainly it. The contemporary possibilities of the Redmondite project, to which Professor Bew has referred and which we have cited (see Introduction, p. 3), must take account of the limits imposed on policy by that reality.

NOTES

1   S. Gwynn, *Ireland*, London, 1924, p. 12
2   *Ibid.*, p. 51
3   P. Bew, *Ideology and the Irish Question*, Oxford, 1994, p. 158.
4   D. G. Boyce, *Nationalism in Ireland*, (4th ed.) London, 1995, p. 43.
5   E. Gellner, *Encounters With Nationalism*, Oxford, 1994, p. 73.
6   T. P. Coogan, *Disillusioned Decades*, Dublin, 1987, p. 242.
7   *Ibid.*, p. 243.
8   G. FitzGerald, *All in a Life*, London, 1992, p. 376.
9   *Ibid.*, p. 378.
10   C. C. O'Brien *Ancestral Voices*, p. 128.
11   R. L. McCartney *Liberty and Authority in Ireland*, Derry, 1985, p. 15.
12   A. Green 'The British Isles' in J. W. Foster (ed.), *The Idea of the Union*, Vancouver, 1995, p. 24.
13   *Ibid.*, p. 25.
14   Cited in Cultural Traditions Group, *Giving Voices*, Belfast, 1995, p. 13.
15   A. Clifford, *The Constitutional History of Éire/Ireland*, Belfast, 1987, p. 310.
16   J. Whyte, *Interpreting Northern Ireland*, Oxford, 1991, pp 157-58.
17   R. L. McCartney, 'Priests, Politics and Pluralism' in J. W. Foster (ed.) *op. cit.*, pp 90-91.
18   Cited in D. Keogh, *Twentieth Century Ireland*, Dublin, 1994, p. 30.
19   D. Kennedy, *The Widening Gulf*, Belfast, 1988.
20   V. Griffin, *Mark of Protest*, Dublin, 1993, p. 223.
21   Cited in Keogh, *op. cit.*, p. 338.
22   *The Irish Times*, 8 March 1995.
23   D. Morrow, 'Church and Religion in the Ulster Crisis' in S. Dunn (ed.), *Facets of the Conflict in Northern Ireland*, London, 1995.
24   *The Irish Times*, 13 May 1995.
25   *The Irish Times*, 19 April 1995.
26   *The Irish Times*, 20 April 1995.
27   *The Irish Times*, 29 September 1995.
28   D. McConnell, 'Regions and Minorities' in P. O Drisceoil (ed.) *Regions: Identity and Power*, Belfast, 1993, p. 130.
29   Board of the Adelaide Hospital, *The Adelaide Hospital: Symbol and Expression of a Pluralist Society*, a submission to the Forum for Peace and Reconciliation, October 1995, p. 4.
30   Cited in Bew, *op. cit.*, p. 27.
31   R. Ferguson, Locality and Political Tradition in M. Crozier (ed.) *Varieties of Britishness*, Belfast, 1990, p. 44.
32   S. Gwynn, *Experiences of a Literary Man*, London, 1926, p. 1.
33   L. Bryson and C. McCartney, *Clashing Symbols*, Belfast, 1994, p. 38.
34   M. Douglas, *Natural Symbols*, Harmondsworth, 1978, p. 58.
35   J. W. Foster, 'Why I am a Unionist' in J. W. Foster (ed.), *op. cit.*, p. 61.
36   G. Adams, *Free Ireland: Towards a Lasting Peace* (revised edition) Dingle, 1995, p. 143.
37   D. Trimble in M. Crozier (ed.) *Varieties of Irishness*, Belfast, 1989, pp 45-46.
38   Bryson and McCartney, *op. cit.*, p. 38.

39 Cited in M. Cronin, 'Sport and a Sense of Irishness', *Irish Studies Review*, no 9, Winter 1994/95, p. 13.

40 A. Bairner, 'The Arts and Sport' in A. Aughey and D. Morrow (eds.) *Northern Ireland Politics* (forthcoming), London, p. 172.

41 Cronin, *op. cit.*, p. 17.

42 M. Holmes, 'Symbols of National Identity and Sport: The Case of the Irish Football Team', *Irish Political Studies*, vol 9, 1994, p. 97.

43 'The Contingency of Language' in R. Rorty, *Contingency, Irony and Solidarity*, Cambridge, 1990, p. 9.

44 G. W. F. Hegel, *The Phenomenology of Mind* (trans. Sir J. Baillie), London, 1966, p. 605.

45 Cadogan Group, *Northern Limits*, Belfast, 1992, p. 14.

46 *Ibid.*, p. 27.

A
UNIONIST LEGAL PERSPECTIVE
ON OBSTACLES IN THE SOUTH
TO BETTER RELATIONS
WITH THE NORTH

BRICE DICKSON

UNIVERSITY OF ULSTER

INTRODUCTION AND SUMMARY

As requested in its terms of reference, this commissioned paper explores some aspects of life and State in the South of Ireland which (a) may present barriers, from a Northern/unionist perspective, to better relations between the South and North or (b) may inhibit the development, for its own sake, of a more pluralist society in the South. The analysis focuses in particular on how those aspects of life and State are reflected in the law, especially the constitutional law, of the South and on whether the relevant legal rules and principles are genuine obstacles to reconciliation within the island as a whole and to meaningful pluralism within that part of it which forms the Republic.

The paper attempts to make an unprejudiced assessment of the alleged obstacles but has been prepared in the knowledge that the quality of any such assessment remains profoundly dependent upon the meaning given to 'better relations', 'reconciliation' and 'pluralism' in this context. Before one can decide that something is an obstacle one obviously needs to be quite clear about what it is that the putative obstacle is supposedly obstructing. As the writer wishes the assessment to have as wide an impact as possible he has deliberately chosen a non-prescriptive interpretation of the terms in question. Thus it is not assumed that 'better relations' or 'reconciliation' are euphemisms for 'federation' or 'unity' nor, alternatively, that they presuppose communication between completely separate peoples. Neither does the paper attempt to provide a fixed set of indicia against which to measure a society's claim to be pluralistic. Its remit is to evaluate the obstacles, or the apparent obstacles, *per se* in order to come to a conclusion as to their significance for future political arrangements within this island. The analysis will be alive to the fact that apparent obstacles may not indeed be real obstacles — either because appearances can be deceptive or because realities are sometimes misidentified.

Pervading the whole of the paper, though, is the realization that in the minds of Northern unionists the main reason for bad relations between the North and South is the belief on the part of most Southerners (mixed of course with that of Northern nationalists) that a united Ireland is preferable to a divided Ireland. Quite simply, it is the existence of this belief that makes unionist-minded Northerners suspicious of Southern actions, especially governmental actions. But the paper also bears in mind that relations between two jurisdictions *can* be excellent even though the jurisdictions may differ greatly as to the way in which they are each constituted, regulated and administered. Canada and the United States of America, for example, differ significantly in these respects, as do Australia and New Zealand, and the inhabitants of these countries are for the most part very proud of their national heritage and loyal to their own political system, yet these jurisdictions remain extremely friendly nations *inter se*. What makes for unfriendliness between the two parts of Ireland — there is no point in gainsaying it — is the basic disagreement over which government, the Irish or the British, should be responsible for governing the area known as Northern Ireland.

The paper's tentative conclusion is that while, for the most part, the constitutional and legal systems in the South do *not* present significant obstacles to better relations between the two parts of Ireland, if there were ever to be a move towards a situation beyond what can simply be described as 'better relations' this *would* require the adaptation of several features of the Southern constitutional and legal systems in order to prevent them endangering the stability of that new situation. In short, the closer one comes to a union of the two parts of Ireland the more difficult it is to describe the troublesome features in the South as mere flies in the ointment — they gradually become real spanners in the works.

UNIONIST FEARS AND CAUTION

To the extent that one of the obstacles to better relations between North and South can be identified as fear, it is as well to recognize that fear can be of at least two varieties. One is fear of the dangerous, which is based on a rational appreciation of the exact nature of what is being confronted, another is fear of the unknown, which is based on ignorance or uncertainty. For Northern unionists faced with the prospect of constitutional change, these two types of fear are not always disentangled: even when the unknown becomes known they still readily assume it to be dangerous. Danger is equated with the unfamiliar and the untried — such an attitude is part and parcel of a conservative disposition. But in this respect Northern unionists do not differ from most other people, whether in the Republic of Ireland or in the rest of the United Kingdom, whatever their party political allegiance. Change, especially constitutional change, is something which almost by definition carries risks and threats. That is one reason why it must be preceded by detailed explanation and consultation.

Unionists seem to have a fear of the Irish Constitution, or if not a fear then at least a serious distrust. This is due not just to Articles 2 and 3, which they know so well, and which are outside the remit of this paper, but to the fact that, unlike the British Constitution, Bunreacht na hÉireann is a single written document of recent vintage. They realize, moreover, that the 1937 Constitution is based largely on the Irish Free State Constitution of 1922 and to the extent that it is not this is because Éamon de Valera took advantage of the British royal family's abdication crisis in 1936 to eliminate all reference to the King in the Constitution and to abolish the office of Governor General.

The reason for unionist *caution* is perhaps even more deep-seated. Conscious that their position within the United Kingdom has been a precarious one for many years, they are wary of supposedly rigid verbal formulae in case these contain traps. The dominant unionist mentality is one which dislikes attributing authority to mere pieces of paper, preferring instead to engage in repeated declarations of allegiance to institutions, traditions and convictions. Theirs is indeed a conservative way of proceeding — *ad hoc,* incremental and evolutionary — and it helps to explain why unionists have been suspicious of so-called 'constitutional guarantees' and of documents such as the Anglo-Irish

Agreement of 1985, the Downing Street Declaration of 1993 and the Framework Documents of 1995. This caution is not based on ideas rooted in an irrelevant past, the view propounded by David Miller in his *Queen's Rebels*.[1] It is based on a more positive outlook which happens recently to have been on the defensive because of the dubious reputation of the unionist administration in Northern Ireland from 1920 to 1972. For an explanation of this outlook — the essence of the modern ideology of unionism — readers are referred to the study by Arthur Aughey entitled *Under Siege — Ulster Unionism and the Anglo-Irish Agreement*.[2]

CONSTITUTIONAL LEGISLATION

Of course unionists themselves have had to live with constitutional legislation since the very inception of the separate entity known as Northern Ireland.[3] But they have done so reluctantly. The Government of Ireland Act of 1920, which partitioned Ireland and created, but at the same time limited, the powers of the Belfast Parliament, was considered by many unionists between 1920 and 1972 primarily as the mechanism by which the South of Ireland left the United Kingdom rather than as the founding document of Northern Ireland. Likewise the Northern Ireland Constitution Act 1973, and the various pieces of legislation shoring up the direct rule arrangements (in particular the Northern Ireland Act 1974), tend to be viewed by unionists as akin to interim nuisances, in place because it has not yet proved possible to set up a new local assembly to replace Stormont. Annual renewal debates on the 1974 Act at Westminster provide good opportunities for unionists to call (at any rate until 1994) for harsher measures against terrorism and (still today) for an enhancement of local democracy in Northern Ireland.

This is not to deny that, like most groups, unionists will rely upon written constitutional laws when it suits them to do so. They have often appealed to the Act of Union of 1800 as a reason for resisting what might appear to be changes to the constitutional position of Northern Ireland. Mr Molyneaux and others challenged the Anglo-Irish Agreement of 1985 on this basis in the courts, though unsuccessfully.[4] Unionists have also taken cases under the European Convention on Human Rights on issues such as voting systems[5] and lack of protection for members of the security forces.[6] But such cases are the exceptions which prove the rule. In general unionists seem averse to putting their eggs into any particular constitutional basket. This may well be because they are only too aware of a crucial weakness in their constitutional creed: they believe in the doctrine of parliamentary sovereignty, because traditionally the English, as well of course as the Belfast, Parliaments have always been dominated by pro-Union parties, yet that very doctrine means that there can be no cast-iron guarantee that shifting majorities or new party policies will not put an end to the Union despite the wishes of unionists themselves. Unionists are reassured, however, by the very vagueness of the British Constitution: they cannot believe that parliamentary sovereignty would be allowed to override majoritarian wishes and centuries of history.

For the time being, therefore, unionists are naturally wary of condensing complex constitutional principles to numbered paragraphs in one written document, as this would risk compromising the position they have gradually won for themselves since the Plantations. In their view, and it is by no means an indefensible one, Northern Ireland, like the rest of the United Kingdom, is a modern democracy which has survived quite well on the foundation of some scattered constitutional laws and numerous constitutional conventions. Many of the latter concern the central core of the British Constitution, the monarchy, which is discussed below. At the heart of this approach to constitution-building is an adherence to historical precedent and a reluctance to introduce fundamentally new concepts. For Northern unionists the Republic of Ireland represents just such fundamental innovation: the break with the United Kingdom in 1920, followed by the exit from the Commonwealth in 1949, are antipathetic to all that unionists stand for and believe in.

Northern unionists are pressured into adopting this stance not just because they border a nation with different traditions. They also feel themselves increasingly isolated within the United Kingdom itself. In fact if they listen to the views of most Europeans and Americans they sense they are beleaguered on all sides. Appealing to the Britishness of their compatriots in Great Britain is no longer a sure way for them to gain support for their cause, a cause which many of them recognize has been almost fatally damaged by the activities of loyalist paramilitary groups, especially in the last three years of the troubles when these groups were responsible for more deaths than were the republican paramilitaries.[7]

Naturally there are advantages as well as disadvantages to being a separate jurisdiction such as Northern Ireland. One of the advantages is supposedly that the particular wishes of the local people can be taken into account when decisions are being made as to what laws to introduce for the area. One of the disadvantages is that the links with the parent jurisdiction inevitably become attenuated. Experience has shown that the former advantage is one which operates erratically: while it has resulted in the non-introduction of laws applicable elsewhere in the United Kingdom but which seemed genuinely unpopular in Northern Ireland (e.g. on abortion or the poll tax), it has not led to the introduction of laws even when there was clear majority support for them among local MPs or the people in general (e.g. on rights for disabled people or on protection against racial discrimination). In addition, the British Parliament has frequently foisted laws on Northern Ireland even when most of its residents and MPs are opposed to them. But the same can be said for regional areas of any unitary State: it may well happen, for example, that laws on divorce will be introduced in the Republic of Ireland even though the majority of people in the west of the country do not want them.

It needs to be acknowledged, furthermore, that Northern unionist perceptions of the South are themselves partly determined by unionists' own experiences of law and justice in the North. And the nature of those experiences can be difficult to internalize, especially if, in accordance with the views of one school of thought, the experiences of today are significantly different from those of twenty years ago. In a recent study Morison and Livingstone contend that the *real* Constitution of Northern Ireland is not at all like the one people read about:

> New forms of international and supranational order as well as the realities
> of the exercise of political power in the last two decades in a changing
> polity are not reflected in a constitutionalism which, even in its
> reforming guise, concentrates almost exclusively on traditional
> parliamentary mechanisms and their capacity to curb excessive power
> exercised by a domestic executive. Public power is now qualitatively
> different from what is described by traditional scholarship. And it is still
> changing.[8]

The authors suggest that lessons learned in Northern Ireland about the manner in which public power is exercised need to be taken on board in the rest of the United Kingdom. Morison and Livingstone label the current 'Constitution' of Northern Ireland, that which has operated since 1985, as a 'communicative' one, that is, one which uses 'communication mechanisms' such as community relations programmes or anti-discrimination laws to implement policies.[9] If there is any substance in this thesis, and many would agree that it bears close analysis, it suggests at the very least that for unionists to be satisfied with 'constitutional' arrangements in the South they will have to be assured that comparable 'communication' mechanisms are in place. There are of course some parallels between, in the North, the British Government's guidelines on Policy Appraisal and Fair Treatment and its Targeting Social Need programme and, in the South, the Irish Government's 'social partners' approach and the Programme for Renewal, but there remains a qualitative as well as a quantitative difference in the two polities in this respect.

So it can be argued that to Northern unionists a principal obstacle in the South to better relations with the North is, simply, the Republic's failure to emulate important features of the British way of doing things, however that may be characterized. In the constitutional sphere the features in question include parliamentary sovereignty (i.e. the fact that courts cannot strike down Acts of Parliament as being unconstitutional), the refusal to adopt a set of constitutional rights, the adherence to a first-past-the-post voting system at general elections and the role of the monarchy. A few words must now be devoted to each of these.

PARLIAMENTARY SOVEREIGNTY

Unionists believe fervently that Parliament (or, more strictly, the Queen in Parliament) has absolute power in the United Kingdom. They do not wish to live in a State where Parliament's pronouncements can be negated by the edict of unelected judges, however eminent or erudite those judges may be. Nor do they want their Parliament to be subservient to any other Parliament (i.e. the Dáil). European law-making institutions are tolerated because, somewhat ironically, they are not perceived as being threatening to the constitutional status of Northern Ireland (even though the power of those institutions to affect the substantive content of Northern Ireland law — and the potential for increasing that power — is immense).[10]

One of the difficulties with this view today is that in the United Kingdom the dominance of Parliament by members of the Government, or at any rate by members of the governing party, means that the former is no longer anything like as omnipotent as in previous times.[11] A startling manifestation of this occurred at the end of October 1995 when a handful of backbench Tory MPs at Westminster succeeded in derailing the Family Homes and Domestic Violence Bill even though the Bill had initially been proposed by the non-partisan Law Commission and had already received an unimpeded and uncontroversial passage through Parliament until the backbenchers' approach to the Lord Chancellor (prompted, even more alarmingly, by a national tabloid).[13]

At the same time the sovereignty of Parliament, or of the governing party, is being attacked from two distinct quarters. On the one hand, legislation and judgements emanating respectively from Brussels and Luxembourg are beginning severely to restrict Parliament's freedom to do what it wishes within the United Kingdom.[13] On the other, judges within Great Britain are themselves proving much more willing than in the past to side with private citizens and organizations when they are in dispute with the Government. The Law Lords currently in post are the most active in the history of the State. They have taken the area of law known as judicial review of administrative action to new heights.[14] They have also been willing to transpose into British domestic law European standards of justice, both those deriving from the European Union and those found in the European Convention on Human Rights (a creation of the Council of Europe in Strasbourg).[15]

The Republic of Ireland is also bound by the legislation and judgements issued in Brussels and Luxembourg. But an important difference is that the ratification of any European Treaty which conflicts with the Irish Constitution requires an amendment to that Constitution. This of course explains the referenda on the Treaty of Rome in 1972 (leading to the third amendment of the Constitution), on the Single European Act in 1987 (leading to the tenth amendment) and on the Maastricht Treaty in 1992 (leading to the eleventh amendment). Perversely, then, Northern unionists might be capable of persuasion that there is more likelihood of the Irish polity being able to resist undue European interference in the internal affairs of the country than of the English polity managing to do so. Ireland, of course, plays a different role in the European Union from that of the United Kingdom.

Northern unionists, if they examined the matter carefully, might well conclude that they stand to gain more, economically, socially and even politically, if they put themselves forward in Brussels as members of the Irish constitutency rather than of the British one.

Here, too, though, severe scepticism currently prevails. One of the most thoughtful of the unionist family, Robert McCartney MP, sees any suggestion of Europeanizing the Northern Ireland problem as mere hoodwinking. He was commenting on an article written for *The Irish News* by Albert Reynolds TD, where he had ventured the view that:

> We [presumably the whole of the people of Ireland] would prosper better by treating Ireland within the European Union as an island economy of five million people. A high degree of North/South economic integration can be achieved under appropriate consensual institutions without any prejudice to continuing differences over sovereignty.[16]

Mr McCartney's riposte was as follows:

> What, therefore, is the value of the so-called guarantee to retain the constitutional link with Britain when Northern Ireland would, in fact, form part of the national economy of the Irish Republic?... The present peace process of which the Declaration [of 1993], and articles such as that of Mr Reynolds, form such a part is not, in fact, a peace process at all. It is merely an organised and well planned progression along a pan-nationalist agenda for a united Ireland.[17]

In the Republic of Ireland, of course, the powers of the courts are already much more extensive than in any part of the United Kingdom. More extensive, indeed, than those of courts in most other liberal democracies, including France and the United States of America. Irish courts can pronounce upon the constitutionality of legislation not only before it is promulgated[18] but also afterwards.[19] By way of contrast, France enjoys only prior review, the United States only subsequent review and the United Kingdom no such review at all. Unionists, it can be safely assumed, are not in favour of judicial interference with democratically expressed wishes. But that stance may hold good only for as long as unionists themselves benefit from the traditional majoritarian form of democracy: if they were to become a minority group, either within the United Kingdom or within Ireland, they may well come to have a better appreciation of the admirable checks which judicial review of the constitutionality of legislation can place on authoritarianism.

NO CONSTITUTIONAL RIGHTS

There was of course a Bill of Rights enacted for England and Wales in 1689. But at no time was this extended to any part of Ireland[20] and in any event its content is not at all similar to that which would be contained in a Bill of Rights today (or even one enacted a century later, such as the first ten amendments to the United States Constitution, agreed in 1791, or the *Déclaration des Droits de l'Homme et du Citoyen*, promulgated in France in 1789). There is now a substantial body of support for the introduction of a Bill of Rights throughout the United Kingdom — voiced not just by civil libertarian pressure groups but also by parliamentarians and even judges — and in Northern Ireland the support is almost unanimous even if there is disagreement amongst political parties as to how precisely the Bill should be worded.[21] The Ulster Unionist and Democratic Unionist Parties have indicated their support in theory for a Bill of Rights, i.e. for constitutional protection of human rights, but have been short on specifics. They are nervous of provisions such as Articles 40 to 44 of the Irish Constitution ('Fundamental Rights') either because those provisions are not balanced by a set of fundamental duties[22] or because the rights conferred are not those to which unionists would themselves accord priority within society.

Unionists may also be suspicious of constitutional rights because they have lived through twenty five years of violence in Northern Ireland and are of the view that when members of the general public, or society's security forces, are truly under threat of indiscriminate attack it may be necessary to sacrifice, or at least qualify, some of the citizenry's human rights in order to achieve a higher goal, namely the elimination of terrorism. Hence the call within some unionist quarters in recent years for the reintroduction of internment without trial. A few unionists would undoubtedly perceive a Bill of Rights as a hindrance to an effective fight against terrorism. They need to be reminded, though, that a Bill of Rights is not automatically inconsistent with the enactment of 'emergency' laws to deal with a terrorist threat. Even the new interim Constitution of South Africa — accepted by members of the African National Congress — makes allowance for certain provisions in its chapter on fundamental rights to be suspended in times of emergency.[23] There are also principles of international law and practice which can be looked to when seeking to make emergency laws compatible with constitutional rights.[24]

The British Conservative Party, however, is against the introduction of a Bill of Rights for the United Kingdom and it is important to know the nature of its principal objection. It is that the present legal position is actually preferable to that which would exist were a Bill of Rights to be enacted. At the moment everyone in the United Kingdom has the right to do anything he or she wishes to do, provided only that it is not prohibited by law; under a Bill of Rights, so the argument goes, people would have the right to do only that which is specifically permitted by the Bill. There are valid counter-arguments to this position, not the least of which is that a Bill of Rights can expressly preserve existing rights while improving the mechanisms for enforcing those as well as newly created rights, but the strength of the Conservative position, probably shared by a large number of unionists in Northern Ireland, needs to be borne in mind. It serves to justify some of the restlessness which unionists feel when they are asked to have better relations with a State where the Constitution does talk about fundamental rights. Even when it is explained that the Republic of Ireland, like the United Kingdom, has introduced emergency laws to combat terrorism — sometimes, as in the case of the media ban, going much further than the United Kingdom's equivalents — unionists often remain unconvinced. This is an indication of the 'laager' mentality which, perhaps understandably, has developed over the last quarter of a century within Northern unionist circles. It will not be easily dismantled.

FIRST–PAST–THE–POST ELECTIONS

Great Britain has chosen to retain a first-past-the-post electoral system and even in Northern Ireland, where proportional representation is used for local authority elections and for European elections, the voting system for general Westminster elections is still on a first-past-the-post basis. There is no certainty that this will be changed anywhere in the United Kingdom even if the Labour Party wins the next general election there, for that party has promised merely to hold a referendum on the issue and its leader, Tony Blair, is himself as yet unpersuaded that proportional representation is to be preferred.

Articles 12.2.3, 16.2.5 and 18.5 of the Irish Constitution require the President, the Dáil and the Seanad all to be elected on a system of proportional representation by means of the single transferable vote. Given the unionists' experience of PR voting in elections in Northern Ireland over the last twenty years and more, this method of choosing political representatives is not likely to be a serious obstacle to better relations between North and South. The problems which arose on this score in the early days of Northern Ireland's history will most probably not recur. Today there is a fair amount of respect within the unionist camp, broadly defined, for the Republic's electoral system, and it has been persuasively defended by academic political scientists within the South.[25] Some unionists even look with envy at the Irish Constitution's provisions guaranteeing Seanad seats to representatives of the National University of Ireland and to Trinity College![26]

THE MONARCHY

There can be little doubt that loyalty to the Crown is still very strong within the unionist community in the North. In spite of the difficulties which the royal family has been experiencing of late in Great Britain, and in parts of the Commonwealth, there is no prospect whatsoever of Northern unionists opting to de-select the House of Windsor as the supplier of the British Head of State. Unionists are also glad to remind nationalists that various institutions in the South — academic, sporting and professional — are not averse to clinging to the epithet 'Royal' in an attempt to add lustre to their name.

It is difficult to be precise about what underpins steadfastness to the Crown amongst unionists, but a possible source is the symbolism the royal family provided during the second world war. The different experiences of the populations of Ireland North and South during that period still influence Northern unionist perceptions of the 'character' of society in the Republic. Unionists continue to look with disdain on the first amendment to the Irish Constitution made in 1939, which paved the way for treating the second world war as 'a time when there is taking place an armed conflict in which the State is not a participant but in respect of which...a national emergency exists affecting the vital interests of the State.'

The Protestantism of the royal family is another obvious reason for unionist loyalty, but perhaps not one that is an absolute prerequisite to continued unionist support: if Prince Charles were to obtain a divorce and marry a Catholic, this would be unlikely to shake the loyalty of many unionists to any great extent. Nor, even, would the disestablishment of the Church of England. Although the disestablishment of the Church of Ireland in 1869 did not go unchallenged in constitutional law,[27] its occurrence had few meaningful consequences for the position of unionists within the United Kingdom.

The flip side of unionist loyalty to the Crown is unionist suspicion of presidencies. This is the case not just with the presidency of the United States, where at least until recently the need to curry favour with Irish voters in that country (who are predominantly of an Irish nationalist persuasion) was deemed both by election candidates there and by unionists in Northern Ireland to be more important than conveying an understanding of the unionist position. The suspicion exists also in relation to the presidency in Ireland. Notwithstanding that the current President made quite clear at the time her opposition to the Anglo-Irish Agreement of 1985, and despite the huge popularity Mrs Robinson still enjoys in the Republic, Northern unionists cannot respect the transience of a presidency, even a figurehead one, to anything like the same degree that they can respect a monarchy. In this respect they have over 1,000 years of tradition on their side so it is hard to gainsay the sincerity of their feelings. At the same time, there is probably nothing in the provisions dealing with the presidency in the present Irish Constitution which Northern unionists would find objectionable *per se*. The oath which the President has to swear when taking up office would not cause any problems,[28] nor, given the limited nature of the President's powers in the first place, would the constitutional provision making the exercise of those powers non-reviewable by the Oireachtas and non-justiciable by the courts.[29]

Unionists, it is submitted, may be confused about the exact nature of their identity. They are most definitely not confused about their sense of loyalty, which is a different thing.[30] And it is possibly because the monarchy is such a central feature of the British Constitution, albeit that that Constitution is not codified in a single document, that Northern unionists harbour such deep distrust of the modern Irish Constitution. This seems to have been partially acknowledged by the Irish Government when, in *A New Framework for Agreement*, the document issued jointly by the British and Irish Governments in February 1995, it agreed to 'introduce and support proposals for change in the Irish Constitution to implement the commitments in the Joint Declaration [of 1993]'.[31] It may be revealing, therefore, to survey that Constitution to see which of its provisions are truly inimical to the unionist perspective. Articles 2 and 3, of course, are excluded from consideration.

BUNREACHT NA hÉIREANN

The Preamble to the Constitution is perhaps one of the most offensive parts in this regard, even though it does not have any substantive content. In particular, not many Northern Protestants or unionists would be impressed by the 'pluralism' of these two passages:

> In the name of the Most Holy Trinity, from Whom is all authority and to Whom, as our final end, all actions both of men and States must be referred...

and

> Gratefully remembering [our fathers'] heroic and unremitting struggle [through centuries of trial] to regain the rightful independence of our Nation...

There are theological and historical problems with these phrases in the eyes of unionists, problems not alleviated by the reference in the opening Article of the Constitution proper to 'the genius and traditions of the Irish Nation.' Such nationalism is unusual in modern democratic constitutions and is not found, for example, in the Grundrecht of Germany of 1949 or the Constitution of the Fifth French Republic of 1958.[32]

Article 7 of the Constitution stipulates what the flag of Ireland will be. While each nation is of course perfectly entitled to devise its own emblem, many Northern unionists are rather cynical about the inclusion of orange in the tricolour in view of the dwindling number of Protestants now living in the South. In any event, precluding any reference whatsoever to the Union Jack is virtually unthinkable for unionists. They also do not see the necessity for Article 8 of the Constitution in so far as it makes Irish the national, and first official, language of the country, especially when this is coupled with the provision in Article 25.4.6 which says that in the case of conflict between the texts of a law enrolled in both Irish and English the text in Irish shall prevail. But this does not mean that unionists are against the Irish language in and of itself. Campaigning for greater use of the Irish language is often seen as an anti-unionist ploy; in fact a large number of unionists can see beyond such tactics and appreciate the linguistic issue for what it is, an aspect of cultural heritage. For these unionists Terence Brown probably struck the nail on the head when he wrote:

> Irish, to be sure, remains and will remain as a resource for the creative imagination, a vital constituent of the life of small groups of committed individuals and local communities, a focus of dissentient radicalism, a humanistic resource and as a symbolic expression of the nation's sense of itself, rightly employed on official occasions. But it seems indisputable to me that for the great majority of citizens W. B. Yeats' famous formulation will increasingly have the ring of personal, regretful truth: 'Irish is my native language but it is not my mother tongue.[33]

Some unionists in the North do, however, treasure the language.[34] To encourage others to do so the challenge for people in the South is to disengage the language from any attempt to hijack it for political ends. As unionist Councillor Chris McGimpsey has written:

> Unionists can point to developments during this century as a period when the demand for the separation of our island from the rest of the United Kingdom was couched in terms of the demand for a Gaelic, Catholic and nationalist Ireland. The language has been linked in the minds of both the Irish majority and the Irish minority with a specific political agenda. This is something which, notwithstanding the rhetoric of Irish republicanism, seems to hold no place for Irish unionists.[37]

In that part of the Irish Constitution ranging from Articles 9 to 39 there is precious little which any Northern unionist could reasonably find objectionable and much that he or she might well applaud. Article 16's provisions on the size of constituencies, Article 18's on the composition of the Seanad and Article 27's on referenda are, it could be argued, forward-looking and imaginative. The express provisions on the Seanad's power to delay legislation, on emergency Bills and on the Government's right to be heard in both Houses of the Oireachtas are also very clear and worthy of imitation. By way of contrast, few today are prepared to defend the composition and powers of Britain's House of Lords, a body certain to be radically reformed if the Labour Party wins the next election.

Unionists might even be heartened by Article 38.3.1, which allows the creation of special courts 'in cases where it may be determined...that the ordinary courts are inadequate to secure the effective administration of justice, and the preservation of public peace and order.' Nationalist criticisms of Diplock Courts in the North (now required to be somewhat muted in view of the ground-breaking research on the courts' operation recently published by Jackson and Doran[36]) are easy to counter by citing equally convincing criticisms of the Special Criminal Court in the South, some of which emanated from Mrs Mary Robinson when she was a legal academic.[37]

ARTICLES 40-44

The part of the Constitution dealing with Fundamental Rights (Articles 40-44) does contain several phrases which grate upon Northern unionists. Although it may only be of academic interest, Article 40.2.1 is objectionable insofar as it disables any person from accepting a title of honour (e.g. 'Alderman', 'the Right Honourable' — designating membership of the Privy Council — or a knighthood) except with the prior approval of the Government. Article 40.6.1.i seems to go too far in requiring the State to endeavour to ensure that organs of public opinion such as the press 'shall not be used to undermine...the authority of the State.'

Article 41, on the family, elevates that institution to one which possesses 'inalienable and prescriptive rights, antecedent and superior to all positive law' and guarantees protection of the family 'in its constitution and authority.' In Section 2.2 the Article requires the State to endeavour to ensure 'that mothers shall not be obliged by economic necessity to engage in labour to the neglect of their duties in the home.'

Section 3, of course, goes on to pledge protection of the family 'against attack' and to prohibit the dissolution of marriage. All of these provisions, it is submitted, are antipathetic to Northern unionists, but not to a degree that stands in the way of the development of better relations.

It is not, of course, that unionists are less prepared to recognize that families can play an important role in any society, or that in practice most mothers do not still play a larger role than fathers within the home, but unionists do not see the necessity for such strongly worded provisions in a modern constitution; apart from anything else the words seem to devalue units that are less than whole families and individuals who do not happen to belong to a meaningful family. The Constitution's bias in this respect is compounded by Article 42.1, which acknowledges that the primary and natural educator of the child is the family, and by Article 42.4, which requires the State to provide educational facilities 'with due regard, however, for the rights of parents, especially in the matter of religious and moral formation.' The result of the November 1995 referendum on divorce, however narrow the majority in favour of reform, will have gone some way towards reassuring unionists and Protestants in Northern Ireland that the Republic's laws on personal matters can accommodate followers of non-Catholic teaching. But, as unionists such as Chris McGimpsey have been quick to point out, the significance of this change can easily be overestimated.

Article 44, although amended in 1972 so as to delete the special recognition given to 'the Holy Catholic Apostolic and Roman Church as the guardian of the Faith possessed by the great majority of the citizens' (as well as the recognition given to other Churches, the Church of Ireland, the Presbyterian Church, the Methodist Church, the Religious Society of Friends and the Jewish Congregations), still opens inappropriately (for a Northern unionist) with the words 'The State acknowledges that the homage of public worship is due to Almighty God. It shall hold His Name in reverence, and shall respect and honour religion.' Certainly Presbyterians do not tend to approve of the inclusion of such sentiments in as vital a document as the nation's Constitution. At the same time it is unlikely that many of them would go so far as to encourage adoption of the formulation used in the first amendment to the Constitution of the United States, agreed in 1791: 'Congress shall make no law respecting an establishment of religion, or prohibiting the free exercise thereof.' This represents a complete hands-off approach to State-Church relations which can itself lead to severe difficulties.

The unionist who reads the remaining sections of Article 44 may be reasonably reassured that religious rights within the Irish Constitution are by no means synonymous with Catholic rights. Articles 44.2.1 and 44.2.3 are quite explicit:

> Freedom of conscience and the free profession and practice of religion are, subject to public order and morality, guaranteed to every citizen.

and

> The State shall not impose any disabilities or make any discrimination on the ground of religious profession, belief or status.

There has not as yet been much litigation in the Republic on these provisions, and in particular the legitimacy of legal provisions which prescribe different conditions for the celebration of a marriage depending on the religion of the parties concerned, or of provisions restricting Sunday trading, has still not been fully tested.[38] As in England, the latter is an area where European Union standards may ultimately have an influence on the way in which laws are framed. Article 44.2.3 may also mean that any restriction on Ministers of religion standing as candidates for Parliament would be invalid: at present Rev. William McCrae and Rev. Ian Paisley are the only Ministers serving as MPs in Westminster because their Church, the Free Presbyterian Church, is not one of the ones grounding exclusion under the House of Commons Disqualification Act 1975.

Northern unionists may worry that the Republic's legal system does not go as far as Northern Ireland's legal system in protecting people against religious discrimination. Article 44.2.3 of the Constitution, for instance, seems to outlaw only discrimination by the State. It should be noted, in addition, that the Republic's legislation on unfair dismissals deems any dismissal from employment on the ground of religious opinion to be automatically unfair.[39] But this does not begin to equate with the Fair Employment (NI) Acts 1976-1989 which, although also confined to the employment sector (unlike legislation on gender discrimination, which extends to education and to access to goods, facilities and services), protects applicants for jobs as well as current employees and prohibits direct and indirect discrimination falling short of outright dismissal. The

Republic, however, can boast better laws on discrimination based on grounds of ethnic origin, nomadism or sexual orientation.

In neither part of Ireland does employment law protect people against religious discrimination within the education sector: just as the Fair Employment (NI) Acts specifically exempt schools from the scope of the Acts' control, so Articles 44.2.1 and 44.2.3 of the Irish Constitution appear to take second place to Article 44.2.5, which guarantees to every religious denomination 'the right to manage its own affairs.' As interpreted by the Supreme Court in *McGrath and O Ruairc v Trustees of the College of Maynooth*[40] the latter sub-section appears to give *carte blanche* to religious educational establishments to discriminate on irrational grounds. In the words of one learned commentator this leads to an odd result:

> The State may not, by statute or administrative action, make continuing religious allegiance a ground for dismissal from the public service or from private employment, since to do so would violate Article 44.2.3. But if it hands over to religious denominations money used for paying teachers' salaries, both it and they are free from constitutional constraints. There is surely something 'Kafka-esque' about such a situation.[41]

JUDICIAL INTERPRETATIONS

However, even though the actual wording of any Article in the Irish Constitution may not present any real obstacle to better relations between South and North, Northern unionists may still be anxious that the way in which the Constitution is interpreted by the judiciary in the Republic could jeopardize unionist trust in the country's commitment to pluralism. In particular there may be an anxiety that principles of 'natural law' will be used by the Irish judges to distort the *prima facie* effect of constitutional provisions. There are, of course, several judgements by Irish judges which provide evidence of the influence of natural law on their reasoning.[42] Kennedy CJ appealed to natural law when, in his dissenting opinion in *The State (Ryan) v Lennon,* he objected to various amendments to the Constitution of the Irish Free State Act 1922:

> ...every act, whether legislative, executive or judicial, in order to be lawful under the Constitution, must be capable of being justified under the authority thereby declared to be derived from God.[43] From this it seems

clear that, if any legislation of the Oireachtas (including any purported amendment of the Constitution) were to offend against that acknowledged ultimate Source from which the legislative authority has come through the people to the Oireachtas, as, for instance, if it were repugnant to the Natural law, such legislation would be necessarily unconstitutional and invalid, and it would be, therefore, absolutely null and void and inoperative.[44]

Another reference is that by Walsh J in *McGee v Attorney-General:*

Articles 40, 41, 42 and 44 of the Constitution all fall within that section of the Constitution which is called 'Fundamental Rights'. Articles 41, 42 and 43 emphatically reject the theory that there are no rights without laws, no rights contrary to law and no rights anterior to law. They indicate that justice is placed above the law and acknowledge that natural rights, or human rights, are not created by law but that the Constitution confirms their existence and gives them protection. The individual has natural and human rights over which the State has no authority; and the family, as the natural primary and fundamental group of society, has rights as such which the State cannot control.[45]

As has been pointed out, there is a logical inconsistency in a written Constitution ceding authority to a vague and unwritten natural law.[46] It could even lead to a situation where the judges might decide that a constitutional amendment which has been approved in a referendum cannot be incorporated into the Constitution because it is in breach of those judges' understanding of natural law.

To some degree unionist and Protestant fears in this regard may have been relieved by the Supreme Court judgement earlier this year in the case concerning the constitutionality of the Regulation of Information (Services Outside the State for Termination of Pregnancies) Bill, where Hamilton CJ stated quite explicitly that the court did not accept the argument that natural law is the fundamental law of the State or that the people could not amend the Constitution unless such amendment were compatible with natural law.[47] Instead he reiterated the view that in interpreting the Constitution the courts must apply 'their ideas of prudence, justice and charity'. A cynical unionist, especially one with legal knowledge, might still not be convinced that this approach totally banishes the influence of Catholic morality from judicial reasoning in the Republic, but it certainly goes some way towards lessening the weight of that influence.

A further difficulty, though, is that many unionists see a gap between the rhetoric of Articles 40-44 and the reality of matters on the ground. This is particularly true as regards Article 40.1, which rather grandly provides as follows:

> All citizens shall, as human persons, be held equal before the law.
> This shall not be held to mean that the State shall not in its enactments have due regard to differences of capacity, physical and moral, and of social functions.

While this section reads well, the fact is that Irish courts have shown a marked reluctance to apply it:

> They have given it a restricted ambit; they prefer to decide cases on other grounds; and they have often justified statutory discriminations by reasoning that does not probe very deeply[48]...[I]n contrast with their United States counterparts the Irish courts have almost invariably shown great deference to legislative judgment...many of the Irish decisions seem to proceed on this basis [that any justification that the courts can conjure up will suffice].[49]

Space does not permit an analysis of the case-law on this point, save to relate that homosexuals,[50] married couples[51] and disabled people[52] have all failed, in different circumstances, to invoke the protection of this section. 'Equality before the law', however, is a notoriously slippery concept to apply, as the Americans have found in the morass of litigation engendered by the 14th Amendment to the US Constitution.

The Irish judges have been more dynamic in relation to Article 40.3 of the Constitution, the first two sub-sections of which have been the foundation for the construction of a whole panoply of so-called 'unenumerated' rights:

> 1. The State guarantees in its laws to respect, and, as far as practicable, by its laws to defend and vindicate the personal rights of the citizen.
>
> 2. The State shall, in particular, by its laws protect as best it may from unjust attack and, in the case of injustice done, vindicate the life, person, good name and property rights of every citizen.'

The law books explain that judges have taken advantage of loose wording in those provisions ('as far as practicable', 'personal rights', 'in particular') to create such constitutional rights as the rights to strike, to privacy, to access to the courts, to travel, to marry and found a family, and to fair procedures in decision-making.[53]

Unionists, I suspect, are wary of such judicial activism, especially when it is grounded, as occasionally it is, in the vague 'Directive Principles of Social Policy' listed in Article 45. Although many other constitutions include similar directive principles, again non-justiciable,[54] anyone of a conservative disposition would be reluctant to see unelected judges given such free rein to interpret Parliament's laws in accordance with those principles: permitting judges to second-guess the policies laid down by Parliament tends to blur the distinction between two discrete functions of government, the legislative and the judicial, thereby undermining one of the basic tenets of common law constitutionalism, the separation of powers. In this respect the strictures mentioned earlier in this paper in relation to conservative opposition to the growth of judicial review in the United Kingdom are applicable here too. It is difficult, on the other hand, to point to any particular decisions of the Irish courts referring to Articles 40.3 or 45 which are guaranteed to raise unionist ire: the decisions on abortion, it is submitted, are *sui generis* and it is to be hoped that the amendments to Article 40.3.3 made as a result of the referenda on that subject in 1983 and 1992 have laid controversy to rest for some time. The law on abortion in Northern Ireland, when closely examined, is none too clear either.[55]

OTHER FEATURES
OF THE SOUTHERN LEGAL SYSTEM

Unionists are prepared to acknowledge that the legal system of the South of Ireland has come a long way in the past seventy five years. It has moved from being a virtual clone of the English system to having its own distinct character. However, there is often considerable annoyance in the North when crticisms are made in the South of aspects of the Northern legal system which, although imperfect and maybe out of step with internationally required standards, are at least more acceptable than corresponding aspects of the Southern legal system. Applying double standards, say unionists, is a common phenomenon when Southerners pass comments on the Northern prison system, on the rights of detainees in RUC stations or on legal aid provision.

Accountability mechanisms for the police and other public authorities are also, generally speaking, not as effective in the South as in the North. Unionist dismay at what they view as Southern hypocrisy has frequently crystallized when extradition requests regarding persons arrested in the South have been refused. Even though lawyers may be able to explain to unionists that such refusals are soundly based *in law,* there is definitely a feeling in that camp, not yet fully dispelled despite the South's ratification of the European Convention on the Suppression of Terrorism, that the Republic's judges have in effect sacrificed a community's cry for justice on the altar of legal technicalities.

'The pot calling the kettle black' is an accusation which unionists can raise against commentators in the South quite regularly and justifiably. South of the border miscarriages of justice are perhaps more frequent, police malpractice more common, the plight of children and other vulnerable groups more serious and access to justice more restricted than in the North. For better relations to be cemented between the two parts of the island it may be sensible to set up some kind of informal commission which could look at ways in which each legal system could learn from the other for their overall mutual benefit. At present the Irish Association of Law Teachers (which comprises legal academics throughout Ireland) is supporting the production of a 'Compendium of Law in Ireland' with such an aim in mind. This may also enable the South and the North to pay greater attention to internationally proclaimed standards of justice.

The 'backwardness', as some unionists would impolitely call it, of the Irish legal system is perhaps best exemplified by the way in which it regulates the education sector. This paper has already briefly referred to the 1937 Constitution's provisions on education, which are extremely general in nature. There are not, however, many other instructive provisions in Irish law. Indeed one commentator sums up the position thus:

> There is no Education Act, but there are a number of legislative measures affecting different parts of the system... Many of the regulations issued by the Department of Education have no statutory basis but are considered to have the force of law. The main administrative consequences of the absence of legislation are that new regulations are not examined or debated by the Oireachtas and official documents are not required to be published. Long-term planning is also made very difficult, because there are no basic aims governing the administration.[56]

It would seem that whatever the strict legal position in the South the education sector is still unduly permeated by a Catholic ethos for any unionist to be comfortable with it. The growth of multi-denominational schools has gone some way towards reducing the discomfort, as of course have the various exchanges and joint ventures which have taken place between Catholic schools in the South and State (i.e. largely Protestant) schools in the North, under the auspices of, amongst others, the Co-operation North organization. But there can be no denying the continuing distrust which lingers in Northern Protestant/unionist hearts concerning the 'pluralist' nature of the Southern education sector. It is worth repeating the conclusion of the Opsahl Inquiry on this issue:

> In the light of the widespread and deep fear and mistrust we encountered
> among Northern Protestants about the Catholic nature of Southern
> society and the intentions of Southern people with regard to Northern
> Ireland, we believe that the government of the Republic of Ireland must
> move — and be seen to move — to make good the claim in the 1916
> Declaration that it cherishes all the children of the Irish nation equally.[57]

SPECIAL LEGAL POSITION
OF IRELAND IN UK LAW

Notwithstanding that the Republic of Ireland is an independent State, it is not treated in the same way as other countries, even other countries within the European Union, in the eyes of United Kingdom law. Technically, Ireland is not a foreign country in those eyes, nor are citizens of the Republic 'aliens' in terms of United Kingdom immigration law.[58] Indeed the British Islands (the United Kingdom, the Isle of Man and the Channel Islands) forms together with the Republic of Ireland, a 'Common Travel Area', which is the reason why journeys within that area by persons resident there have not been subject to immigration requirements (except those applied under the Prevention of Terrorism Acts).[59] Likewise, although citizens of the Republic of Ireland are not automatically citizens of the United Kingdom, they are entitled to vote, subject to residence requirements, in British elections and to stand as candidates for election. (Of course the same applies *vice-versa.*) Under legislation passed in 1976 certain acts committed in either part of Ireland constitute criminal offences triable in either jurisdiction[60] and under a little known provision peculiar to Northern Irish law the judges in Northern Ireland are presumed to know the law of the Republic of Ireland in the same way as they are presumed to know the law of England and Wales (but not of Scotland).[61] There have also, of course, been special arrangements for extradition between the two nations, even if these have not always operated smoothly.[62]

One lesson which can be drawn from these special legal arrangements between the United Kingdom and Ireland is that their existence does not in any way undermine the independence of either nation. Nor was this the case when there was a monetary union throughout these islands. It could be contended that the effects of membership of the European Union, especially after the Maastricht Treaty of 1992, are much more far-reaching for both countries in this regard. At present a lot more could be done to cement the links, especially between the Republic of Ireland and Northern Ireland, without in any way endangering either jurisdiction's legal and constitutional autonomy. This was recently acknowledged, though not elaborated upon, in the inaugural professorial lecture of Northern Ireland's leading expert on local constitutional law.[63] But soundings taken within the various unionist communities would suggest, as would a study of relevant writings, that Northern unionists may first need to be further reassured of their jurisdiction's autonomy and *raison d'être* before they will be persuaded to develop better relations with, or make meaningful gestures of reconciliation towards, their neighbours in the South.

NOTES

1   Dublin: Gill and Macmillan, 1978.

2   Belfast: Blackstaff Press, 1989, see pp. 20-24.

3   For an account of this legislation see Brigid Hadfield, *The Constitution of Northern Ireland*, Belfast: SLS Legal Publications (NI), 1989.

4   *Ex parte Molyneaux* [1986] 1 W.L.R. 331.

5   *Lindsay and others v UK* Applic. No 8364/78; 15 *DR* 247 (1979).

6   E.g. *X v UK and Ireland* Applic. No. 9348/81, (1983) 5 *European Human Rights Reports* 504 and *M v UK and Ireland* Applic. No. 9837/82, 47 *DR* 27 (1986).

7   The Annual Reports of the Chief Constable of the RUC for 1992-94 show that loyalist paramilitaries killed 123 persons while republican paramilitaries killed 96.

8   J. Morison and S. Livingstone, *Reshaping Public Power: Northern Ireland and the British Constitutional Crisis*, London: Sweet & Maxwell, 1995, at p.viii.

9   They contrast this period with that of the 'mechanical' Constitution 1922-72 and the 'organic' Constitution 1972-85.

10   Unionists cannot have thought much of the European Court of Justice's decision in *Johnston v Chief Constable of the RUC* [1987] QB 129, where the court held that the Secretary of State for Northern Ireland could not rely solely upon 'national security' as a ground for exempting Sir John Hermon from his legal duty to treat female police officers in the same way as male police officers as regards access to firearm training.

11   For a recent and perceptive examination of this trend see Andrew Marr, *Ruling Britannia*, London: Michael Joseph, 1995.

12   *Daily Mail*, 23-27 October 1995.

13   For an example see the case decided in October 1995 involving Mr Richardson, a male pensioner who successfully argued before the European Court of Justice that it was unlawful discrimination for him to be charged for his medical prescriptions.

14   See, most recently, Brigid Hadfield (ed.), *Judicial Review: A Thematic Approach*, Dublin: Gill and Macmillan, 1995.

15   See *R v Secretary of State for Employment, ex parte EOC* [1994] 1 All ER 910, where the Law Lords struck down a provision of the Employment Protection Consolidation Act 1978 for being in breach of European Union standards on sex equality, and the judgement of Dyson J in the case of the five IRA men who challenged the Home Secretary's decision to delay a parole decision after they had spent nearly twenty years in prison. *The Times*, 30 September 1995.

16   *The Irish News*, 15 September 1994.

17   'Sovereignty and Seduction' in John Wilson Foster (ed.), *The Idea of the Union*, Belfast: Belcouver Press, 1995, at p.67.

18   Article 26.

19   Article 34.

20   Geoffrey Lock, 'The 1689 Bill of Rights', *Political Studies* (1989), XXXVII, 540-561.

21   See the coverage of this topic in Andy Pollak (ed.), *A Citizen's Inquiry — The Opsahl Report on Northern Ireland*, Dublin: Lilliput Press for Initiative '92, 1993.

22   Article 9.2 provides that 'Fidelity to the nation and loyalty to the State are fundamental political duties of all citizens' but mention of 'nation' and 'State' simply serve to exacerbate unionist opposition in this context.

23   Section 34 of the 1994 Constitution (to be revised in 1996). A state of emergency must be expressly declared, but the need for the declaration can be challenged in court. A valid declaration can permit detention without any appearance before a judge for up to ten days.

24   See, for example, the Paris Minimum Standards of Human Rights Norms in a State of Emergency, approved by the International Law Association in 1984 (and setting out the non-derogable rights and freedoms to which individuals remain entitled even during states of emergency): Richard B Lillich, (1985) 79 *American Journal of International Law* 1072-81.

25   E.g. Michael Gallagher, 'Does Ireland Need a New electoral System?' in *Irish Political Studies*, 2, 1987, pp.27-48.

26   Article 18.4.1 (each institution has three seats within the sixty-member body).

27   *Ex parte Selwyn* (1872) 36 *JP Jo* 54. This was an application by a Canon of the Church for a court order requiring the Lord President of the Council to petition Queen Victoria to obtain a judicial decision regarding the validity of her assent to the Irish Church Disestablishment Act 1869. Under this Act nearly half of the property owned by the Church of Ireland (£7 million) was confiscated by the Government.

28   'In the presence of Almighty God I do solemnly and sincerely promise and declare that I will maintain the Constitution of Ireland and uphold its laws, that I will fulfil my duties faithfully and conscientiously in accordance with the Constitution and the law, and that I will dedicate my abilities to the service and welfare of the people of Ireland. May God direct and sustain me.' (Article 12.8)

29   Article 13.8.1.

30   Cf. Terence Brown in 'British Ireland', in Edna Longley (ed.) *Culture in Ireland — Division or Diversity*, p.74: 'The Unionist is loyal to the British Crown as the symbolic expression of the constitutional reality of the British state in whose commonwealth the citizen and subject feels his or her interests are most likely to be protected. His or her identity is a different matter. And a rather confused matter it is.'

31   Para.21.

32   See S. E. Finer, V. Bogdanor and B. Rudden, *Comparing Constitutions*, Oxford: Clarendon Press 1994.

33   'British Ireland', note 31 above, pp.78-9.

34   As was evidenced to the Opsahl Inquiry: see note 22 above, p.122.

35   *The Irish Language and the Unionist Tradition*, proceedings of a seminar held at the Ulster People's College, Belfast, 9 May 1992, p.8.

36   *Judge Without Jury — Diplock Trials in the Adversary System*, Oxford: Clarendon Press, 1995.

27   See 'The Protection of Human Rights in the Republic of Ireland', ch.6 in Colin
      Campbell (ed.), *Do We Need a Bill of Rights?*, London: Temple Smith, 1980. See
      too Desmond Clarke, 'Emergency Legislation, Fundamental Rights and Article
      28.3.3 of the Irish Constitution' [1977] *Irish Jurist* 217.

28   See James Casey, *Constitutional Law in Ireland*, London: Sweet & Maxwell, (2nd
      ed), 1992, pp.557-563.

39   S.6(2)(c).

40   [1979] I.L.R.M. 166.

41   Casey, note 39 above, pp. 571-2.

42   The main proponent in recent times is Mr Justice Roderick O'Hanlon, now
      retired. See, for instance, his 'Natural Rights and the Irish Constitution' (1993)
      11 *Irish Law Times* 8 and 'The Judiciary and the Moral Law' *ibid.* 129.

43   See now Article 6.1 of the 1937 Constitution: 'All powers of government,
      legislative, executive and judicial, derive, under God, from the people, whose
      right it is to designate the rulers of the State and, in final appeal, to decide
      all questions of national policy, according to the requirements of the common
      good.'

44   [1935] I.R. 170 at p.204.

45   [1974] I.R. 284 at p.310.

46   See Desmond M Clarke, 'Natural Law and Constitutional Consistency', chap.2
      in G. Quinn, A. Ingram and S. Livingstone, *Justice and Legal Theory in Ireland,*
      Dublin: Oak Tree Press, 1995. Also Clarke's 'The Role of Natural Law in Irish
      Constitutional Law' [1981] *Irish Jurist* 187.

47   See the judgement set out in full in *The Irish Times,* 13 May 1995.

48   Casey, note 39 above, p.360.

49   *Ibid.* p.363.

50   *Norris v Attorney-General* [1984] I.R. 36.

51   *Murphy v Attorney-General* [1982] I.R. 241.

52   *Draper v Attorney-General* [1984] I.R. 277.

53   See generally J. M. Kelly, *The Irish Constitution*, (3rd) ed Dublin: Butterworths,
      1994.

54   For instance the Constitutions of India and Namibia.

55   See Ann Furedi (ed.), *The Abortion Law in Northern Ireland: Human Rights and
      Reproductive Choice,* Belfast: Family Planning Association, 1995.

56   David Alvey, *Irish Education — The Case for Reform*, Dublin: Church & State
      Books, Belfast: Athol Books, 1991, at p.79.

57   *A Citizens' Inquiry*, note 22 above, p.120.

58   British Nationality Act 1981, s.50(1).

59   Immigration Act 1971, s.1(3), s.9 and Sch.4.

60   Criminal Law Jurisdiction Act 1976 (UK) and Criminal Law (Jurisdiction) Act
      1976 (Ireland). The former Act was used for the first time in October 1995 to
      justify a visit by three Irish judges to Enniskillen for the purpose of taking
      evidence from a witness in Northern Ireland in a case involving a defendant
      charged in the South with attempted murder in the North.

61   S.114(2) of the Judicature (NI) Act 1978 reads: 'Without prejudice to any other statutory provision or to any rule of law or practice, in proceedings before a court in Northern Ireland judicial notice may be taken of the law of England and Wales or of the law of the Republic of Ireland.'

62   See Colm Campbell, 'Extradition to Northern Ireland: Prospects and Problems' (1989) 52 *Modern Law Review* 585-621.

63   Lecture by Prof. Brigid Hadfield at Queen's University, Belfast, 31 October 1995.

THE ROLE OF THE CATHOLIC CHURCH IN THE REPUBLIC OF IRELAND

1922 – 1995

DERMOT KEOGH

UNIVERSITY COLLEGE, CORK

PROVINCES AND DIOCESES OF IRELAND
Irish Catholic Directory

CONTENTS

INTRODUCTION

THE IRISH CATHOLIC CHURCH, or more specifically the activities of certain individuals, came to command in early autumn 1995 a large number of column inches in the quality and in the 'yellow' press. Programmes on television and radio, including the main news bulletins, have been led by stories which might, earlier in the history of the State, have been described as 'giving scandal' to the laity. There was much discussion in the media of a 'Church in crisis' and of a Church 'in decline'. While it may be too early to speak of a paradigm shift in the place of the Catholic Church in Irish society, it was clear that a high level of demoralization existed among the laity, male and female religious, and the diocesan clergy. It was unlikely that at times members of the hierarchy were immune from such feelings of demoralization.

The cumulative impact of the various scandals — and more particularly the collective episcopal response to the handling of the scandals — had created a major credibility problem for the Irish hierarchy, probably unprecedented in the history of twentieth century Irish Catholicism.[1] An opinion poll in *The Sunday Tribune* on 1 October 1995 headlined: '75% lack confidence in Bishops'. Whatever about the scientific accuracy of the survey, it presented as fact the finding that only 25 per cent of people had total or a great deal of confidence in Church leaders.[2] The paper stated that 'a staggering 75% of people have mixed, or little or no confidence at all in their church leaders'.[3] Based on a survey of 1,200 adults, it also revealed that only 11.5 per cent of people between the ages of eighteen and thirty four had total or great confidence in Church leaders.[4] The table, reproduced below, shows in greater detail the data covering 'confidence by age group'.

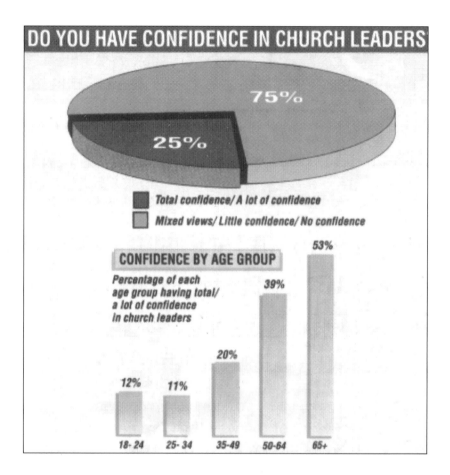

While opinion poll results are all too easily converted into 'facts', such findings could not be lightly dismissed as an aberration. In the mid-1990s the leadership of the Catholic Church was in crisis. The depth of that crisis was reflected in a letter I received from a religious who has devoted a lifetime to the work of the Church: 'What do you make of the problems that have overtaken the church (and society) in Ireland? .... Is it all in full decline?' That such a person should be formulating such a question is evidence of the gravity of the crisis which continued to grow in the autumn of 1995. Irish Catholicism appeared to be a long distance from the celebratory mood of autumn 1979 when John Paul II became the first Pope to visit Ireland.

CHURCH AND STATE IN IRELAND
PRELIMINARY OBSERVATIONS

In his widely esteemed work *Church and State in Modern Ireland 1923-1979*, Professor John Whyte concluded that Ireland was not a theocratic State.[5] He also rejected the view that the Church was just another interest group (like the farmers or the trade union movement). Professor Whyte did not find it easy to provide a satisfactory intermediary model:

> The difficulty is that the hierarchy exerts influence not on a *tabula rasa* but on a society in which all sorts of other influences are also at work. Party traditions can affect the bishops's power; so can change in the climate of opinion; so can the nature of the issues on which they are seeking to exert pressure. The best answer to the question 'how much influence does the hierarchy possess in Irish politics?' is that no simple answer is possible: it depends on the circumstances. This may sound an answer disappointingly lacking in precision, but it corresponds to the reality of things: any more definite answer would do violence to the evidence. [6]

This passage appeared far too cautious and tentative when it was first published in 1971.

Mr Noel Browne, a former Minister for Health in the inter-party Government between 1948 and 1951, has presented the argument frequently that the hierarchy exercised extensive influence over the political life of the Irish State. He puts forward the view in his memoirs that in 1950–51 there existed a 'conspiracy to subvert my implementation of the free no-means-test mother and child scheme which the 1947 Act had authorised.' He identified John Charles McQuaid, who was the Archbishop of Dublin from 1940 to 1971, as one of the main actors in that conspiracy.[7] This episode — known as the Mother and Child crisis — is perceived by Browne to have been the most flagrant and most blatant example of the use of episcopal power to have been comprehensively documented in the entire history of the State. This view has been disputed by a number of his contemporaries.[8] It will be referred to in greater detail later in the paper (see pp. 130 – 134) John Whyte and Noel Browne have influenced very significantly images of Church-State relations in the country.

Yet, for an area of such central importance, the topic has not attracted that many academic studies. Among the most important recent studies, Dr Tom Inglis has provided a sociological view of the Catholic Church in Ireland. His work looked at the Church:

> … not as a voluntary institution to which people are freely committed, but as a coercive and dominating power to which people have become allied in their own rational, instrumental struggle to attain more immediate, worldly ends. In other words, although Irish Catholics may adhere to the rules and regulations of the Church in order to attain salvation, this can be analytically separated from the more immediate, instrumental struggle to attain possessions, positions and prestige.[9]

Dr Inglis presents a view of a coercive institution where 'a rigid adherence to the teachings and practice of the Church has been the dominant type of ethical behaviour among modern Irish Catholics.' More recently, sociologist Dr Tony Fahey, has made an important contribution in his essay 'Catholicism and Industrial Society in Ireland'.[10]

Professor Patrick Corish's *The Irish Catholic Experience* is an important work.[11] In the context of historical scholarship, I might mention two of my own books on Church-State relations: *The Vatican, the Bishops and Irish Politics, 1919-1939* and *Ireland and the Vatican — the Politics and Diplomacy of Church-State Relations, 1922-1960*.[12]

Professor Desmond Clarke, a leading Irish philosopher, has written a series of important essays on Church and State which raise fundamental questions.[13] Professor Patrick Hannon, Professor of Moral Theology at Maynooth, has written an excellent and timely study on Church, State, Morality and Law.[14] In a more popular vein, Fr Joe Dunn, published *No Lions in the Hierarchy — An Anthology of Sorts*.[15] Seán Mac Réamoinn's edited volume of essays, *Authority in the Church*, was added to a growing body of literature providing a series of critiques of the Catholic Church in Ireland in the mid-1990s.[16] Many other essays and titles could be added to this list.[17]

The Catholic press has also provided a range of critical reflections on the progress of the Church. (See Appendix II for a list of religious press in Ireland.) The leading Catholic magazines in Ireland set a consistently high standard. They deservedly enjoy a wide and critical readership.[18]

Despite the publication of a range of work — memoirs, historical monographs, sociological studies and philosophical theses — scholars have yet to bring to public attention findings based on new State archival material and the personal papers of politicians which could inform contemporary debate in this country on Church-State issues.[19]

A large number of Catholic bishops are to be congratulated for the progressive approach that they have taken towards the preservation of historical records. Resources have been made available for the cataloguing of diocesan archives. Scholars have been warmly encouraged to work on those papers.[20] However, historians are still hampered in their work by the continued closure of archival collections central to a comprehensive analysis of this area. Where myth so easily substitutes for empirical findings, it is important to advance the study of Church-State relations as expeditiously as possible.[21] It is incumbent upon every citizen to remain open to new historical findings, even when such findings challenge us to question and to modify our respective positions.

DESCRIPTION AND PURPOSE
OF THIS OVERVIEW

This paper will attempt to provide a brief overview of the role played by the Catholic Church in the foundation and in the building of the Irish State. It will focus on:

- The development of the relationships between Irish radical nationalists and the Church.

- The role played by the Catholic Church in the securing of popular legitimacy for the Irish State and in the shaping of Irish society under the administration of William T. Cosgrave.

- The development of Church-State relations in de Valera's Ireland with particular reference to the writing of the Constitution and the place of tolerance in that society.

- A brief overview of the role played by the Catholic Church during the inter-party Government, 1948-1951 and a fresh look at the Mother and Child crisis.

- A study of the Catholic Church and tolerance in the 1950s — the story of Maria Duce; and the Fethard-on-Sea episode revisited.

- The changing role of the Irish Church in the wake of Vatican II.

- Competing models of Church in the 1970s and 1980s.

- Options and alternatives for the Catholic Church in the 1990s.[22]

Four factors are identified which have enabled the Catholic Church to wield a strong influence over the shaping of the dominant philosophy of the Irish State and over the legislation of that State:

- The Catholic Church has been responsible for educating a majority of successive generations of Irish leaders and elites; individual members of the clergy have maintained a close personal relationship with many of those leaders — be it in politics, in industry or in the public service.

- A closeness between priests and people helped preserve a form of populist Catholicism in the country; the corollary of that was the sometimes antagonistic attitude of members of the hierarchy towards the Holy See particularly when the Vatican sought to intervene in Irish politics.

- The hierarchy developed a corporate identity through the operations of the national episcopal conference.

- The Catholic Church and a majority of the politicians who came to power in the first fifty years of the State's existence shared a common objective — the building up of a State based on the philosophy of Catholic nationalism.

Possessing a strong popular base, exercising a profound ideological influence over the leaders of the new Irish State, and speaking as one voice through the National Conference of Bishops, the Catholic Church was traditionally in a position to mobilize its resources to protect its interest. This position lasted virtually unchallenged until the 1960s. However, the changing nature of Irish society in the 1970s, 1980s and 1990s has radically changed the relationships between Church and State. Those decades also witnessed a radical shift in the way in which many Catholics came to view the institutional Church. In the mid-1990s it was perceived to be in a state of crisis. Professor Mary McAleese, who was a member of the episcopal delegation to the New Ireland Forum on 9 February 1984, wrote eleven years later:

Instead of a modern debate using all the modern modes of insight from empirical research, market testing, consumer feedback and the like, we have had imposed on us a vision designated by the church authorities, designed exclusively within a celibate male paradigm, a rigidly hierarchical structure which is monarchical in tone. It is a church which has yet to come to terms with Newman's educated laity, with its consumer rights ethos, its burgeoning jurisprudence on individual rights and remedies for their infringement. It is a church which is currently in a crisis over authority.[23]

Such swingeing criticism, and many other voices might be added, comes out of a deep sense of religious conviction, and commitment to finding solutions which will bring about radical Church reform. The crises in the Catholic Church in the mid-1990s, and this point will be developed later, are a serious indirect obstacle to the achievement of peace and reconciliation on this island. Swamped by crises, the Catholic Church may find itself becoming more and more self-absorbed and less equipped to cooperate with the other Churches in the process of reinforcing the path to peace.

THE CATHOLIC CHURCH
AND THE FOUNDATION OF THE IRISH STATE
SOME GENERAL OBSERVATIONS

The Catholic Church in Ireland has long had a sense of its own pastoral independence — an independence which has been jealously protected from any untoward 'interference' by the Holy See in the politics of the island. Perhaps William Walsh, who was Archbishop of Dublin from 1885 to 1921, provided the clearest expression of that determination to preserve pastoral sovereignty in the handling of Church-State relations when he wrote as follows to the much respected Tobias Kirby, Rector of the Irish College, Rome, on 28 January 1891:

> We are still in the midst of our difficulties here — the prospect of an amicable solution being now apparently further off than ever. It would be well if Your Grace [Archbishop of Ephesus] would tell any persons who presume to offer you advice about the details of Irish affairs, that they had better keep to matters of which they are capable of forming an opinion. *Above all, let them look at home.* We here mean to strain every nerve to keep our people safe from such a fate as that which has befallen the Catholics of Rome and Italy.[24]

The political context in which the letter was sent provides the key to understanding the reason for the vehemence of the Archbishop's sentiments. It was a unique and troubled time in the relationship between the Catholic Church and the Irish Parliamentary Party. (For different reasons, the leadership of the Catholic Church is facing a crisis of authority of a similar kind at the end of the twentieth century.) The Parnell divorce crisis had radically weakened, if not undermined, the nationalist consensus. The hierarchy, having survived the unhelpful intervention of the Holy See with its condemnation of the Plan of Campaign, faced open revolt in the early 1890s. Bishops were finally compelled to speak out against Parnell on the divorce issue.

The task of having to rebuild a consensus between Church and 'nation' was made all the more difficult because of the continuation of the split in the Irish Parliamentary Party throughout the last decade of the nineteenth century. But even when unity was restored in that party the Catholic hierarchy had then to face the new challenge presented by the rise of radical nationalism and of the physical force movement.

Unity was preserved with difficulty on the bench of bishops as a new consensus was forged between 1916 and 1922 between the Church and the embryonic Irish State. The solidifying of that relationship facilitated the building of the Saorstát on the foundations of Catholic nationalism. That marriage of Catholicism and nationalism endured into the 1960s. It was an alliance of mutual convenience.

In an important article on 'Priests and People in Modern Ireland', Professor John A. Murphy wrote as follows:

> It is hardly an exaggeration to say that the Irish revolution of 1913-1921 completely bypassed the priests, and it was carried through without benefit of clergy. In so far as its roots were urban, its independent development is understandable. The great majority of the clergy were, of course, opposed to revolutionary methods. If the younger priests came out for Sinn Féin, their elders stood by the Party. ... It is a facet of the priest's ambivalent position in secular society that he should throw the revolutionary a rope only when the latter reaches dry land.[25]

That thesis does not allow sufficiently for the significant developments which occurred in the thinking and allegiances of the hierarchy and clergy during the period of growing 'people power' between 1918 and 1921. In my book, *The Vatican, the Bishops and Irish Politics 1919-1939*, I attempt to trace the gradual conversion of the hierarchy and clergy to the cause of Sinn Féin. Due to the determined leadership of the Archbishop of Dublin William Walsh, who died in 1921, the Catholic Church came to form an integral part of the campaign for independence.

It is not sustainable, therefore, to argue that radical nationalists like Monsignor John Hagan, Rector of the Irish College, Rome, merely threw the nationalist revolutionaries a rope *after* they had achieved — or were on the point of achieving — political success. Rather it should be stressed that Sinn Féin leaders, like Éamon de Valera, depended greatly on the advice and upon the friendship of priests, prelates and nuns during those revolutionary years. (Many of those friendships were sustained through de Valera's lifetime.)

This was not merely a question of friendship or nationalist dependence upon the infrastructure provided by the Irish clerical diaspora in Europe, Canada, the United States, Australia, New Zealand and South Africa; rather the different strands of Catholic thinking and teaching had a major influence on the intellectual formation of most of the 1918-1921 generation.[26] For example, Seán T. O'Kelly, who became President of Ireland in 1945, was in a unique position to appreciate and understand the importance of the Catholic Church, both nationally and internationally, in that struggle for national self-determination. His position as Sinn Féin head of mission in Paris in 1919 — and his six month stay at the Irish College in Rome in 1920 — allowed him to witness at first hand the frenetic actions of senior Irish clergymen at the Holy See as they sought to prevent a papal condemnation of the actions of the representatives of Dáil Éireann.[27] At least, that was the perception of, among others, Éamon de Valera. It was also a view shared by William T. Cosgrave who later appeared on the opposite side to de Valera in the anti-Treaty divide.

Indeed, most leading members of Sinn Féin proved to be very devout and loyal members of the Catholic Church. For example, William T. Cosgrave, who was to take over as the leader of the Saorstát at the end of 1922, suggested the setting up of a 'theological senate' in March 1921:

> The suggestion contained in it, is that there should be a sort of 'Upper House' to the Dáil consisting of a Theological Board which would decide whether any enactment of the Dáil were contrary to Faith and Morals or not. There is also a suggestion that a guarantee be given to the

Holy Father that the Dáil will not make laws contrary to the teachings of
the Church, in return for which the Holy Father will be asked to
recognise the Dáil as a body entitled to legislate for Ireland.[28]

Éamon de Valera wrote on 4 March 1921: 'Tell L. MacC. [William
T. Cosgrave was then Minister for Local Government] that I read his
theological proposal, and there is no necessity at the moment to
consider it further.'[29] The recommendation, on the face of it, appeared
to wish upon the bishops the power to vet the legislation of Dáil
Éireann. But Cosgrave's overriding concern may have been to secure
official papal recognition of Dáil. Nevertheless, this archival fragment
revealed Cosgrave's willingness to give the Irish Catholic bishops a
position of prominence in the life of the new State. Contrary to popular
perceptions, that was a position which prominent Sinn Féiners like
Cosgrave, de Valera and O'Kelly felt that most of the bishops had
earned. The extent and the importance of episcopal support, which had
been extended in 1920 to Dáil Éireann, was not that widely known
within Dáil Éireann. But as far as both Cosgrave and de Valera were
concerned, the Irish Catholic Church had proven its commitment to
the achievement of self-government, even if a minority of the bishops
and a number of the senior clergy were less than enthusiastic about the
project of full independence.

ORGANIZATION OF THE IRISH HIERARCHY

Before developing the analysis further, it is necessary to provide a brief
description of the evolution of the organization and governing structure
of the Catholic Church. Dr Seán Cannon has produced an important
study on the origins of Irish episcopal meetings between 1788 and
1882.[30] There were meetings at two levels: the metropolitan resumed
the practice of meeting every three years 'to deal with matters that
concern the spiritual government of the Catholic flock committed to
their care.' John Thomas Troy, who became Archbishop of Dublin in
1786, was responsible for a new plan for regular episcopal meetings at
national and provincial levels. In 1788, he invited the archbishops to
meet in Dublin between 10 and 18 November in order 'to preserve the
unity of the Spirit in the bond of peace and to promote uniformity in

carrying out ecclesiastical laws.' The Secretary of Propaganda was informed in 1801 that:

> The four archbishops of this area have, since the year 1788 resumed the ancient and praiseworthy practice which had been interrupted for more than a century, of assembling every three years in the city of Dublin to deal with matters that concern the spiritual government of the Catholic flock committed to their care.

The meeting of the National Conference of Bishops evolved from there into the structure which is in existence today.[31]

As the country was divided into twenty six dioceses (see map p. 86), it proved difficult for the bishops to meet regularly in the turbulent post-1916 period. However, they made a determined and successful effort to conduct business as usual; and the cohesion of the leadership of the hierarchy during the war of independence was helped greatly by the fact that the bishops continued to meet throughout the period. The Irish hierarchy met twice yearly in June and October between 1919 and 1922. Special meetings of the hierarchy were held on 13 December 1921 and 26 April 1922. During the years just prior to the foundation of the State the Standing Committee of the hierarchy met four times each year:

- On the third Tuesday in January at 12 noon in University College Dublin.
- On the Tuesday in the second week after Easter Sunday at 12 noon in University College Dublin.
- On the Monday preceding the June meeting of the episcopal conference in Maynooth College at 12 noon.
- On the Monday preceding the October meeting of the Episcopal Conference in Maynooth College, at 12 noon. If 1 January fell on a Tuesday the meeting of the Standing Committee was held on the fourth Tuesday of January.

The Standing Committee was empowered to deal with any urgent matter arising between the general meetings of the Conference by a resolution of the June 1887 general meeting. At a general meeting in October 1890 it was decided that the Standing Committee could be asked to consider any matter which an individual bishop considered urgent and involved interests wider than diocesan scope. The Chairman would consider such a request and, if necessary, consult with the other archbishops. If a meeting was called in response to such a request, the bishop making the request would be invited to attend the meeting. There is no evidence that any meeting was held as result of this resolution, but since the four meetings were held almost at three-monthly intervals it was hardly necessary to call a special meeting. The January 1922 meeting was brought forward to December 1921 as a special meeting of the whole episcopal conference was called for December 1921 to discuss the Treaty proposals.

The members of the Standing Committee consisted of the four archbishops *ex officio* (Armagh presiding, Dublin, Cashel and Tuam), the Secretary of the Conference and the Second Secretary (he later became the Financial Secretary, and that rule has changed), also *ex officio*, plus one bishop from each of the four ecclesiastical provinces. The membership in 1918 was three archbishops, the Bishop of Cloyne as Secretary, the Bishop of Ross as Second Secretary and the Bishops of Raphoe, Galway and Kildare and Leiglin.[32] The Rules of Procedure were first adopted in 1882.[33]

Ireland was very much among a minority of the Churches in Western Europe to have a national episcopal organization. This structure served the Irish Church well during the early decades of the twentieth century — and particularly during the turbulent period between 1919 and 1923. The hierarchy had a structure through which it could communicate with the leaders of Sinn Féin. The centralization of the hierarchy was also to work to the advantage of the Provisional Government of Saorstát Éireann in 1922.

COSGRAVE, DE VALERA
AND THE CATHOLIC CHURCH

In 1922, the Catholic Church was well positioned to play a significant and welcome part in the process of State building. Professor Murphy has noted, in his article cited above, that the alignment of the bishops and the majority of priests with the new Free State was 'a predictable stand for order and moderation'.[34] But that did not mean that the Catholic Church lacked independence or was little more than 'Cumann na nGaedheal at prayer'. The Catholic hierarchy had taken the Treaty side quite emphatically in 1922, but that had not prevented leading members of the episcopacy from criticizing the policy of executions carried out by the Free State Government during the civil war.[35]

While the hierarchy supported Cosgrave and wished to see the Free State achieve popular legitimacy, other leading churchmen saw de Valera as a prophet and future leader of the Irish people. Therefore, when de Valera was returned to office in 1932 he had come to enjoy by that date excellent working relations with the hierarchy as a whole — with not more than two exceptions on the bench of bishops.

It is also worthy of note that elements in the clergy retained close contact with the dissident revolutionary 'republicans' who continued on their path of parliamentary abstentionism after de Valera had split with them in 1925 and had entered the Dáil two years later as the leader of Fianna Fáil. Fr Michael O'Flanagan is a good example of one among a small group of clergy who chose to live their lives as part of the Church's loyal opposition.[36] Peadar O'Donnell, who devoted a lifetime to revolutionary politics and literary achievement paid a particular tribute to a number of like minded priests who stood by him during the 'Red Scare' days of 1931 when Ireland was allegedly faced with the threat of a communist conspiracy. He wrote:

> But the strange thing is that I do not believe I could have lived through the Red scare that made me its mad dog only that I spent much of my time in priests' houses. We had to be careful no word leaked out that some voteen [a Donegal term for a pious fraud] could carry to the bishops. The simple fact is that bishops do not count, except in their bullying power over priests, as an influence on Irish life. They don't know and likely couldn't be made realize that their pastorals, and especially their joint pastorals, are little more than a joke to a great many priests; always providing that no word of any priest's irreverent crack gets back to his bishop. And this is the nub of the matter. It's the conservatives among the laity that the priest has to be on his guard against. A great many experiences have led me to the conclusion that this is not a clerical-ridden country but a yahoo-ridden Church. I have rarely seen an unthreatened priest make himself the mouthpiece for reaction.[37]

The Irish revolutionary elite which de Valera led to power in 1932 may not have been overly pious but, with very few exceptions, no hostility was shown to the Church, even by the men who had been excommunicated a decade earlier. Anti-clericalism was perceived as being a form of political indulgence which no minority government had the luxury of flaunting. Tight party discipline masked the range of 'anti-clerical' feelings which were usually directed at the episcopacy as a whole. More usually, the antagonism was reserved for a particular bishop or a specific member of the clergy. The leadership of the Catholic Church was traditionalist and conservative. But so, too, were Cosgrave and de Valera. Once friends and fellow 1916 veterans, they were divided politically by the civil war. But their general intellectual formation made them into statesmen who shared a common Catholic outlook. That, ultimately, was of greater importance in providing a continuity of policies after de Valera and Fianna Fáil came to power in 1932.

THE CATHOLIC CHURCH
AND THE RELIGIOUS MINORITY
IN NORTHERN IRELAND

While the Catholic hierarchy had supported the coming into existence of the Irish Free State, bishops viewed with considerable apprehension the future of the minority in Northern Ireland. Comprising six counties of the traditional province of Ulster, its 5,238 square miles are about one sixth of the land area of Ireland. Northern Ireland had a population of 1,256,561 according to the 1926 census. Catholics were 33.5 per cent, Presbyterian 31.3 per cent and the Church of Ireland 27 per cent. Partition had immediate implications for the Church leadership. While the administrative structure of the Church continued on an all-Ireland basis, the Primate and leader of the Church resided in Armagh. Moreover, the ecclesiastical province of Armagh stretched south to below Mullingar in the midlands while a number of northern dioceses were on both sides of the border. The Primate had to do business with two different Governments as had the bishops of Kilmore, Derry and Clogher.[38]

Northern bishops faced a period of great uncertainty and turmoil in 1922. In May of that year, the Bishop of Down and Connor, Joseph MacRory, wrote to a friend in Rome: 'If you want to give His Holiness an idea of the Orange spirit, get him to dip into the song-book I send, but have a look through it first yourself. It will give some idea, though faint, of the spirit of these savages.'[39] MacRory and his fellow Northern bishop, Edward Mulhern of Dromore, feared for their lives in June 1922, so unsettled was the situation in Northern Ireland following the

IRA shooting on 22 June 1922 of Sir Henry Wilson. The latter, born in County Longford, had been made adviser to the Northern Prime Minister, Sir James Craig. He was also elected MP for County Down in 1921. Both MacRory and Mulhern felt obliged to remain on in Dublin for a few days after the meeting of the hierarchy fearing what might happen if they returned to their respective dioceses immediately after the shooting.[40] The situation in Northern Ireland gradually settled down. But the Catholic leadership continued to feel vulnerable and afraid of what might befall the minority in a Protestant-dominated State.[41]

Therefore, the Catholic Church in the two States was to have diametrically opposed experiences. In Northern Ireland, the Catholic Church was in a minority. In the Irish Free State, the Catholic Church was in the overwhelming majority. Did the minority status of the Catholic Church in Northern Ireland have any influence on the operations of the bishops in the South? While only further research will answer that question comprehensively, the dominant perception in Northern Ireland was that the Catholic Church came to exercise an inordinate influence over successive Irish Governments. Reporting in 1984, the New Ireland Forum stated:

> There is a widespread perception among unionists that the Roman
> Catholic Church exerts or seeks to exert undue influence in regard to
> aspects of the civil and legal organisation of society which Protestants
> consider to be a matter for private conscience.[42]

The historical validity of this perception will be examined in the following sections.

CHURCH AND STATE
IN THE IRISH FREE STATE

The 1926 census recorded that there was a total of 3,171,697 Catholics on the island of Ireland, 2,751,269 of whom were in Saorstát Éireann and 420,428 in Northern Ireland. There were in the Saorstát 164,215 members of the Church of Ireland, 32,429 Presbyterians, 10,663 Methodists, 3,686 Jews, 717 Baptists and 9,013 'others'. That was a total of 220,723 non-Roman Catholics. Religious homogeneity south of the border contributed to relative political stability while politico-religious rivalry in the North was the cause of endemic sectarian tension.[43]

The reason why the Catholic Church came to wield influence in the South is not merely attributable to its having the 'big battalions'. The support given to the leaders of Dáil Éireann between 1919 and 1922 has already been mentioned as has also the role played by the hierarchy during the civil war. Once that war was over, the newly independent sovereign State sought to rebuild. The prosecution of the war had cost the State about £17 million. Material destruction was estimated to be about £30 million. In April 1923, the Dáil was told that there was a deficit of £4 million which had to be met by borrowing. Defence took up 30 per cent of national expenditure in 1923-4 while 7 per cent went on personal injuries claims and compensation for loss of property in the fighting. Payment of those claims continued well into the 1920s.

A State weakened at birth by civil war, depended all the more upon the Catholic Church to help it achieve popular legitimacy. The State found the well organized infrastructure of the Catholic Church a great strength in those difficult times. There were, according to the 1926 census, 13,105 Catholic clergymen and nuns in Ireland — 9,209 nuns and 3,898 clergymen. There were also 1,111 Christian Brothers and monks and 358 religious lay brothers and sisters. There were also 2,752 Catholic theological students. The clerical role in education was extensive as will be explained in this paper. The place of the Church in the running of the voluntary hospitals, foster homes, and other institutions in the service sector was often a further hidden subsidy for the State.

The vitality of the various Churches in Ireland in the 1920s was manifest in the thriving missionary movement which sent clergy and religious to various parts of the world. The Columban Fathers, founded in Maynooth for the conversion of China in 1916, was a leading example of that outward-looking spirit.[44]

Irish Catholicism at home sought in the 1920s, as one of its major objectives, to reinforce the legitimacy of the new State. The political climate of Saorstát Éireann suited and reassured members of a Catholic hierarchy who had lived through the dangers of the revolutionary period. When law and order broke down some bishops found that their very lives had been threatened by Crown forces.[45] The President of the Executive Council between 1922 and 1932 was William T. Cosgrave; he was a devout Catholic and a close friend of Archbishop Edward Byrne of Dublin who gained special permission from the Holy See to have an altar built in the President's home where Mass could be said on a regular basis for his family. However, his personal devotion to his religion did not blind him to his responsibilities under the Constitution to uphold the rights of minorities.

Economic stringency, the close relationship of the Government with the Catholic Church and a State philosophy of minimal interference have been identified as three constraining factors on the development of educational reform in the 1920s where the main emphasis was on curriculum rather than structural change.[46] The Minister for Finance, Ernest Blythe (the only non-Catholic minister in the Executive Council) cut national teachers' salaries by 10 per cent in 1923. This reflected the poverty of the country at the time. However, despite the limited State resources during their respective tenures, the two Ministers for Education Eoin MacNeill (1923-1925) and John Marcus O'Sullivan (1926-1932) were responsible for significant administrative initiatives.[47] Ó Buachalla argues that the policies pursued by the Cumann na nGaedheal government were 'singularly important in that they established a model which the education system followed with minor modifications for almost forty years.'[48] That educational system was based on the religious pillars in the State. All of the Churches sought to preserve a denominational educational structure. The State respected the views of the various Church leaders. In return, the Churches were expected to play a major role in the building of national character and identity.

The desire to build a national consciousness and the general suspicion which both Church and State shared about the evils of foreign influences helped to shape a strongly conservative attitude towards sexual morality in Ireland in the 1920s. The influence of the foreign press and foreign dances came under special attack. Archbishop Harty of Cashel said on 25 April 1926 that the 'quantity of such horrible papers circulating in the country was simply appalling.'[49] Modern dancing and foreign fashion were frowned upon by bishops who feared that continental moral laxity might reach Irish shores through the medium of cinema, radio and the British yellow press. A joint pastoral, issued on 6 October 1925, warned against the 'occasions of sin' which were attendant on night dances in particular:

> To say nothing of the special danger of drink, imported dances of an evil kind, the surroundings of the dancing hall, withdrawal from the hall for intervals, and the dark ways home have been the destruction of virtue in

every part of Ireland. The dancing of dubious dances on Sunday, more particularly by persons dazed with drink, amounts to woeful desecration of the Lord's Day wherever it takes place.[50]

A number of members of the hierarchy believed that native dancing had salvific powers: 'Irish dances do not make degenerates.'[52] On 9 May 1926 Archbishop Gilmartin of Tuam condemned foreign dances, indecent dress, company-keeping and bad books. He spoke of a 'craze for pleasure — unlawful pleasure.' He warned that family ties were weakened and in other countries where there were facilities for divorce 'the family hardly existed'.[52] The same prelate warned his flock on 8 December 1926:

> In recent years the dangerous occasions of sin had been multiplied. The old Irish dances had been discarded for foreign importations which, according to all accounts, lent themselves not so much to rhythm as to low sensuality. The actual hours of sleep had been turned into debasing pleasure. Company-keeping under the stars of night had succeeded in too many places to the good old Irish custom of visiting, chatting and story-telling from one house to another, with the Rosary to bring all home in due time.[53]

Further research may reveal the extent to which Irish society in the 1920s underestimated the indigenous causes of 'occasions of sin'.[54] The 'Garden of Eden' before English intervention theory has been addressed by Tom Maxwell, aged eighteen, a character in David Thomson's *Woodbrook*:

> Tommy said that the English were damned and taking that in a secular sense I did not care whether they were damned or not and told him so and that I was Scottish anyway. But I was damned too, he said. All Protestants were. However well they behaved on earth, they could not get into heaven, only to purgatory at the best and most of them to hell for the terrible crimes they continued to commit of which he mentioned some that had been reported lately in the papers. It astonished me to hear him talk as if serious crime did not exist in Ireland. He believed that there had been in Ireland no rape, no murder, no abuse of children in his or his father's time.[55]

Tommy held rather extreme views. But it was not uncommon for future generations in Ireland to preserve without any justification an element of that naiveté. Garda reports and the data compiled by the

Department of Justice demonstrate that the basis for such naiveté was completely unfounded.[56]

Legislative initiatives on censorship, the curtailing of drinking hours and the blocking of divorce were not taken merely under pressure from the bishops.[57] The majority of politicians shared as Catholic an outlook as the hierarchy. The extent to which the other Churches supported those measures is a subject for further research. What, for example, were the views of members of the Church of Ireland, the other Christian Churches and the Jewish community toward the non-availability of divorce in the 1920s?

The Cosgrave Government's handling of the question of divorce revealed a pattern which was to repeat itself in Church-State relations in subsequent decades. There had been no explicit provision for divorce in Irish law. The Matrimonial Causes Act of 1857 was never extended to Ireland. The Irish citizen could only get a dissolution of his or her marriage by the costly procedure of a private Bill in Parliament.[58] Soon after independence three private divorce Bills were introduced. The Attorney General sought a decision from the Executive Council as to whether legislation would be promoted to set up the necessary procedures. It seemed to him that while the religious and sacramental aspect of the matter was outside the purview of the Government, it might be considered necessary to consult the Church. Aware that divorce was against the teaching of the Catholic Church, Cosgrave immediately sought the advice of his friend, Archbishop Edward Byrne. The latter offered his personal view:

> ... that under no circumstances could the church give any sanction to divorce. That the church regards Matrimony as a Sacrament only, and claims sole jurisdiction in regard to it. That they could not even sanction divorce for non-Catholics for the reason that all persons who had been baptised are member of the church and under its jurisdiction.

Byrne said that it was a matter for the bishops as a whole. The Archbishop said that he would have the matter brought before the next meeting of the bishops upon receipt of a memorandum from Government. Therefore, the matter was formally referred to the bishops as a body. Meeting in October 1923, the hierarchy stated:

> The Bishops of Ireland have to say that it would be altogether unworthy of an Irish legislative body to sanction the concession of such divorce, no matter who the petitioners may be.

Cosgrave took note of this advice and he had further consultations in early 1924 with Byrne from whom he received a memorandum on the divorce question. He wrote to a bishop concerning the situation: 'I was a child so far as my information and knowledge of the subject [divorce] was concerned.'[59]

Cosgrave followed the advice of the bishops. He sought to pass in the Dáil a resolution preventing the introduction into the House of private Bills for divorce. The Senate was then asked to pass the same resolution. W. B. Yeats opposed:

> It is one of the glories of the Church in which I was born that we have put our bishops in their places in discussions involving legislation.... I think it tragic that within three years of this country gaining its independence we should be discussing a measure which a minority of the nation consider to be grossly oppressive.[60]

On the other side of the debate, Professor William Magennis made the memorable remark: 'You cannot be a good Catholic if you allow divorce even between Protestants.'[61] Here was a clear manifestation of the majoritarian mentality which was to characterize aspects of Irish public life during the following decades. The Catholic hierarchy had taken a particularly strong line on the question of divorce. While there may have been some unease in Government circles about the emphatic nature of the episcopal advice, the Executive Council did not resist. But Cosgrave did not get the outcome he desired in the Senate. Lord Glenavy ruled that the resolution was unconstitutional and there the matter rested until the introduction of Bunreacht na hÉireann in 1937.

The Catholic Truth Society (CTS) and a number of prominent clergymen had been campaigning since the foundation of the State for the introduction of stricter censorship laws. A Committee of Enquiry on Evil Literature was set up in 1926. The report was quite nuanced and ought to be quoted extensively to demonstrate that there were citizens in the Irish Free State who sought to protect basic liberties:

> The difference of opinion between two witnesses having the same aims probably arose from the fact that one was applying the test virginibus puerisque, while the other was thinking of what would be demoralising to persons of mature minds. But the State could not accept the former test for what is permissible without destroying a liberty that authors have always enjoyed. The censorship that should protect the young from

literary influences pernicious to the immature is the censorship exercised in the home, the school, and through the spiritual director. But literature has never been restricted in any country to writings that meet the standard to be observed in works intended only for the youth and the maiden. And in fact unless all the agencies of moral culture are constantly and effectively employed for the maintenance of a healthy public taste amongst the young it is certain that no effort of the State can prevent the public taste from becoming corrupt. ....the law therefore apparently imposes little restriction on a writer's selection of matter. A charge of obscenity will depend to a great extent on the manner in which his subjects are dealt with, and it would be difficult to frame a law prohibiting books of an immoral tendency that would not impose restrictions on authors from which literature has ever been free.

Nevertheless, it ought not to be difficult for a group of citizens selected for their culture, good sense and respect for morality to recognise books written with a corrupt intent, or aiming at notoriety and circulation by reason of their appeal to sensual or corrupt instincts and passions, and to discriminate such books from those having a purely literary aim in view but which, as part of their reflection of the world, admit representation of the vices or the passions that exist.[62]

But the latter reflections were not the guiding sentiments of the new legislation as it came to be applied. A Censorship Bill was introduced in summer 1928. Leading Irish literary figures, William Butler Yeats, George Bernard Shaw and George Russell all attacked the legislation as being far too restrictive.[63] But their collective wrath and reputation were not sufficient to prevent the passage of the Bill and the first censorship board was established on 13 February 1930. The committee had the power to prohibit the sale and distribution of 'indecent or obscene' books. The publishing, selling or distribution of literature advocating birth control was also deemed an offence under the Act.

However, a 'censorship mentality' had been in evidence in Ireland for many years before that legislation came into force. Brinsley MacNamara published *The Valley of the Squinting Windows* in 1918. It was considered unacceptable by many people in the village of Delvin, County Westmeath. The result was the public burning of the book and the humiliation of the author. The author's father who was a local schoolmaster was boycotted and driven into exile. This was followed by a bitter legal battle in 1923. MacNamara was made Registrar of the

National Gallery of Ireland in 1925, a post that he continued to hold until 1960.[64] The publication of James Joyce's *Ulysses* in 1922 was also a shock to romantic nationalists. Molly Bloom's luxuriation in her own sensuality did not meet with approval in either Ireland or abroad.[65] Paradoxically, the book was never banned in Ireland. But Seán O'Casey did not fare quite so well. His plays *Shadow of a Gunman* (1923), *Juno and the Paycock* (1924), and *The Silver Tassie* (1928) did not set out to flatter the revolutionary generation of 1916-1923. When the Abbey Theatre performed *The Plough and the Stars* (1926) there were vocal protests against the bringing of the tricolour into a public house. Objection was also taken on stage to the presence in the pub of a prostitute, Rosie Redmond. The play ran for two weeks but with the lights on in the theatre and with gardaí lining the passages at the sides of the pit.[66] The social realism of the play caused deep offence, just as earlier Lennox Robinson's short story in *Tomorrow* had caused upset; it concerned an Irish farm girl who was raped and then imagined herself to be the Madonna. For his literary efforts, Lennox Robinson was sacked from his job as secretary of the Carnegie Library Trust.[67] By the early 1930s, the censorship board was operating a system based on the test of *virginibus puerisque* with the most serious consequences for foreign and Irish authors alike.

In attempting to measure resistance to change in the Irish Free State, it might be observed that the Catholic Church could be a source of reaction and of innovation. But it was not the only source of reaction as may be noted by the manner in which the Royal Hibernian Academy treated innovators in the visual arts. It was appropriate that two women painters — who later developed strong religious themes in their work — were responsible for bringing Cubism to Dublin. Mainie Jellett and Evie Hone mounted a joint exhibition in 1924. The former had two of her abstract works severely criticized when she showed them in the capital the previous year.[68] They both continued to run the gauntlet of the critics for many years until local provincial prejudice was finally overcome and well-deserved recognition followed.[69]

A young London-born Jewish painter, Harry Kernoff, had made his home in Dublin in the 1920s. He was influenced by the Neue Sachlichkeit, or New Objectivity movement, which was a reaction against Expressionism. Kernoff's early work was a quest to understand reality in the style of this new movement.[70] Jellett, Hone and Kernoff were three of a group of younger Irish painters who sought to develop their talents in the wider framework of contemporary developments in European art. Some members of the younger generation had a role model in the individualism of Jack B. Yeats. The continued hostility to innovation was a characteristic of Irish society in general. Conservatism remained a feature of most aspects of Irish administrative, cultural and social life in the 1920s. The emphasis was on the need for continuity and conformity.[71]

By the end of the 1920s Cumann na nGaedheal had taken note of the fact that its stock had declined among the minority religious groups in the country. Its political popularity generally had fallen as de Valera's Fianna Fáil (founded in 1926, its members entered the Dáil in 1927) became better organized. The Government was to receive a strong injection of popular support by the holding of the Catholic emancipation centenary celebrations in 1929. A successful attempt to establish diplomatic relations with the Holy See that year had complicated relations between the bishops and the Government. Paradoxically, a number of the Irish bishops were very unhappy with the idea of having a nuncio resident in Dublin. Firstly, it was feared that he would be running with tales to Rome all too frequently. Secondly, it was believed that the nuncio would interfere with the process of episcopal appointments. Thirdly, it was believed that British influence would be extended over the Irish Church as a consequence of the perceived subservience of the Vatican towards the Court of St James.[72] However, the arrival of the papal nuncio in January 1930, was to have a stabilizing effect on Church-State relations. This was due to the sensitivity, the high intelligence, and the prudence of the first nuncio, the Dublin-born Franciscan, Paschal Robinson. Had the task been entrusted to a less professional person, the outcome might have been far less satisfactory for both the Church and for the State.[73]

It would be wrong to conclude that both the Catholic Church and the State were oblivious to the rights of religious minorities during the first ten years of the Free State. While Church authorities sought to curtail the activities of the more extreme anti-Protestant elements in its ranks, it enjoyed a position of great privilege relative to the minority Churches. It grew comfortable in the role of being called upon to offer its opinion on pieces of pending legislation which had a direct impact

on the activities of the Church. Government contact with the Catholic
episcopacy was rarely put on a formal footing. Cosgrave knew the
Archbishop of Dublin very well. Matters were often settled informally.
Thus developed what I have termed the politics of informal consensus.
But there was a confessional point beyond which Cosgrave was not
prepared to pass; his reasons were motivated by both political
pragmatism and a concern for the defence of the rights of religious
minorities.

A number of episodes towards the end of his term in office illustrate
the complexities of his political approach. Concerned by the availability
of contraceptives, the National Conference of Bishops in 1929 sought a
meeting with the Minister for Justice, J. Fitzgerald Kenney. The Bishop
of Ossory, Patrick Collier, told the Minister that the hierarchy considered
the law governing the sale of contraceptives to be quite inadequate.
Contraceptives were available in pharmacies. This complaint resulted in
a frank exchange of views in which the Minister stressed the electoral
vulnerability of the Government and its concern not to alienate further
members of the minority Churches following their negative reaction to
the Immoral Literature Bill. The banning of the sale of contraceptives
required an amendment to the Criminal Law Act.

Collier, in his report to the June 1930 meeting of the hierarchy,
repeated what the Minister had said that 'they [Government] considered
another dose would be dangerous'. This was a reference to what the
Minister had said concerning the political dangers inherent for the
Government in introducing legislation which was liable to provoke the
wrath of the other Churches. But Bishop Collier concluded in his
report that the inference was plain and that were the Government in a
safe position there would be no hesitation. (That was not a correct
assumption, as subsequent events were to show.) The hierarchy were
told that the Minister had conceded the strength of the case but argued
that Protestants strongly objected to having what they called 'Catholic
morality' forced upon them by law. To the obvious objection by Collier
that they lived in a Catholic State, the Minister for Justice responded by
stressing the instability of the Government, the danger of alienating
more Protestant support and said that the Government would not be
justified in running risks which would result in a grave upheaval in the
country, at least not for the next few years. The Minister promised,
however, to prevent the distribution of literature on contraception.[74]

Perhaps as a means of deflecting further episcopal pressure, the Government established a committee to investigate reform of the Criminal Law Amendment Acts 1880-1885. The committee reported in 1931. But that was a matter of bad timing. At the Lambeth Conference in 1930, the Anglican Church ruled on the question of the use of contraceptives:

> Where there is a clearly felt moral obligation to limit or avoid parenthood the method must be decided on Christian principles. The primary and obvious method is complete abstinence from intercourse (as far as may be necessary) in a life of discipline and self-control lived in the power of the Holy Spirit. Nevertheless in those cases where there is such a clearly felt moral obligation to limit or to avoid parenthood, and where there is a morally sound reason for avoiding complete abstinence, the Conference agrees that other methods may be used, provided that this is done in the light of the same Christian principles. The Conference records its strong condemnation of the use of any methods of contraception control from motives of selfishness, luxury or mere convenience.

Resolution 15, quoted above, was carried by 193 votes to 67. This decision by the Anglican Church only helped reinforce the resolve of the Irish Catholic Church to have the laws reformed governing the sale of contraceptives. Cosgrave was out of office by 1932 and it fell to de Valera to introduce the necessary amending legislation to ban the importation and sale of contraceptives. But if the hierarchy had to wait a few years for the banning of contraception, the Vocational Education Act (1931) was heavily influenced by Catholic thought.[75]

Yet Cosgrave ought not to be dismissed as a confessional politician willing to do the bidding of the bishops. His sense of fair play was tested two years before leaving office by the Letitia Dunbar-Harrison case. The latter had been appointed to the post of librarian for Mayo after winning in open competition. She was a Protestant and an honours Trinity College graduate in languages.[76] When the Mayo library committee refused to give approval to the appointment — a stand supported by the local County Council, the Government stood by the decision of the Local Appointments Commission. It ordered the disbandment of the County Council. Despite local protests, Dunbar-Harrison took up her post. A number of the local clergy were outspokenly against her appointment. A Christian Brother, M. S. Kelly argued that her 'mental constitution was the constitution of Trinity College.' Mgr D'Alton of Tuam told the local library committee that they were not appointing a 'washerwoman or a mechanic but an educated girl who ought to know what books to put into the hands of the Catholic boys and girls of this county which was at least 99 per cent Catholic.' D'Alton stressed the difference between the two Churches on birth control: 'supposing there were books attacking these fundamental truths of Catholicity, is it safe to entrust a girl who is not a Catholic, and is not in sympathy with Catholic views, with their handling?' he asked.[77]

These comments reveal the degree of mistrust which some members of the Catholic clergy had for Protestant institutions such as Trinity College. The appointment of Dunbar-Harrison was part of a far greater concern which Catholics had for the employment of Protestants in 'sensitive' positions. Those fears were often expressed in the pages of Catholic journals noted less for displays of prudence than for intemperate comment. The *Catholic Bulletin* — never regarded by the bishops as automatically reflecting the views of the hierarchy — spoke out frequently against Trinity: 'Is not the title of Catholic, assumed and used by such a Catholic Medical Graduate of Trinity College, Dublin, simply an added danger for the morality of our Catholic population, rich and poor?'[78] The conclusion appeared to be that Catholic graduates of Trinity could not be trusted.

Soon after that article appeared the Minister for Education, John Marcus O'Sullivan, had an interview with the Archbishop of Cashel, John Harty. Much to the relief of the Minister, he was assured that the bishops were not going to make any pronouncement on the question of librarians. Meanwhile, Cosgrave made a number of efforts to enlist the support of the bishops to kill off the embarrassing case. But the bishops did not want to have the issue formally raised at a meeting of the hierarchy. It was a matter for the local ordinary who was the Archbishop of Tuam, Thomas Gilmartin. Cosgrave met him on 25 February 1931. But the meeting did not solve much. There was an imminent danger that the question was now being broadened to include the appointment of dispensary doctors. Gilmartin made the unhelpful suggestion to Cosgrave that the Government should sign a concordat with the Holy See.[79] That was not a position with which many members of the hierarchy would have agreed. The idea would have met with far less enthusiasm in the Executive Council. There is no evidence that future Irish Governments reversed this position. A concordat was not considered either necessary or relevant for Ireland.

Cosgrave had secured the strong backing of his ministerial colleagues to take a tough stance on the Dunbar-Harrison case. Fearing the possibility of a general challenge to appointments made by the independent Local Appointments Commission, he abandoned his placatory tone and confronted the hierarchy. A memorandum was prepared for Cardinal Joseph MacRory and sent to Armagh on 28 March 1931 outlining the 'considerable anxiety' which 'certain matters' had given rise to in the minds of members of the Executive Council and himself. That was due to the fact 'such matters' might have possible reactions upon State institutions, 'and upon the happy relations which exist between the Church and the State in this country.' The text of this letter, which is quoted in full in Appendix I, is of great significance. It showed Cosgrave's respect for the Church. But it also demonstrated his determination to uphold the workings of the Constitution:

> We feel confident that Your Eminence and their Lordships and bishops appreciate the effective limits to the powers of government which exist in relation to certain matters if some of the fundamental principles on which our state is founded are not to be repudiated. Such repudiation, direct or indirect, by any Irish government would, we are convinced, entail consequences very detrimental to the country's welfare.

Cosgrave regarded any attempt to impose a religious test on a candidate for the post of dispensary doctor as being unconstitutional:

> The system of appointment of medical officers now in operation was devised to prevent grave abuses which were, unfortunately, far from uncommon in the past. It has been recently conveyed to us that if a non-Catholic doctor, or indeed a doctor not qualified in the National University is appointed as a dispensary doctor, some of the bishops may feel it to be their duty to denounce the appointment.

Cosgrave believed that such a denunciation would be regarded and represented as a denunciation, by implication at least, of the Government under whose agency the appointment was made. He held that the Maynooth Synod statutes 256 and 257 had been adduced 'in support of the contention that action of this nature is a duty incumbent on the bishops.' He firmly rejected the idea that it would be possible to discriminate by way of religious test against non-Catholics as such or against graduates of Trinity College or Queen's University, Belfast. That rejection was rooted in the 'fundamental principle upon which the state is based'. The same principle was operative 'in regard to the position of county librarians'.

Cosgrave drew attention to the delicate question of marriage dispensations on grounds of non-consummation which were granted by the Church and 'of which the civil authorities receive no notification'. He warned:

> That these and other difficulties exist is not open to question. That in the
> present circumstances, they are capable of a solution which could be
> regarded as satisfying, at once, the requirements of the church and the
> state is, I fear, open to grave doubt. Any failure following an attempt to
> solve these problems would only add to the difficulty, and if it came to
> public knowledge, might prove a source of unrest, if not a scandal.

Cosgrave warned that those considerations made the Government all the more fearful of the danger that might be precipitated if the attention of the public were to be focused on those questions in an unauthorized way.[80]

On receipt of the letter Cardinal MacRory sought an interview with Cosgrave. They met in mid-April but details of the meeting are not available. But Cosgrave and O'Sullivan met Gilmartin of Tuam within days of seeing the Cardinal. The Archbishop was on the defensive from the outset. He meekly suggested that Cosgrave might consider transferring Dunbar-Harrison at a suitable time. She was moved finally in January 1940 to become librarian in the Department of Defence. The outcome was, according to the Irish correspondent of *Round Table*, 'fair to the lady, soothing to the Mayo bigots and good for the government.'[81]

The Dunbar-Harrison episode, at one level, displayed an absence of tolerance in Irish society for the rights of the members of minority religions. But it also showed the determination of the Cosgrave government to maintain the principles of tolerance in which the Constitution was rooted. Jack White, writing about that episode in 1975, concluded:

> What is most remarkable, perhaps, at a range of over forty years, is that
> the government of the day was prepared to face such pressures, political
> and clerical, in order to assert the equal rights of the minority.[82]

The uncertainty of the politics of the 1920s contributed to the closeness of the working relationship between Church and State in the decade 1922-1932. There was further evidence of the intimacy of that relationship in 1931 when the Irish Government, fearing the existence of a left wing conspiracy in the country, wrote to each of the bishops requesting action by the hierarchy. Each of the bishops was supplied with confidential Department of Justice memoranda which gave details of the conspiracy. Writing to MacRory, Cosgrave said:

> We are confronted with a completely new situation. Doctrines are being taught and practised which were never before countenanced amongst us and I feel that the influence of the Church alone will be able to prevail in the struggle against them. Only through the powerful influence of the Church will innocent youths be prevented from being led into a criminal conspiracy, escape from which is impossible because it involves the certainty of vengeance and the grave danger of death.[83]

MacRory took that invitation very seriously as did the vast majority of the bishops. A joint pastoral was read in every Catholic church in the country on 18 October 1931. It condemned subversive groups and Saor Éire — a newly founded organization — which was held responsible by the Government for giving the lead in the politics of conspiracy.[84] Constitutional politics prevailed and de Valera and Fianna Fáil were returned to power in 1932 as a minority government. Jack White wrote of the period:

> ...as the shadow of Mr de Valera loomed larger, Protestants found themselves increasingly hemmed in by the three orthodoxies — the republican orthodoxy, the Gaelic orthodoxy, and now the Catholic orthodoxy. It is all the more remarkable that, within twenty years, they found themselves in the position of supporting Mr de Valera, because he was seen as the only man strong enough to take a stand against the bishops.[86]

IRISH CATHOLICISM AND THE STATE
1932-1948

The handling of Church-State relations was marked more by continuity than by change with the arrival in power of de Valera. Educated by the Christian Brothers and by the Holy Ghost Fathers at Blackrock College,

Dublin, his political thinking was heavily influenced by his Catholicism.[86] That influence was sustained through the lifelong friendships which he retained with a number of his teachers and with other leading religious in the Holy Ghost order. He was to develop a close working relationship with Dr John Charles McQuaid, the Dean and later President of Blackrock College.[87] The significance of that friendship will be developed later in this paper. De Valera was also very friendly with a number of leading Carmelites, Franciscans and diocesan clergy. His relationship with the hierarchy was potentially problematical. But the majority of the bishops had come to realize that in government de Valera might be expected to maintain the same close relationship with the hierarchy as had existed during the Cosgrave Government. This was quickly demonstrated by the manner in which de Valera and Fianna Fáil helped handle the Eucharistic Congress which was held in Dublin in the summer of 1932. The occasion proved to be an organizational triumph for both Church and State.[88]

While the 1930s witnessed the emergence of a Church characterized in more strident form by clericalism, juridicalism and triumphalism, this did not mean that the hierarchy capitulated to pressure from extremist groups. The bishops sought to hold the middle ground and avoid giving encouragement to those who wished to embark upon radical political projects for the root and branch restructuring of Irish society. The temptation to view *Catholicism* as a monolith is not a supportable historical proposition. It is important, therefore, to stress the existence of the different currents in Irish Catholicism.

The corporatist current was very strong in the 1930s. It ranged in degrees of radicalism from those who wished to adapt existing structures to accommodate the vocationalist model of Pius XI to those who favoured the Italian fascist model.[89] A number of distinguished lay and clerical academics contributed to the literature of the movement: Professor James Hogan, University College Cork, Professor Michael Tierney of University College Dublin and Fr Edward Coyne were among the most prominent and the most moderate.

Vocationalism was very much in political vogue in the 1930s. But there was also a clerico-fascist wing to the movement. Mistrust of liberal democratic institutions was taken to an extreme by the Blueshirts who sought to corporatize Irish society on the model of Mussolini's Italy.[90]

This movement was decisively defeated by de Valera. A remnant of the Blueshirt movement emerged in the form of the Irish Christian Front (ICF) in July 1936 during the first weeks of the Spanish civil war, demanding recognition of the rebel forces of General Francisco Franco, large public demonstrations were organized to pressurize if not intimidate the Fianna Fáil Government into changing its position of maintaining relations with the Republican Government in Madrid. A leading member of the hierarchy and large numbers of the Catholic clergy identified with the ICF cause. The strong clerical presence on ICF platforms appeared somewhat incongruous in view of the fact that the hierarchy had successfully conducted a policy of preventing clergy from becoming involved in politics. The priest on the political platform — so much a feature of nineteenth and early twentieth century Ireland — was a rarity in the latter part of the 1920s and early 1930s. The early months of the Spanish civil war witnessed a return to the old practice. But the leaders of the Catholic Church came to realize that that was a mistake and quickly reverted to the original policy. A weaker political leader, faced as de Valera was with a general election in the near future, might have been stampeded into precipitous action. The Government stood firm. Franco was recognized by Dublin in early 1939 after the war had ended.[91]

Catholic journals and periodicals in the 1930s represented the thinking of different currents in the Church. In their cruder manifestations of Catholic populism, a number of these journals continued to speak insultingly about Protestantism and Judaism. The idea of a world conspiracy — made up of Freemasons, Jews and communists — was a recurring theme in a number of those publications. *The Catholic Mind*, a short-lived journal in the late 1920s and early 1930s, manifested the cruder side of populist Catholicism. There were oft-repeated claims in its columns that all of the founders of communism and socialism were Jewish. In dealing with Nazi persecution of the Jews, a contributor in *The Irish Mind* wrote in 1933:

> Neither have we heard a single word of protests from Jewish communities regarding the cruel and invidious persecution perpetrated by the Jewish government of the Soviet Union. We have protests in plenty from Jews throughout the world on behalf of their co-religionists in Germany, but not a word of protest against the treatment of Catholics and Protestants there. Their silence is eloquent.[92]

The Holy Ghost Father, Fr Denis Fahey, paid much attention in his writings to the alleged role of Jews in world conspiracies. This disturbing feature of his writings allegedly catalogued the nefarious role of the 'Jewish nation' in global affairs. Although he claimed not to be anti-Semitic, he opposed the spread of Jewish 'naturalism':

> ... accordingly the world-wide power of the strongly organised Jewish nation, in international finance, in the Press, in the cinema-industry and in the Freemasons, coupled with their skill in becoming members of the different political parties everywhere, tends inevitably to the disruption of the whole order of things...[and] will lead to the ruthless imposition of one national form.[93]

Fahey did not see this as an abstract threat; he felt that the IRA had come under the influence of that world conspiracy. It was nothing more than a cover for the Communist International. The IRA were preparing for the establishment of a communist republic from which private property in land and the means of production would be excluded. His conclusion was as follows:

> Thus if ever a Communist Republic is set up in Ireland, we shall be trampled under foot in another world-empire ruled from Moscow or — Jerusalem.[94]

Fahey's version of Catholicism was adversarial, confrontational and divisive. He represented a combative form of Catholicism which sought to be polemical. While Fahey's influence will be further assessed later in this paper, it must be stated here that he did not attract a particularly wide following in his lifetime. His works were available and widely read. His ideas were treated with scepticism by many members of his own Holy Ghost order. De Valera, who knew Fahey personally, did not have any sympathy for his ideas. The hierarchy disliked extremists. Despite the fact that Fahey's works were passed by the ecclesiastical censor — and one carried a preface from Dr John Charles McQuaid — he finally ran into difficulties with Church authorities in the 1940s. Nevertheless, his followers reconstituted themselves in an organization called Maria Duce [Under the Leadership of Mary] in 1945 (see pp. 135–142).

The Jesuit, Edward Cahill, who was a contemporary of Fahey's, shared many of the same obsessions as the Holy Ghost priest. His focus of attack was more the role of the Freemasons and the communists in

Irish society. His views, too, were never considered to be particularly relevant by de Valera and his Government. Neither, it must be added, did mainstream Irish Catholicism respond favourably to Cahill's desire to establish militant continental-style Catholic Action in Ireland.[95] He had founded An Ríoghacht [the Kingship of Christ] on 31 October 1926 in the hope of emulating the Italian experience. But it did not succeed for a number of reasons, the most obvious one being that there was little need for an assertive, mass Catholic Action movement in a country where the overwhelming majority of the population was loyally Catholic. It is instructive that the more moderate, tolerant and ecumenically-minded layman, Frank Duff, had much more success than either Cahill or Fahey. A civil servant, Duff founded the Legion of Mary on 7 September 1921. This remarkable figure felt little sympathy for the antagonisms of Fahey or Cahill. Under his leadership, the Legion of Mary was to became a national and then an international organization. A measure of his ecumenism — quite unusual in those years — was his determination to dialogue with, and not confront, other religions. Duff helped establish the Pillar of Fire society and the Mercier Society in the 1940s. The former sought to provide a forum for dialogue between Catholics and Jews. It had two meetings before being closed down on the instructions of the new Archbishop of Dublin, Dr John Charles McQuaid. The Mercier Society, which was established to allow for discussion and an exchange of ideas between Protestants and Catholics, survived for a longer period than the Pillar of Fire society. But it, too, was closed down by the new Archbishop.[96]

The above examples have been chosen to illustrate the diversity of the currents within Irish Catholicism in the 1930s and 1940s. The plurality of ideas and pressure groups made the writing of the 1937 Constitution more difficult than might first be realized. Were the ideas of Fahey and Cahill to have predominated — and that was always unlikely — Ireland would have become a confessional State with the Catholic Church established as the one, true Church. However, de Valera did not give an opportunity to the competing Catholic currents to influence the drafting of the new Constitution. That was a job he reserved for himself, a small number of civil servants and Dr John Charles McQuaid. The legal adviser to the Department of External Affairs (now Foreign Affairs), John Hearne was instructed by de Valera on 30 April 1935, and again on 2 May, to prepare draft heads for a new Constitution. He submitted those to de Valera on 18 May together with a memorandum outlining the preliminary method adopted in the preparation of the draft. With the help of Arthur Matheson, who drafted Government legislation, Hearne continued with his task into 1936. The Secretary of the Department of the President, Maurice Moynihan, was also centrally involved.

In the summer of 1936, Edward Cahill SJ, was in correspondence with de Valera. News of the most closely guarded secret had reached his ears. He offered to give de Valera the benefit of his advice. De Valera accepted. But the Jesuit Order in Dublin preferred to take the matter out of Cahill's hands. The Provincial established a sub-committee to bring the best brains of the Jesuits in Ireland together to work on the project. A draft was duly produced and sent to de Valera by Cahill on 21 October 1936. It contained a draft preamble and a number of articles covering the topics of education, the rights of the family, marriage etc.[97] This document had an influence on the drafting process. It was used very extensively by Dr John Charles McQuaid who was perhaps the most central figure in the writing of the Constitution.

Two observations might be made about the drafting of the new Irish Constitution: firstly, there was really only one clergyman directly involved in the process and that was McQuaid. (The role of the Jesuits was confined to the presentation of a submission which de Valera had incorrectly identified as being primarily the work of Cahill.) Secondly, the role played by individual Church leaders appears to have been confined to a consultation on Article 44 on religion. By contrast, on the basis of the most recent historical research, McQuaid was involved from a very early stage in the drafting process. He heavily influenced the substance and the wording of a number of Articles.[98]

How had McQuaid come to exercise in the 1930s such an important position of influence in de Valera's political world? The de Valera family had moved from Sandymount to Springville, Cross Avenue, in spring, 1930. The two men lived a few minutes from each other on foot. During the latter part of 1936, de Valera frequently employed his son, Vivion, to take documents to McQuaid. The future Archbishop of Dublin was the main architect of the Articles on family and marriage. In an early draft, McQuaid had sent the following wording to de Valera:

1. The State guarantees the constitution and protection of the family as the basis of moral education and social discipline and harmony, and the sure foundation of ordered society.

2.1   The Constitution of the family depends upon valid marriage.

2.2   Marriage, as the basis of family life, is under the special protection of the State; attacks on the sanctity of marriage or of family life are prohibited.

2.3   *Contraception and advocacy of the practice of contraception are prohibited and the possession, use, sale and distribution of contraceptives shall be punishable by law.* [My emphasis]

2.4   No law shall be enacted authorising the dissolution of a valid consummated marriage of baptized persons. No law shall be enacted authorising the annulment of marriage save on the following grounds, namely, that either or both of the parties did not agree to enter into the marriage contract, or was or were not free to enter, or did not freely enter into the marriage contract, or that the marriage was under the law for the time being in force invalid in form. Subject to the foregoing, the contract of marriage shall be regulated by law.

2.5   The State shall encourage early marriage and foster the production of large families by appropriate grants of remission of taxation in respect of children, by the promotion of saving and thrift schemes and by facilitating the provision of housing accommodation on reasonable terms.

2.6   Maternity is under the special protection of the State. Provision may be made by law for the supervision and inspection of lying-in hospitals and maternity nursing homes.[99]

De Valera, who had taken care of the contraception issue with the passage of the Criminal Law Amendment Act in 1935, was not persuaded by McQuaid to include a ban on contraception in the Constitution. The second draft of the Family Article (then Article 36) did not include any reference to contraception.

McQuaid was much more successful on the question of divorce. But de Valera was obliged again to modify the views of the Holy Ghost father. One of McQuaid's early drafts read as follows:

No person whose marriage has been dissolved under the civil law of any other State but is a subsisting valid marriage under the law for the time being in force within the jurisdiction of the Government and Parliament established by this Constitution, shall be capable of contracting a valid marriage within that jurisdiction during the lifetime of the other party to the marriage so dissolved.[100]

A note to de Valera outlined McQuaid's outright hostility to divorce. It was, he wrote:

> ... hardly possible to describe how great are the evils that flow from divorce. Matrimonial contracts are by it made variable; mutual kindness is weakened; deplorable inducements to unfaithfulness are supplied; harm is done to the education and training of children; occasion is afforded to the breaking up of homes; the seeds are sown of dissension among families; the dignity of womanhood is lessened and brought low, and women run the risk of being deserted after having ministered to the pleasures of men. .... So soon as the road to divorce began to be made smooth by law, at once quarrels, jealousies, and judicial separation largely increased, and such shamelessness followed, that men who had been in favour of these divorces repented of what they had done, and feared if they did not carefully seek a remedy by repealing the law, the State itself might come to ruin.[101]

De Valera accepted the substance of McQuaid's argument against divorce and he repeated those sentiments in the Dáil when he spoke on the subject.

It is possible to take other Articles — personal guarantees, private property and directive social principles, and education — and demonstrate the significant influence which McQuaid exercised on the drafting process. He practically wrote the Article on education, and he also had a major intellectual impact on the drafting of the preamble. Being from Cavan — a border county — it may not be so surprising to find that McQuaid also had a significant role to play in the drafting of Articles 2 and 3.[102]

Paradoxically, de Valera encountered the greatest difficulty with McQuaid in the drafting of Article 44. I have written on this matter elsewhere. There I describe how de Valera had relatively little contact with Church leaders while writing the Constitution. He felt obliged to seek advice from that quarter, and ultimately from the Holy See, only after he had found that McQuaid insisted on the placing of a 'one, true Church' formula in the Constitution. De Valera felt that such a course was neither right nor politically defensible. He did the rounds of Church leaders during the first two weeks in April 1937.

TABLE 2
DE VALERA'S NEGOTIATIONS
WITH THE CHURCHES, 1937

April 3	Called on the Nuncio *(Saturday)*
April 5	Saw the Cardinal at the Nunciature *(Monday)*
April 5	Called on Archbishop Byrne *(Monday)*
April 10	Saw the Nuncio, who promised to see Cardinal *(Saturday)*
April 10	Saw Archbishop Byrne *(Saturday)*
April 10	Saw Dr Irwin *(Saturday)*
April 11	Saw the Nuncio at Sean T's *(Sunday)*
April 12	Called on the Nuncio *(Monday)*
April 12	Saw Dr Irwin *(Monday)*
April 13	Phoned the Nuncio *(Tuesday)*
April 13	Saw the Rev. W. H. Massey, head of the Methodist Church in Ireland *(Tuesday)*
April 14	Saw Dr Irwin *(Wednesday)*
April 16	Saw Dr Irwin, the Moderator, and the Moderator Designate, who travelled from Belfast (Friday)
April 16	Saw the Nuncio at Sean T's *(Friday)*
April 16	J.P.W. [Walshe] went to Rome *(Friday evening)*
April 22	Called on the Nuncio *(Thursday)*
April 23	Nuncio phoned to say Cardinal approved Christian Churches *(Friday)*
April 24	Saw Nuncio and Cardinal *(Saturday)*
April 26	M. Moynihan say Arch. Gregg to D'Arcy *(Monday)*
April 27	Robinson goes to see D'Arcy *(Tuesday)*

Sourte: De Valera's account of his contact with the Churches: de Valera papers.

The outcome was the original draft Article 44 which recognized 'the special position of the Holy Catholic Apostolic and Roman Church as the guardian of the Faith professed by the great majority of the citizens.' The same section went on to include recognition of the Churches of the religious minorities, including the Jewish Congregations. Section 2 of Article 44 read:

> Freedom of conscience and the free profession and practice of religion are, subject to public order and morality, guaranteed to every citizen.

Overall, the 1937 Constitution was written at a time when clericalism, juridicalism and triumphalism was very prevalent in Irish society. Nevertheless, Church leaders played only a very small role in the drafting of the document. However, de Valera's strong Catholicism was the most dominant influence. It was fortunate that he represented a current of Catholicism which, albeit conservative, was not as radical or as extreme as were many of the ideas prevalent in Irish society in the 1930s. Both Cosgrave and de Valera — devout conservative Catholics — recognized that the laws and the Constitution of the country had to be inclusive. Being Irish and being Catholic were not synonymous.[103]

It ought to be mentioned here that the Chief Rabbi, Isaac Herzog, did not appear on the list of Church leaders that de Valera consulted. However, it is almost certain that he did do so. Herzog left Ireland in April 1937 to take up an appointment as Chief Rabbi in Palestine. There was a public ceremony to mark the occasion of his departure held in the Mansion House, Dublin, on 8 April 1937. According to an oral tradition in the Jewish community, Herzog is believed to have discussed the matter of the religious article with de Valera. The question of the inclusion of a formal mention of the Jewish community was discussed and agreed upon.[104]

In view of the anti-Semitic writings from the 1930s mentioned earlier, it might be appropriate to quote a section from an editorial in *The Irish Times* referring to the place of the Jewish community in Irish society:

> We claim no special credit for Ireland because she never has persecuted — for therein she has behaved merely as any civilised country ought to behave. On the other hand, it is difficult to read the speeches which were delivered at the Thursday function [farewell reception for Herzog] without, at least, a faint glow of pride. ..... Here in Ireland the Jews are not a separate people; they are part of the nation to whose welfare they

have contributed in large measure. They have done fine service to our industry, our commerce and our art, and, if we have tolerated them — to use an objectionable phrase — we have been more than repaid by their presence in our midst.[105]

The Constitution was described in 1957 by Pius XII in the following way:

Grounded on the bedrock of the natural law those fundamental human prerogatives which your constitution undertakes to assure to every citizen of Ireland, within the limits of order and morality, could find no ampler, no safer guarantee against the godless forces of subversion, the spirit of faction and violence, than mutual trust between the authorities of Church and State, independent each in its own sphere, but as it were allied for the common welfare in accordance with the principles of Catholic faith and doctrine.[106]

How did the other Churches view the new Constitution? *The Irish Times* regarded it as being 'largely bunkum, and to that extent it is harmless.' *The Church of Ireland Gazette* stated: 'The whole thing will not make us any freer, will not indeed make the slightest difference to our affairs.'[107] The introduction of a Constitution which would not 'make the slightest difference' to the affairs of the Church of Ireland was a small victory for tolerance. As Jack White noted, de Valera had stood up to the Church militant over Spain: 'This first indication that he was willing to stand firm against pressure from the Catholic Church was not lost on Protestants.'[108] The Church of Ireland may have considered de Valera's stance on the drafting of the Constitution even more significant. He had, as Cosgrave had done before him, stood out against confessionalism.

The new Constitution was framed at a time when confessional lobbies in Irish society were vocal. Influential Catholic laymen wished to see de Valera establish the Church as the 'one, true, Church'. But that was not what de Valera chose to do. He gave recognition to the 'special position' of the Catholic Church while recognizing the other Churches together with the Jewish congregation. That document, framed in difficult times, did not bear the hallmark of extremist confessional influence.[109]

Fianna Fáil was returned to power by a very slender majority in a general election on 1 July 1937. The Constitution had been passed in a referendum held on the same day by 685,105 to 526,945. On 27 April 1938 the new Seanad met and on 4 May Douglas Hyde was elected unopposed as the first President of Ireland. Entering office on 25 June, it was fitting that the first holder of that position should be a member of the Church of Ireland. De Valera was securely in power as world war approached, and he was to remain in office until 1948. Ireland remained a liberal democracy despite the gravest intrusion into the life of the citizen during World War II.

The Government did not have to face any wartime challenges from political Catholicism. Only Frank Duff's Legion of Mary and Muintir na Tire exhibited any healthy signs of attracting a greater mass following. De Valera was a strong leader who had worked out a clear *modus operandi* with the hierarchy. It was in the interest of neither the Church nor the State to encourage the radical projects of political Catholicism. As all the political parties in the Oireachtas were Catholic, the challenge which faced social Christians in other European countries was not in evidence.

Reviewing the early de Valera years, it might be stated that emphasis on the role of the bishops and the clergy in the policing of sexual morality has tended to negate the positive part played by many of the clergy in the formation of the nation's cultural life. Seán Ó Faoláin bemoaned the fact in the 1940s that the Church continued to rely upon 'the weapon of authority'. But that, in his opinion, could only be done for as long as Ireland was sheltered from the world:

> The writers see clearly that this isolation is now a dream. Walls of Censorship have been erected to keep out books and films that raise awkward questions. Practically every Irish writer of note has at one time or another been thrown to the lambs, i.e., in the interests of the most unsophisticated banned in his own country, some over and over again. But the air is uncensorable. Vulgarity and cheapness are not censored. Films are censored only for blatantly objectionable things; their triviality, their debasing cheapness of thought, their tinsel dreams infect the most remote villages. Above all a constant flow and reflow of emigrants flood the world outside with all its questions, challenges and bright temptations.[110]

The Ó Faoláin jeremiad is only part of the truth. The Catholic Church did favour censorship. But the laity also shared a desire to keep nationalist Ireland pure and uncontaminated from the ways of the world. However, to focus on the cultural authoritarianism of the Church is to neglect to point to the role of the Church as an intellectual innovator and agent of cultural change. This is a theme which may only be stated here as being worthy of exploration. The danger of trying to reduce the intellectual conflicts in Irish society to a lay/modernist-clerical/traditionalist cleavage is one that ought to be avoided. Notwithstanding the authoritarianism, the puritanism, the sexual repression and the radical individualism which characterized dominant aspects of Irish Catholicism, the controversy over a painting by Georges Rouault illustrates the range of thinking within the Church as a whole. This controversy began in 1942 when the advisory committee of the Municipal Gallery of Modern Art, Dublin, refused to accept the gift of a Rouault painting entitled 'Christ and the Soldier'. It had been purchased by the Friends of the National Collection for £380. The claim was made that the painting was blasphemous. Seán Keating, a distinguished Irish painter, did not consider the Rouault to be a work of art; it was 'naive, childish and unintelligible'. The poet Patrick Kavanagh declared against the painting but he also condemned those who rejected it.

Myles na gCopaleen ridiculed the opposition:

... the picture is executed in the modern manner, and could not be expected to please persons whose knowledge of sacred art is derived from the shiny chromo-lithograph bondieuserie of the boulevard Saint Sulpice, examples of which are to be found in every decent Irishman's bedroom.

A distinguished Holy Ghost father, Edward Leen, was asked to deliver a lecture on Rouault at which the painting of 'Christ and the Soldier' would be on display. He asked:

Is the picture blasphemous? The truth cannot be blasphemous even when it lays bare relentlessly, even cruelly, the inner sense of a reality which crashes through our miserable conventionality.

The intellectual argument in defence of Rouault was somewhat one-sided. But the controversy continued only to be resolved in a novel way: the national seminary of the Catholic Church, St Patrick's College, Maynooth, was delighted to accept the painting on loan. It was placed in the library. Today the painting hangs, where it ought to have done from the outset, in its rightful place in the Municipal Gallery.[111]

Perhaps this controversy will help to show how diverse a group were Catholic clergy and religious. Conservatism — religious and artistic — could be found in Irish lay life. The range of human experience of the members of the Irish Catholic Church differed greatly and some members of the laity were fortunate to find that their encounters with clergy and religious could be life-enhancing and enriching. Unfortunately others had the experience of finding themselves the victims of authoritarianism — an authoritarianism which was also manifest in the way the institutions of the State often treated its citizens.

The legislators did, however, avoid extremist solutions propounded by overheated Catholic lobbies who were concerned about the need to corporatize that society and keep it safe from the nefarious influence of the triple alliance of communists, Freemasons and Jews. Neither Church nor State welcomed the idea of extremists playing a commanding role in Irish society. De Valera had shown his hostility to intemperate religious advocates. The Catholic hierarchy, notwithstanding the injudicious acts and utterances of individual bishops, also sought to protect Irish society from the zealots.

IRISH CATHOLICISM
AND THE MOTHER AND CHILD CASE

De Valera and Fianna Fáil lost power in 1948 and were replaced by a five-party Government led by John A. Costello. One of the first actions of the new Government, which included Seán MacBride as Minister for External Affairs, was to send a telegram to the Pope:

> ... desiring to repose at the feet of your Holiness the assurance of our
> filial loyalty and of our devotion to your August Person, as well as our
> firm resolve to be guided in all our work by the teaching of Christ, and
> to strive for the attainment of a social order in Ireland based on Christian
> principles.[112]

There was no precedent for this decision. Neither Cosgrave nor de Valera had sent a telegram to the Pope upon assuming office.

The text of the telegram accurately reflected many of the actions of the inter-party Government between 1948 and 1951. Within weeks of coming into office, the Irish Ambassador to the Holy See, Joseph Walshe, had offered Ireland as a refuge to Pius XII in the event of his having to flee Rome following a socialist/communist takeover. The Minister for External Affairs, Seán MacBride was responsible for arranging or helping to arrange — through the good offices of the

Catholic Church — the collection of funds to help the Christian Democrats win the general election in Italy. The Archbishop of Dublin, John Charles McQuaid, who had been appointed to that office in 1940, was encouraged to lead this appeal by MacBride. During the years 1948-1951, McQuaid was encouraged to become much more actively involved in the affairs of Government than ever had been the case under de Valera.[113]

From autumn 1948 until the following summer, the Irish Government attempted to reverse the decision of the Holy See to send an Italian to replace the papal nuncio, Paschal Robinson, who had died on 27 August. It was unlikely that the Government could ever have expected to win but MacBride — advised by Ambassador Walshe — persisted. Finally, the Government was forced to capitulate and the original nominee, Ettore Felici, came to Ireland. Those events again brought Archbishop McQuaid into the Government decision-making process. He was invited to advise throughout the crisis. On at least one occasion he was asked to review a government document in order to make suggested changes before it was sent to the Holy See. Moreover, the Irish bishops were requested by the Government to intervene at the Holy See in order to support its stance. This self-generated crisis demonstrated the closeness of Church and State during the term of office of the first inter-party Government.[114]

Ironically, it is commonly accepted that that Government fell because of a Church-State crisis — the only Government in the history of the State to go out of office for that reason.

The Mother and Child crisis, as it was called, was less a Church-State crisis than an internal government crisis. But what the crisis does reveal was the growing integralist impulse of the leadership of the Catholic hierarchy — a desire to secure certain Catholic principles as the underpinning for social legislation.

The motivation for such an intransigent stance sprang from a growing mistrust of the independence of the State. Behind the actions of the bishops — and here it might be more appropriate to speak of the leadership of the hierarchy — was the fear that the State might one day be controlled by a secular socialist Government. Therefore, it was necessary to make a determined stance in order to defeat the 'socialistic' project known as the Mother and Child scheme. The frontiers of the State had to be rolled back.

Another old fear also manifested itself at that time. During the course of the Dunbar-Harrison episode, the Government had to take measures to prevent the possible episcopal boycott of doctors trained elsewhere than in the constituent colleges of the National University of Ireland. The Minister for Health in the inter-party Government, Noel Browne, was a graduate of Trinity College. He had taken over the implementation of the Mother and Child scheme from the previous Fianna Fáil Government. From the vantage point of the mid-1990s it is hard to imagine what possible objections there could have been to a scheme which proposed to introduce a free, non means tested programme to take care of all mothers, and children up to the age of sixteen. But the secretary to the National Conference of Bishops, Bishop Staunton wrote to Costello on 10 October 1950 in his official capacity stating that the scheme was in direct opposition to the rights of the family and of the individual and was liable to 'very great abuse'. If adopted, the letter continued, it would 'constitute a ready-made instrument for future totalitarian aggression'. It was the view of the hierarchy that the right to provide for the health of children belonged to parents and not to the State. The State had the right to intervene only in a subsidiary capacity, to supplement and not to supplant. Staunton continued: [my emphasis] '*It may help indigent or neglectful parents; it may not deprive 90 per cent of parents of their rights because of 10 per cent necessitous or negligent parents.*' The Bishop, on behalf of the hierarchy, told Costello that it was not sound social policy to impose a state medical service on the whole community on the pretext of relieving the necessitous 10 per cent from the so-called indignity of the means test. Staunton also wrote that the right to provide for the physical education of children belonged to the family and not to the State:

> Gynaecological care may be, and in some other countries is, interpreted to include provision for birth limitation and abortion. We have no guarantee that State officials will respect Catholic principles in regard to these matters. Doctors trained in instruction in which we have no confidence may be appointed as medical officers under the proposed service, and may give gynaecological care not in accordance with Catholic principles.

Staunton further claimed, on behalf of the hierarchy, that the proposed scheme destroyed the confidential relationship between patient and doctor. It also meant for the hierarchy the elimination of private medical practitioners by a State paid service.[115]

The vehemence of the sentiments in the letter might have been better addressed to an anti-clerical Government. But Costello and his ministerial colleagues were devout Christians — most of whom had made a pilgrimage to Rome in 1950 for Holy Year.

During the course of the crisis, Costello told the Dáil: 'I am an Irishman second; I am a Catholic first.' MacBride, in notes he put on file, stated that due weight had also to be given to the heads of other religious denominations: 'In this case [the mother and child issue] we are dealing with the considered views of the leaders of the Catholic Church to which the vast majority of our people belong; their views cannot be ignored.' Noel Browne was also prepared to defer to the ruling of the bishops in moral matters. He felt, however, that there was room for an alternative opinion when dealing with social policy. Browne was forced to resign on 10 April 1951. In the end, he had not been supported by a single member of the cabinet.

A united Government might have been able to stand up to the episcopal challenge. That was what happened when Fianna Fáil returned to power. The new Minister for Health, James Ryan, took over the implementation of the scheme. He was again confronted by episcopal intransigence. The hierarchy went so far as to issue a letter in April 1953 to all the national papers — with the exception of *The Irish Times*. De Valera confronted his former schoolfriend, Cardinal John D'Alton and the letter was withdrawn. A strong denunciation of the Ryan scheme, it was couched in somewhat less robust language than the Staunton missive referred to above.[116] Ambassador Walshe provided an unsolicited commentary on the text which was forwarded to him in Rome:

> The declaration is fearfully ill-digested. In no country, not to speak of a Catholic Country, would the Bishops make so many general assumptions about the possibly unchristian and immoral or amoral attitude of State Servants. The 'principle' quoted from Quadragesimo anno is so vague and so little in accord with the growing complexity of social problems, in every State, that I feel quite sure it would not be referred to by any sociological expert today in Rome. The declaration is so biased, ill-prepared, badly written that it must have been a last minute decision, perhaps taken under pressure from the Doctors Group — and the Bishops put themselves in the position of being protectors of privilege. As I read the position, they owe a lot to the Taoiseach for having taken their heads out of the noose. Had he allowed the situation to develop as

it was surely going to develop, helped by Jack Costello's unparalleled bad judgment, their prestige and power would have received a great blow indeed.[117]

The hierarchy had indeed cause on that occasion to be grateful to de Valera. He had prevented a Church-State crisis which the bishops would have lost decisively. It was clear that the leadership of the Church in the 1950s — notwithstanding the presence of John Charles McQuaid — was very weak. The hierarchy sought to block. A number of its leaders had excellent negative minds. But besides showing themselves to be out of touch with contemporary developments in Catholic social teaching, they had made a significant error of judgement by allowing themselves to be manipulated by the medical profession. The late Bishop of Ferns, Donal Herlihy told me: 'We allowed ourselves to be used by the doctors, but it won't happen again.'[118] With the growth of special interest groups inside and outside the Church in the latter part of the twentieth century, the wisdom of Bishop Herlihy's comment has enduring relevance.

The Mother and Child crisis had exposed serious deficiencies in the decision-making structures of the hierarchy. It also showed up a basic lack of good judgement. Therefore, the 1950s might have been used profitably by the Irish hierarchy to engage in serious stocktaking but only further research will reveal whether that occurred. A preliminary survey of Government files shows that Archbishop McQuaid was involved in at least one other major conflict with de Valera — on this occasion in early 1953 over an increase in capitation grants for secondary schools.[119] Other evidence shows that various Government departments — Health, Justice, Education, Taoiseach, External Affairs — had begun to take a more independent and assertive position during the latter part of a decade which is often mistakenly noted for economic, social and cultural stagnation.[120]

DEALING WITH INTOLERANCE

I have sought to emphasize in this study the intellectual and cultural diversity of Irish Catholicism. The intolerance and bigotry of a number of Catholic publications were as offensive to other Catholics as they were to the members of the other Churches or religious communities who were the victims of the attacks. But how did the Church and the State deal with displays of intolerance? I have chosen to illustrate my answer by using two case studies:

1. The rise and fall of Maria Duce,

2. The Fethard-on-Sea controversy.

The first involves an analysis of Archbishop John Charles McQuaid's response to the emergence after the war of a rightwing confessional grouping, Maria Duce. Their ultimate demise was due to the withdrawal of episcopal approval for their activities.

The Fethard-on-Sea episode, involving the boycotting of members of the Church of Ireland by their Catholic neighbours, reveals the manner in which Éamon de Valera and his Fianna Fáil Government reacted to deescalate a serious community situation in Wexford in 1957. This laid down a benchmark against intolerance — even at the expense of having to speak out against the position of a former episcopal friend.

CASE STUDY 1:
THE RISE AND FALL OF MARIA DUCE

Bloodied but unbowed, a loyal group of Fahey followers established Maria Duce in the summer of 1945. The inspiration for the establishment of that organization came also, according to its members, from the dissatisfaction of a group of laymen who had corresponded with the press on matters of Catholic interest but 'repeated rebuffs' made them aware of the need to unite:

> Truth, it seems, is poor propaganda, and the vested interests who direct the policies of these papers are careful that its startling and naked reality should not obtrude itself on the public attention.[121]

There was little need for Maria Duce activists to identify those hidden forces. The war against Jewish-inspired naturalism was declared yet again. In the words of its founders this organization pledged 'to vindicate the Social Rights of Christ the King.' Its purpose was to foster among its members 'a knowledge of and a zeal for Christ's Kingly Rights in every sphere of human activity.' Membership was open to all Catholics seventeen years of age or over. After a three months probation, if judged worthy, they would be 'enrolled at one of the ceremonies of consecration that take place at regular intervals.' Maria Duce had a six-point integralist programme for the establishment of social order which, in essence, favoured the establishment of a confessional State:

1   The Catholic Church is the One True Church and ought to be acknowledged as such by States and nations. The non-Catholics ought always to be treated in accordance with the teaching of the Church and the principles of Christian Charity, so that the rights of all human persons be respected.

2   The state must recognise the Catholic Church as Divinely appointed to teach man what favours or hinders his supernatural destiny.

3   The Unity and Indissolubility of Christian Marriage ought to be most carefully maintained, as symbolising the union of Christ and His Mystical Body.

4   The Education of Youth ought always to envisage Youth as members of the Mystical Body.

5   The Social Doctrine contained in the Papal Encyclicals ought to be reduced to practice in such wise as to promote the virtuous life of individual members of the mystical Body of Christ organised in families, Vocational Associations and States.

Maria Duce's charter went on to outline the need to organize society along vocational lines in order to 'avoid the pitfalls inherent both in the unbridled individualism favoured by Capitalism and in the excessive State-control sponsored by Communism.'[122]

Dissatisfied with the national press, Maria Duce established *Fiat*. It was first produced on a hand duplicating machine and appeared about every six weeks. The paper pursued many of the old themes familiar to readers of Fahey's work. An article in issue number 10 entitled ' "Anti-Semitism" at Oberammergau', reproduced many of the arguments earlier advanced by Fahey:

We may be able to do little to foil the Jewish attempt to use Russia as a means for Bolshevizing Europe, but we must resist all attempts to impose Jewish Naturalism here. We must particularly oppose the Jewish control of money and credit and the powerful Jewish campaign for Naturalism in the Press and the Cinema, all of which are weapons in the 'softening up' process for Bolshevism. ....

If we wish to survive as a Nation and preserve our Catholic civilization, we must, however, combat the undeniable Judeo-Masonic attempt to promote Naturalism in this country, whatever form it may assume.[123]

Fiat also reproduced articles on the alleged Judeo-Masonic control of the United States, of the United Nations and of other international organizations. An article in *Fiat* (no 27) listed the 'Jewish Rulers of UNO', the 'Jews on the Atomic Energy Commission', and the 'big three' who comprised the 'secret government of the U.S.A.' *Fiat* also wrote in defence of Senator Joseph McCarthy;

...no political figure in the United States to-day, or possibly even in the whole history of the great Republic, has become the target of so much organized slander and vilification as Senator McCarthy. No bounds are known to the venomous attacks made daily on his person by apologists of subversive and anti-Christian elements.

That 'campaign of hate' had even been in evidence, according to *Fiat*, in *The Irish Press's* editorial on 31 March 1953.

On the home front, *Fiat* attacked the Irish Association for Civil Liberties (IACL). Seán Ó Faoláin was the President of the IACL at the time and other members included Senator Owen Sheehy Skeffington, the painter Louis Le Brocquy and prominent Irish academics and public figures. In issue 29, the Maria Duce paper inferred that there was a Masonic connection between the local association and its sister organizations in Paris and in New York. A rival organization to the IACL, the Irish Theatre and Cinema Patrons' Association, was supported by Maria Duce. It regularly expressed great concern over the negative impact on local society of such alien forms of mass culture.

Who joined Maria Duce? It had a core membership in Dublin and, apart from the enthusiasm of a few individuals in rural towns, it did not spread to the countryside. Despite its earlier ambitions, it proved to be little more than a study group which met on a Sunday to listen to a lecture by Fahey. Its president was a tailor called Tom Agar. The vice president, Thomas Roseingrave was the organization's major intellectual force. His membership of Maria Duce remained somewhat anomalous and may have had more to do with his personal friendship with Fahey than his espousal of its views. Roseingrave tended to exercise a moderating influence over his Holy Ghost mentor.

Maria Duce did, for a time, enjoy the recognition of John Charles McQuaid. A member of the Holy Ghost order before becoming Archbishop in 1940, McQuaid had been a highly intelligent member of a younger generation of seminarians. There was mutual respect between the two men. But if anyone knew the shortcomings of Fahey it was McQuaid. The Archbishop of Dublin was not unappreciative of the lifelong efforts and dedication of Fahey. Neither was he unsympathetic to Fahey's mariology and his theology of Christ the King. But he was cautious and the relationship in the post war period was never particularly close. Nevertheless, McQuaid was prepared initially to give a qualified sanction to the work of Maria Duce. His initial response may have been partly conditioned by the Archbishop's deep concern over the onset of cold war, the growing power of communism and the dangers of an outbreak of a third world war.

By March 1949, membership forms for Maria Duce also contained the line 'permissu Ordinarii Dioecesis Dublinensis'. But the stridency of Maria Duce and its confrontational style had placed it in some difficulties by the end of that year. This arose, in part, out of a public controversy with the theatre critic of *The Standard*, Gabriel Fallon, who was also a personal friend of Archbishop McQuaid. Fallon wrote critically about Maria Duce. That organization, in turn, alleged that Fallon had said they were conducting a 'totalitarian academy' and that it was 'anti-Semitic'.[124] Despite a visit by a Maria Duce delegation to the editor of *The Standard,* Fallon stood his ground. He said that concerning anti-Semitism and the nature of Article 44 of Ireland's Constitution, he had been a consistent follower of Jacques Maritain. In the course of the exchanges, Fallon wrote:

> I have never made any secret of this fact. Until M. Maritain's teachings are proved in error, or until expressly forbidden to accept them by the proper Ecclesiastical authority, I shall continue to accept them.

Fallon also wrote:

> Unfortunately, the members of this organisation appear to think that there can be only one theological opinion on any question and that no differences of opinion are tolerated by the Church. They make the mistake of believing (to use the phrase of the Rev. Editor of *America*) "that the whole body of Catholic thought is cut and dried."[125]

McQuaid did not wish to see a continuation of feuding between Catholics and he called in the leaders for a serious talk at the end of November. Roseingrave wrote to Fahey on 25 November 1949 explaining that the Archbishop had told the four-man delegation

> ... that 'Maria Duce' was doing splendid work, that it was a great power for good, but that we were not doing enough good work!! He did not express any disapproval with any of our activities.

Roseingrave then added that the Archbishop felt that the work being done by the Catholic Cinema and Theatre Patrons' Association was 'very necessary'. Fahey was further informed that 'His Grace hears many stories about us. Some say we are building up the city, others say we are tearing it down. But his grace told us *that he will not condemn us.*' Roseingrave concluded: 'All activities will continue as usual.' [126] While the Maria Duce delegation interpreted what the Archbishop had said very positively, there was a warning to professionalize their activities. Whether the leadership of Maria Duce realized it or not, McQuaid had issued a stern warning. It may have been as a consequence of this particular encounter that a memorandum was drafted, probably by Roseingrave, which offered a radical self-criticism of the activities of Maria Duce. It argued:

> In concrete terms, the main duty of M.D. is to organize itself so as to be able to work assiduously for the realization in practice of its positive 6-point programme — NOT THE ASSAULT ON COMMUNISM, FREEMASONRY AND THE JEWS, NOT THE ORGANIZATION OF AN ALL-OUT OFFENSIVE OF THE PUBLIC SINNERS AND FELLOW-TRAVELLERS OF HOLLYWOOD — LET ALONE AN OFFENSIVE AGAINST SUCH CATHOLICS WHO (LIKE THE JOURNALISTS OF THE STANDARD) ACCEPT AND RECOGNIZE CHRIST AS PRIEST BUT WHO DO NOT YET REALIZE THE FULL IMPLICATIONS OF HIS KINGSHIP.[127]

While that was what the Archbishop might have wished to hear, it did not come to pass. Maria Duce remained a movement obsessed by its own ghosts.

Maria Duce made its most serious strategic mistake when it directed its activities towards the removal of Article 44, the religious Article in the Constitution. This involved an organized letter-writing campaign to the Department of the Taoiseach. McQuaid, who had been a central

figure in the drafting of the original Article, acted vigorously against
Maria Duce. His secretary, Christopher Mangan, wrote to Tom Agar on
14 February 1951:

> I am asked by His Grace the Archbishop to inform you that he has decided
> to withdraw the — Permissu Ordinarii Diocesis Dublinensis — from your
> six-point programme. The Archbishop bids me therefore to request you to
> refrain from printing this permission on any further literature, which you
> may have printed.
>
> His Grace would also appreciate it if you will kindly refrain from styling,
> in your literature, your organisation as a Catholic Action body, since an
> essential requirement of a body being Catholic Action is that it be
> approved by the Bishop of the Diocese; this approval has not been given
> by the Archbishop to your organisation.[128]

Maria Duce received this blow soon after the picket on the Royal
Theatre against Danny Kaye whom they accused of being a friend of
communists. Maria Duce had also attacked Gregory Peck. Orson Welles
had also fallen foul of that organization. In 1952, it was criticized by the
much respected philosopher, Mgr Arthur Ryan, Queen's University,
Belfast.

Ironically, McQuaid took further action against Maria Duce over the
tone and content of its statement which was handed to the anti-Catholic
author, Paul Blanshard on 29 November at the Gresham Hotel.[129]
McQuaid 'disapproved of the terms of the statement'. It read, in part:

> Your attempt, by your writings, to alienate the Catholic laity from the
> Hierarchy and priests, finds its significant counterpart in the present
> activities of Atheistic Communist governments. Your activity is the activity
> of Stalin and Tito. The history of the Penal Laws in this country might
> convince you of the futility of your task.

The Archbishop made it known that while 'Mr Blanshard may be
hostile to the Catholic Church, any answer made to him ought to be
dignified and restrained.' Requesting to see Fahey, Agar wrote: 'The
sting is in the last paragraph, which is a terrible blow to us.' It read:

> Further, His Grace wishes to declare his emphatic disagreement with the
> use of the name of the Blessed Virgin Mary in your activities.[130]

McQuaid subsequently sent two priests to help guide the organization.
Both priests said they wanted to be of help, 'but we fear they are looking

at events through different spectacles', Roseingrave wrote to Fahey. He felt that the two men had 'rather a *Standard* outlook on matters'. Reviewing activities for Fahey, Roseingrave told him that Regina Publications had sold 23,000 books and pamphlets including 2,300 encyclicals (2,000 of *The Kingship of Christ and Organized Naturalism*). Maria Duce, he claimed, had distributed 400,000 copies of *Fiat*. 'So please God, the work will go on', he wrote. In March, Fahey had a meeting with the Archbishop. 'Perhaps and please God', wrote Roseingrave, 'it indicates a turning in the tide against all the adverse criticism.'[131] But that was not to be the case.

The cause of Maria Duce received indirect help from an unlikely source. Cardinal Alfredo Ottaviani delivered a speech, to mark the occasion of the fourteenth anniversary of Pius XXII's election as Pope, at the Lateran University in Rome on 2 March 1953. Its contents on the relationship between Church and State greatly pleased the leading members of Maria Duce. Fahey immediately sought and obtained permission to translate it into English and publish it as a pamphlet. In a letter to Ottaviani on 6 September 1953, he congratulated Ottaviani on his 'luminous, timely and courageous lecture on the duties of a Catholic State in regard to religion.'

Roseingrave, too, was enthusiastic about the project. He wrote to Fahey on 14 September 1953:

> Now, however, that Cardinal Ottaviani has spoken so clearly I think the new argument of the supporters of Art. 44 will be that Ireland cannot apply the doctrine enunciated by the Cardinal because Ireland today cannot be considered a Catholic country. It cannot, they will say, become a *confessional state*. Alternatively, they will put forward the argument advanced by the *Irish Monthly* (*Donal Barrington*) and which has 'caught' on very well in Catholic circles here namely that Art. 44 does *place all religions on the same level*.

The hierarchy, and the Archbishop of Dublin in particular, must have been concerned about the divisiveness of having the 'Article 44' debate raised again. It had been resolved in 1937 not entirely to the satisfaction of McQuaid. But he was prepared to live with the compromise. Moreover, there was neither political support nor widespread enthusiasm among Irish Catholic intellectuals for any reversal to a confessional State model.

But if Fahey and Roseingrave had developed the hope of using Ottaviaini's speech as the basis for a new campaign, they were again disappointed by the Archbishop. The archdiocesan censor refused permission to publish the pamphlet. Roseingrave wrote to Fahey on 9 December 1954 suggesting why this had happened:

> The one point that came into my mind again and again was : The Hierarchy for some good reason must be prepared to accept the status quo. That policy must be to tolerate the evil of Art. 44.

Maria Duce had been marginalized by its own extremism. The hierarchy had come to accept Article 44. Archbishop McQuaid had removed his ecclesiastical approval and the organization had withered away. There was to be no integralist revival in Ireland in the 1950s. Fahey died in 1954 and Maria Duce quickly diminished in membership. But it never completely disappeared. A cadre of the old guard continued to meet through the 1960s. The works of Fr Fahey were kept in print by the devout. In 1972, following the retirement of John Charles McQuaid, remnants of the Maria Duce group met to mourn the departure of the Archbishop.[132] While Maria Duce had always been a fringe group, the philosophy they represented, and the tactics they had espoused, remained part of a wider integralist current in Irish Catholicism which was to manifest itself at a later date in the century. But there was to be one essential difference: the new right of the later period was far less dependent upon episcopal goodwill than Maria Duce and the other confessional organizations of the 1930s. The withdrawal of McQuaid's support from Maria Duce fatally wounded that organization. In the later period, the 'imprimatur' was neither sought nor offered. It was relatively easy to contain extremism within a strong authoritarian and hierarchical Church. That was no longer possible later in the century.

CASE STUDY 2:
FETHARD–ON–SEA

Irish Catholics continued in the 1950s to articulate their views through the major political parties as they had done in the earlier decades of the State. Irish Catholic nationalism remained very strong in the 1950s and both Church and State, having marked out their respective civic spaces, were content to persevere in the politics of accommodation and containment. However, the extremist stance taken by the leadership of the hierarchy in 1950-51 and again in 1953 over the Fianna Fáil Mother and Child scheme had damaged Church-State relations seriously. The underlying assumption on both occasions — a radical mistrust of the Irish State and of its willingness to protect Catholic values — had offended de Valera. There was a further serious Church-State difficulty over education involving de Valera and McQuaid in 1953-4. What was missing on the Church side in both the Mother and Child crisis and in subsequent conflicts was a spirit of compromise. The intimacy of the Church-State relationship in earlier decades had to be placed on a more formal footing after the events of the Mother and Child crisis. The Catholic Church leadership on that occasion had exhibited little understanding of the need for change. The failure to restructure the workings of Church-State relations in the 1950s was to have serious long-term consequences for the Catholic Church in later decades. It is quite evident from an examination of a number of episcopal statements that the hierarchy did not have a strategic pastoral plan. If economic planning had only recently been adopted by governments in post war Europe, the Irish Church leadership remained reactive and suspicious of Government actions — at a time when ministers exuded good will for the Church.

The lack of strategic planning by the Catholic Church in the 1950s left it open to being consumed by the politics of the present moment. By failing to look to the future no realistic appraisal was made of the direction in which Irish society was heading. That left the bishops and senior clergy open to reactive politics. Furthermore it helped preserve the false impression that there was need for little or no change. It also fostered the unrealistic expectation that the position of strength enjoyed by the Church since the foundation of the State could be preserved indefinitely. A critical evaluation of the future role of the Church in Irish society — in the light of religious developments in continental Europe — would have indicated that there would have to be a greater emphasis on accommodation rather than on confrontation.

Despite its overwhelming majority status, the Catholic Church in the 1950s felt radically insecure. Mistrust of the State has been discussed above. There was a strong suspicion about the bona fides of other Churches and there was also a radical mistrust of lay people. The Bishop of Clonfert, William Philbin, said in 1957:

Reluctant as we are to criticise other religious groups, it seems necessary to point out that at present a concerted effort is being made by the religious minority to secure a dominating position in our public life. .... I suggest that this is an explicit challenge to a Catholic nation which it would be unwise to overlook. Even if it does not succeed in making us desert our faith it may do much towards neutralising our Catholicity, and preventing the application of its principles. It may have done much to this effect already. We are opposed by an extremely efficient propaganda machine. We may have reached a stage when calling Ireland a Catholic nation will itself be regarded as a challenge, and even deplored by some Catholics.[133]

It is hard to discover any evidence which would have proved the basis for such a statement. But the explicitly stated belief that 'Ireland' was 'a Catholic nation' had been challenged with determination throughout the 1950s by Senator Owen Sheehy Skeffington and others.[134] De Valera, too, tried to work out in practice the essence of his compromise in the formulation of Article 44. His politics sought to accommodate and to contain. But there were occasions when he was obliged to make explicit his belief in a pluralist Ireland. The Fethard-on-Sea episode was one such occasion.

The wife of a local County Wexford farmer disappeared from home in 1957 with their two young children. Her husband was a Catholic and she a member of the Church of Ireland. There had been disagreement over the education of the eldest child. When she left home, rumours circulated in the locality that she had been persuaded to leave her husband by Protestant friends. This resulted in a boycott of shops and farms owned by Protestants and the affair turned into an ugly sectarian incident. It received wide coverage in the national press.

The woman and her two children disappeared on 27 April. The husband secured a writ of *habeas corpus* in the Northern Ireland High Court for the production of the two children. The boycott began on 13 May in a village which had a population of about 100. The local Church of Ireland school with eleven pupils closed on 15 May after, according to *The Irish Times*, 'its Catholic teacher was advised by a number of women in the village that it "would be better for her if she did not give any more lessons".' The sexton of St Mogue's Church — also a Catholic — was advised by her neighbours to give up the duties she had been carrying out for a number of years.[135] When a temporary teacher arrived to take over the school, he found a notice on the door which read: 'Beware of lead in this boycott village.'[136]

The boycott was discussed informally at a government meeting on 3 June. The Secretary of the Department of the Taoiseach, Maurice Moynihan, recommended afterwards to de Valera that he should, before taking any further action, discuss the matter with Archbishop McQuaid. De Valera, however, decided to postpone action for the present.[137] In the following weeks, the national press carried a large number of stories about the episode. Moreover, the press in Northern Ireland also carried reports of what was happening in Fethard.

De Valera sought a meeting with McQuaid on 21 June 1957. Uppermost in his mind was the fundamental injustice of the boycott and of the damaging effects it was having on the country's reputation in Northern Ireland and abroad. The Taoiseach saw the Archbishop in Drumcondra that afternoon.

No detailed minute of the conversation was put on the file as McQuaid had requested that the meeting should be treated as 'strictly confidential'. De Valera therefore instructed his secretary Maurice Moynihan to keep the record of the meeting apart from the official file. Nevertheless, Moynihan did write on the file that McQuaid appeared to agree generally with the Taoiseach's views:

> ... as to the inadequate justification, or lack of justification, on the
> available information, for the attitude taken up by members of the
> Catholic community at Fethard and as to the damaging effect on the
> national reputation for religious tolerance and fair play which is likely to
> result from the publicity given to the matter.[138]

Archbishop McQuaid was in a position to take some action. Fethard was in the diocese of Ferns which was in the ecclesiastical province of Dublin. But there was little McQuaid could do if he did not have the support of the local ordinary. Bishop Staunton of Ferns declined to make any comment on the matter in public. But the local clergy in the parish of Fethard were sympathetic and supportive of the boycott. The clergy would not have been in a position to continue their support without the tacit support of their Bishop.

However, the Bishop of Galway, Michael Browne, showing neither reticence nor prudence, spoke at the end of June on the boycott in Wexford at the annual conference of the Catholic Truth Society. He said that there seemed to be a concerted campaign to entice or kidnap Catholic children and deprive them of their Faith. Non-Catholics, with one or two honourable exceptions, did not protest against the crime of conspiring to steal the children of a Catholic father, he said. But they tried to make political capital when a Catholic people made a peaceful and moderate protest. 'Do non-Catholics never use this weapon of boycott in the North?' he asked in the presence of Cardinal D'Alton, Archbishop McQuaid, Bishop Staunton of Ferns, Bishop Collier of Ossory, Bishop Kyne of Meath and Bishop Dunne of Nara.[139] Browne was not speaking on behalf of the hierarchy. He was merely expressing his own views. But those views, which were quite inflammatory in the circumstances, were not contradicted by Staunton.

Given the apparent abdication of responsibility by the hierarchy, de Valera told the Dáil on 4 July 1957 in answer to a question from Noel Browne:

> I have made no public statement because I have clung to the hope that good sense and decent neighbourly feeling would of themselves bring this business to an end. I cannot say that I know every fact, but if, as head of the Government, I must speak, I can only say, from what has appeared in public, that I regard this boycott as ill-conceived, ill-considered, and futile for the achievement of the purpose for which it seems to have been intended; that I regard it as unjust and cruel to confound the innocent with the guilty; that I repudiate any suggestion that this boycott is typical of the attitude or conduct of our people; that I am convinced that ninety per cent of them look on this matter as I do; and that I beg of all who have regard for the fair name, good repute and well-being of our nation to use their influence to bring this deplorable affair to a speedy end.[140]

De Valera received a large number of letters in support of his statement. A J. Monahan from Clontarf wrote on 5 May:

> There will not be one Mass said to-day in Ireland at which the celebrant will not open the Gloria with ever greater fervour than usual, and there is no Irishman anywhere who will not to-day carry his head higher. Indeed, I feel that men everywhere, frightened by the trend of recent events — whether they attempt to express it as I am doing or not — will find in your Fethard statement a hopeful promise of fulfilment to their secret prayers.[141]

Archbishop McQuaid wrote on 5 July:

> It was in Rockwell — where I am for a few days — that I read your letter and the enclosed Parliamentary reply. I am grateful for your

courtesy in sending me the reply that you feel bound to express on the incident at Fethard-on-Sea.

I am, dear Taoiseach...[142]

De Valera's covering letter was not placed on the file. It is not possible to determine from the text of McQuaid's letter whether or not the Taoiseach was happy with the Archbishop's actions.

If he had intervened, the local curate remained quite intransigent. On the Sunday following Valera's statement, he told the local Fethard congregation:

> The priests of this parish, with a full sense of their responsibility and realising the Catholic issue at stake, assure the faithful, loyal Catholics of this parish that, in the stand they are taking in defence of Catholic principles, not now, nor in the near future, nor in the distant future, will their priests let them down by asking them to withdraw one inch or to apologise for their actions. Their priests have the utmost confidence and conviction that the people will persevere unflinchingly, and will not allow anything to happen to mar or besmirch this grand, dignified, noble, loyal, profession of their faith. In view of some of the things that have been said recently, I am going to read this last part again. I want you all to take it to heart, and to listen to it very carefully and put it into practice. It is more necessary now than ever before.

That was exactly the same statement, according to *The Irish Times*, that had been read out in the church three weeks before.[143]

Neither was Bishop Browne of Galway in a mood to moderate his earlier statement. On 7 July he said that the resentment shown by the people of Fethard-on-Sea was also moderate in extent and quality and he had no reason to doubt that. There had been vague statements about a large number of people being victimized. Bishop Browne, dealing with the morality of boycotts, said:

> I will merely point out that it is not against justice or charity to refuse special favours such as one's money or custom to those whom one regards as responsible for, or approving of a grave offence. ..... It is a gross misrepresentation to represent the events in Fethard-on-Sea as due to intolerance or hatred for Protestants. They are not. They are due solely to justified indignation at a grave wrong.[144]

But an editorial in *The Irish Times* on 15 July had no doubt about what was happening in Fethard. The boycott was 'undemocratic, unchristian and in every way detestable.'[145]

The boycott had provoked great outrage in the South. The Government was made fully aware of the displeasure of many citizens who denounced such bigotry in letters to the Department of the Taoiseach. The Minister for Finance, Dr James Ryan (who was from Wexford), discussed the episode with a deputation from the Irish Association of Civil Liberty. The delegation said that they deplored the boycott. Ryan sought to discourage the association from becoming involved at a local level. He felt that a deputation by the association to Fethard at that time would not be helpful. The Minister said that he hoped that there would be an early solution.

The Government again discussed the Fethard boycott on 12 July where the Taoiseach suggested the possibility of the Minister for Justice setting up a judicial inquiry to investigate the matter. The Department of Justice advised that that would not be possible. The minutes of the meeting read that the Minister 'is not invested with any powers that would enable him to set up a tribunal'.[146] The idea was dropped.

However, de Valera had not been inactive over Fethard-on-Sea but he found that he did not get the cooperation he expected from the Church authorities immediately concerned in the area. But that will only be discovered when the ecclesiastical archives become available to historians. The Bishop of Kildare and Leighlin, Thomas Keogh, said on 23 February 1958:

> Sectarianism is not in our minds nor in our bones; there are those who do not accept our Faith in its entirety but in spite of differences we are all bound together by the bonds of charity and it is the same charity that inspires the Catholic apostolate.[147]

He was one episcopal voice. There may have been others. But Keogh is the only one recorded upon the Government file.

The woman in the crisis returned with her two children to her husband in January 1958. The Fethard-on-Sea boycott — undemocratic, unchristian and in every way detestable — did considerable damage to the reputation of the South in Northern Ireland. But to the many fair-minded observers, North and South, the unsavoury episode showed how much out of step were such expressions of intolerance with official thinking and with public opinion in general. De Valera had taken a stance and had tried, behind the scenes, to bring the boycott to a quick end. Those weeks of boycott, however, displayed an ugly side of Irish life and a fundamental lack of any spirit of ecumenism on the part of one prominent Catholic bishop who spoke out on the issue and by another who remained deafeningly silent. Inter-Church dialogue had yet some distance to travel at the end of the 1950s.

IRISH CATHOLICISM, VATICAN II
AND THE STATE IN THE 1960S

It might be helpful at this point to secure the views of an outside observer on the matter of the Church's role in Ireland. A French scholar writing about the Irish Catholic Church in the 1950s and early 1960s noted that the 'exceptional importance and influence of the Bishops, and respect that is paid to them' was a 'unique aspect' which usually impressed foreigners. Bishops were nowadays usually appointed to their native dioceses and were rarely transferred outside their ecclesiastical province. Jean Blanchard, the author in question, also noted the resemblance to the medieval Church 'whose traditions she has almost completely preserved.' He was struck, too, by the large number of dioceses:

> ... and their relatively small areas, their irregular boundaries and the manner in which they frequently inter-penetrate. These peculiarities originated in the distant past, and their cause is often forgotten.[148]

Blanchard contrasted the stability and intimacy of the Irish diocesan system with France where 'the bishops are liable to be appointed to any of the seventeen metropolitan provinces.' He saw as a further strength the 'coherent clerical education' which was given by the national seminary at Maynooth.[149] Another salient feature Blanchard isolated was that 'parish priests are permanent' and it was customary to exclude religious orders from parish or diocesan administration. He noted that the parishes were large and had many curates who usually were given a district of their own to work in. He was struck by the practice of the 'stations' which brought the parish priest into houses in remote parts of the parish to say Mass and hear confessions: 'Ireland rightly preserves and values its many traditions', he wrote.

Blanchard saw Ireland as being 'one of the most ancient and loyal countries of the Catholic World':

Despite the fact that she is traditionalist, nationalist and conservative, she remains the Church of the ordinary people, not of any privileged class. Once a ferment of revolt, she now appears as the guardian of order. The symbol of liberty among a free people, she is prone to direct public opinion; she has a strong hierarchical structure and her clergy wield an unrivalled authority. While she insists on being the 'social conscience' of a Catholic nation, yet she remains democratic in spirit, and her missionaries plant the seeds of liberty in distant continents.[150]

Blanchard's work, despite the hyperbole, owed much to the supervision of the distinguished French religious sociologist, Gabriel Le Bras.[151] His pupil's implicit comparison with the Catholic Church in France provides a valuable insight into the reasons for the strength of Catholicism as a popular force in Irish society during the earlier decades of the State.

Blanchard correctly identified the *local* nature of the Irish Catholic Church. The bishop was a local, the clergy were local and very often the men and women religious in a diocese were also local. There was a closeness between priests and people even if that relationship was unquestionably hierarchical and sometimes authoritarian. There were 1,141 parishes in Ireland administered, according to Blanchard, by 1,090 parish priests. In all, there were 3,798 secular priests for about 3.28 million Catholics in Ireland. That was a ratio of one priest for about 860 laity. The ratio, was of course, much lower if priest members of religious orders were included. There were 2,514 parish churches and chapels, 110 in Kerry, 159 in Armagh and 184 in Dublin. That Ireland was a Catholic country could not go unobserved for long by the outsider. In the 1950s, Heinrich Böll watched as people left St Andrew's Church, Dublin after evening benediction: '.... so I was left with the impression of an overwhelming piety as it flooded Westland Row after the *Tantum ergo*; in Germany you would not see that many people coming out of church after Easter Mass or at Christmas.'[152] Blanchard had caught that mid-century reality when he wrote, as quoted above, that despite the fact that the Irish Catholic Church 'is traditionalist, nationalist and conservative, she remains the Church of the ordinary people, not of any privileged class.' In terms of Western Europe, the Irish Church was quite distinct in that respect. It was much better positioned to respond to the reforming voice of the Second Vatican

Council. Peter Birch, who was appointed Bishop of Ossory in 1964, sought change in the Church. He left the following picture of a Church he wished to leave behind:

I grew up with the idea that a bishop was an old man. I thought age was a necessary part of the office — he had to be old, he had to be severe, and he had to be stern. He came to the parish once in a while and everybody fussed over him. He examined children for Confirmation and, as far as the children were concerned, his chief function seemed to be to reject as many as possible and to admit the others grudgingly.

He gave a bad time to the priests, and they were afraid of him because he would put them off to the missions if they did not do what he wanted. He published a long document at Lent which was read at the Masses on Sundays. It told people what they should not, or could not, do. The sum total of all this was to make a bishop a very forbidding person. That was the image of a bishop that I think I had; I think I still have it and, for that reason, I find it difficult to see myself in the role.[153]

Michael A. Harty was ordained Bishop of Killaloe on 19 November 1967. Two years later he gave a speech in which he attacked the widespread political practice of clientelism:

It is of the utmost importance that the recipients of services or grants should not be led to believe that they are getting a favour when in fact they are merely getting their rights. Occasionally one fears that some of our elected representatives do mislead some of our people in these circumstances. Ugly practices should be called by their proper ugly names and not passed off as endearing Irish eccentricities and this particular practice is one example of corruption.

Bishop Harty added:

Personally, I hold the view that deputies and senators have more than enough to do in being legislators, in explaining both government and opposition policies, in creating the framework in which we can all work effectively, and that they should not be asked to act as messenger boys for local problems, but if they insist on being messenger boys and doing the work of voluntary bodies, what can we do about it.[154]

He also attacked the underlying philosophy of developmentalism:

All our planning at national level seems to be based on the assumption that as material resources grow, there will be a fair distribution of these increased resources. To me that seems an unwarranted assumption, and the evidence from affluent countries proves this.[155]

Both men reflected a willingness to enter difficult territory — Birch was self-critical of the stereotypical Irish bishop while Harty challenged the central economic orthodoxy of the decade. Without wishing to romanticize the 1960s, the Irish Church in that decade was partially characterized by a growing openness and by a willingness to change. This was not uniformly the case and I do not wish to present a unilinear view of history. But the Second Vatican Council had obliged all, conservatives and liberals alike, to enter into the spirit of change.

That theological shift was exemplified by the adoption of a biblical image of Church as 'the People of God'. A model of Church based on the concept of the People of God required the institutional Church to become more open, more participatory and more democratic. That was the spirit of *Gaudium et Spes*. However, having to shift from the majoritarian mind set to a concept of Church in a pluralist society was a quantum leap for those raised and formed within the traditional model of the Irish Church. Many Irish bishops may have found it very difficult to accept the content of the speech of Bishop de Smedt of Bruges on 2 December 1962 in which he denounced in forceful and eloquent terms the clericalism, juridicalism and triumphalism of the institutional Church.[156]

The Jesuit, John Courtney Murray was, in his influential writings, a leading opponent of clericalism, juridicalism and triumphalism. His ideas strongly influenced the deliberations of the Second Vatican Council, particularly in regard to the concept of religious freedom. He had grappled during his lifetime with the question of how one could locate the saving presence of God in historical society. Courtney Murray's work has been carried forward by a new generation of theologians who have learned their theology in the United States where Catholics are a religious grouping.[157]

Another American Jesuit identified the dominant insight of the Second Vatican Council as the presentation of the Church as the People of God. Avery Dulles has written how that 'paradigm focused attention on the Church as a network of inter-personal relationships, on the Church as community.' To that, he argues, has been added the notion of the Church as servant and as healer. That model had increased, he said, the Catholic's sense of solidarity with the whole human race in the struggles for peace, justice and prosperity.[158] Pope Paul VI developed the idea of what was expected from Catholics in *Evangelii Nuntiandi*:

The world calls for and expects from us simplicity of life, the spirit of prayer, charity towards all, especially towards the lowly and the poor, obedience and humility, detachment and self-sacrifice. Without this mark of holiness, our world will have difficulty in touching the heart of modern man. It risks being vain and sterile.[159]

That was a major intellectual challenge and it required a root and branch change of the way of 'being Church' in Ireland.

However willing and open the elderly Archbishop of Dublin John Charles McQuaid felt he was to adapt to the changes sought by the Second Vatican Council, he clung to old ways and his concept of Church was to prove much more enduring and resilient than his numerous critics in the 1960s anticipated. Returning from the Vatican Council, Archbishop McQuaid reassured his flock gathered in the Pro-Cathedral in 1965: 'One could not but feel that the Holy Spirit had guided our deliberations.' To those who might have been worried, he said: 'Allow me to reassure you. No change will worry the tranquillity of your Christian lives.'[160]

McQuaid represented the traditional, clerical model of 'being Church'. Rooted in the majoritarianism mentality, Ireland was perceived as being a Catholic country and this was reflected in her laws — an accommodation reached by the Church with successive Irish governments. The dominant position of the Church in Irish society could only be preserved, according to the above school of thought, if the practice of the politics of informal consensus were continued. Church-State relations were a zero sum game. There could be no concessions as the State could not be trusted. Neither would there have to be any concessions.

In the first half of the 1960s, the Catholic Church underwent a renaissance in the numbers entering seminaries and religious orders. It was a period of great optimism about the future of the Irish Church which had again proved itself to be the exception in Western Europe. The 1961 census showed Ireland to be 94.9 per cent Catholic. In the early 1960s, Professor John Whyte believed that 'a practice rate of 90 per cent is plausible for Ireland'.[161] By 'practice' is meant that a person claims to go to church at least weekly. In Northern Ireland, the 1961 census put the number of Catholics in the State at 34.9 per cent. A survey in 1968 found that that 95 per cent of Catholics claimed to go to church at least once a week. Whyte is inclined to round that figure down to about 90 per cent — the same as in the Republic of Ireland.[162] Mass attendance in other 'Catholic' countries on the continent was much lower. In Austria, Whyte estimates that, at its highest, about 40 per cent attended Mass weekly. In Belgium, he gives the figure of 50 per cent; in France, he accepts the figure of about 25-6 per cent; in Italy, Whyte puts the practice rate at around 45 per cent; in West Germany and Australia about 50 per cent; in New Zealand, about 60 per cent; and 65 per cent in the United States and in English-speaking Canada. The figure for Quebec he gives as 85 per cent.[163]

The 'healthiness' of the Irish situation cautioned men like Archbishop McQuaid to hold the ship on a steady conservative course. However, confronted by the defensiveness of the previous decade, a large section of the Irish Catholic Church began to lay down a challenge to its conservative wing or wings. While there were forces within the Church which opposed change and fought a strong rearguard action, it appeared that new forces were liberating the institution from the vestiges of the old siege mentality. The Church reformers were greatly supported and buoyed by the teachings of Vatican II. Their desire for change was also reinforced by the creative political leadership of Seán Lemass, Taoiseach between 1959 and 1966. Having brought to an end Fianna Fáil's adherence to the sacred doctrine of protectionism, he guided the country to accept free trade, and membership of the Common Market as soon as possible. That latter plan was frustrated in 1963 by the veto of General Charles de Gaulle. Economic growth in the 1960s turned around the emigration flow of the 1950s. People returned to the country to take up positions in new factories or to work in the booming building trade. Education reform led to the introduction of free secondary education in 1967. The liberalization of censorship laws contributed to a growing climate of greater freedom of expression. This trend had been underpinned with the establishment of a national television station (RTÉ) in 1962.

The government of Seán Lemass was anxious to address a number of the unresolved constitutional problems which affected the principle of parity of esteem between Churches in the eyes of the State. His all-party committee on the Constitution reported in the mid-1960s and tackled a number of the thorny issues which still confront Irish society in the mid-1990s. The report recommended a change in Article 3 of the Constitution to read: 'The Irish nation hereby proclaims its firm will that its territory be re-united in harmony and brotherly affection between all Irishmen.' On divorce, the committee felt that it could be argued that Article 41.3 which stated that 'no law shall be enacted providing for the grant of a dissolution of marriage' was 'coercive' and 'unnecessarily harsh and rigid and could, in our view, be regarded as being at variance with the accepted principles of religious liberty as declared at the Vatican Council and elsewhere.'

On Article 44, it was felt that the decisions of the Vatican Council also had a direct impact:

It is clearly to be inferred from these documents, and the comments made on them by competent persons, that the Catholic church does not seek any special recognition or privilege as compared with other religions and that her primary interest is to see that all citizens enjoy equal freedom in the practice of their religion whatever it may be.

That formula reflected the growing parity of esteem in the 1960s between the different Churches.

Cardinal William Conway, who was appointed Archbishop of Armagh in September 1963, stated in a speech in 1966 that the State should allow the maximum of freedom that was compatible with the common good. It was a carefully worded speech. But it might be read as an indirect apology for the hierarchy's stance in the Mother and Child crisis. Speaking about the expanded role of the State, he said 'I think it is true to say that people understand this problem more clearly now than they did twenty years ago, and that some of the fears which were widely held at that time now appear to have been exaggerated.' This reflected the growth of a parity of esteem between Church and State.

Evidence in support of that judgement was found in Cardinal Conway's statement in September 1969: 'I personally would not shed a tear if the relevant sub-section of Article 44 were to disappear.' A month later a meeting of the hierarchy in Maynooth endorsed the Cardinal's statement as representing the bishops' view. Article 44 was amended by referendum in 1972.

Thus ended a debate which had first developed in 1937 between de Valera and John Charles McQuaid (he became Archbishop of Dublin in 1940). The old guard of Maria Duce may have felt betrayed. But the 'special position' clause was gone forever from the Constitution. But how much further was the leadership of the Catholic Church prepared to go to help bring pluralism to Irish society? The appointment of Professor Dermot Ryan, aged forty seven, as Archbishop of Dublin in 1971 further reinforced the perception that a 'progressive' had been appointed to what is, arguably, the most important archbishopric on the island.

Ryan, who had been supportive of moves to get theology accepted in the constituent colleges of the National University of Ireland, was an academic, an intellectual of high standing, and a person likely to be sympathetic to those who sought significant change in the structures of the Church and in the relationship between Church and State.

There was a strong current in the Irish Catholic Church which felt that the Church must change with the times. Ryan inherited an archdioceses where many members of the clergy and laity had responded enthusiastically to the teachings of Vatican II. Indeed, the hierarchy had in the 1960s shown a willingness to implement many Council ideas. The Catholic Communications Institute of Ireland was established; the Catholic Press and Information Office was set up. Episcopal commissions were established to cover the following areas: justice and peace; laity; emigration and the liturgy. Catholic agencies such as CURA and Trócaire and were also set up in the 1960s and 1970s.

In the Catholic print media, *Studies*, *The Furrow*, *Doctrine and Life*, *The Irish Theological Quarterly*, *Herder Correspondence*, *Christus Rex*, *Reality* and *The Word* (See Appendix II) had opened up their pages to debate on Church reform, the liturgical renewal and the changing place of religion in Irish society. There was a Catholic contribution to the new world of Irish television. The early films made by Radharc, one of the longest running documentary programmes on RTÉ, showed a freshness of approach and a willingness to tackle difficult religious, social and political problems. That early generation of Catholic film makers, Joe Dunn, Tom Stack, Dermod McCarthy, Peter Lemass and Billy Fitzgerald, examined issues of great local social sensitivity in Ireland in films entitled *The Young Offender*, *Honesty at the Fair*, *Smuggling*, *Down and Out in Dublin* and *The Boat Train to Euston*. Many of these programmes gave insights into the inequalities in Irish society and the urgent need for reform.[164]

Lay Catholic voices in the 1960s were strong in their support for the social change which many of the Radharc films implied was necessary. Declan Costello wrote, for example, about the need for the Church to use:

> ... its greater moral authority in the cause of social reform. It must act as a social conscience and speak out, not with a still quiet voice, but if necessary a large and strident one. If civil authority has failed to bring about social justice, it can, and I suggest should, point out that failure.

A young economist, Garret FitzGerald, also employed his pen to argue in favour of Church reform and social change.[165] He wrote in *Studies* in 1964:

> If we can successfully graft these liberal and socialist ideas, themselves largely Christian in their origin and inspiration, on to the particular form in which the Christian tradition displays itself in our country in this generation, we may succeed in developing an internally consistent philosophy of our own, appropriate to the needs of the time in which we live, and clearly superior to the excessive conservatism sometimes found in Catholic attitudes, as well as to the wishy-washy liberalism common in Britain, and the doctrinaire socialism of other countries.[166]

FitzGerald, later to enter Irish politics and become Minister for Foreign Affairs (1973-1977) and Taoiseach twice in the 1980s, was searching for a synthesis which put him very much in sympathy with reforming clergy. An example of the work of the latter may be found in a major sociological study undertaken by Professor Liam Ryan. He provided a profile of the social problems prevalent in an unnamed housing estate in Ireland of the 1960s:

> Drink, family, quarrels, bad management, sickness and unemployment; mental and physical difficulties, each one of those alone is sufficient to create endless problems for the families that experience them. When they are found in combination or all together, the resulting misery is unbelievable.

He then went on to describe the experience of one woman caught up with moneylenders:

> The money-lenders were there in their thousands; well, thousands is a bit too many, but they were nearly there in their hundreds and many still remain today. It was fierce. You could be short of money — I knew one

woman who borrowed £5; until she paid back the £5 in one piece she had to pay £2 a month interest. She was paying for one and half years and she had paid back £30 before she cleared the debt.

When voices of protest were raised by Church people about the lack of public housing in the capital, they felt the brunt of public criticism from a number of politicians.

Fr Austin Flannery, then editor of *Doctrine and Life*, was also the producer of a successful television programme, Outlook. When the Jesuit, Michael Sweetman, shared a TV studio with the leader of the Irish Communist Party, Michael O'Riordan, to discuss the housing crisis, Flannery was called a 'gullible priest' by Charles Haughey. The Minister for Local Government, Kevin Boland, called him a 'so-called cleric'. In response, Flannery said that his only intention as a Christian and as a priest was to speak on behalf of people who were in need. He was not alone in that task. Members of the Catholic Church, lay and clerical, contributed to the growth of a radical social critique of Irish society in that decade.

National economic choices had been made and they had significant social consequences. The planning of Irish cities and urban development was to have a profound effect, as Liam Ryan had already pointed out, on the development of a sense of community in the new housing estates around the major cities and towns. But there is little evidence that this area engaged the collective energies of Church and State in Ireland. If the physical environment was to play such an important part in influencing the behaviour of young people, why were estates developed in such an anti-social manner totally lacking in aesthetic or community infrastructure. Many people, raised in rural areas or in parishes in small towns, found themselves — often the parents of young families — citizens of nowhere.

The mistakes in urban planning made in other European countries were repeated in Ireland after they had been made elsewhere. The absence of any community nucleus made it very difficult to reconstruct the parish model in these new areas. The building of very large churches was not done with much foresight or pastoral planning. In turn, this urban expansion was to place severe pressures on the educational infrastructure. These developments occurred in a pastoral planning vacuum. 'Modernization' — a word used here with some reluctance —

would challenge and test religious loyalties to Church leadership and to Church.

In summary, large sections of the Irish Church responded very favourably to the teachings of the Second Vatican Council. The deliberations of the Council fathers had provided a model for change. However, it was up to the local Churches to adapt that model to their own particular situation. While the Vatican Council stressed the universality of the Catholic Church, it also emphasized the importance of the cultural identity and particularism of the local Church. Pope Paul VI stressed this latter dimension in his pronouncements. In particular, reference should be made to his *Octogesmia Adveniens* of 15 May 1971. Paul VI, according to the late Peter Hebblethwaite, 'declared himself "incompetent" (in the technical sense) to offer a universally valid message on social justice.' The Pope wrote: 'In view of the varied situations in the world, it is difficult to give one teaching to cover them all or to offer a solution that has universal value. This is not our intention *or even our mission*' [Peter Hebblethwaite's emphasis].[167] That placed the onus on the local Church to seek solutions pertinent to its particular historical and social situation.

The introduction of a model of Church based on the concept of the 'People of God' required root and branch change in structures. There was a need to make the Church more open and its decision-making processes more democratic and transparent. That was very much in keeping with the democratic promptings from within the Irish Church. There was need, at that point, to develop a long-term pastoral strategy which would have taken into account the changing role of the Church in a changing society. But were some Church leaders transfixed by the idea that Ireland was atypical in Europe — *Hibernia semper fidelis?*

VIOLENCE IN NORTHERN IRELAND

In any general discussion about Church-State relations in Ireland in the 1960s, it is important to emphasize the disruptive and destructive influence of the outbreak of violence on society in the North and in the South. The divisiveness of the violence in Irish politics was evident in the South within twelve months. The traumas of 1970 tested the democratic resolve of the Taoiseach, Mr Jack Lynch, and he was not proved wanting.[168] Reflecting on the 1970s, historians of the future will be in a better position to determine the impact of successive security and diplomatic crises on the quality of decision-making in other areas. Many cabinet ministers had far less time to devote themselves to the management of their respective portfolios. The members of the different Governments were also placed under further pressure because of Ireland's membership of the European Economic Community (EEC) in 1973. The pace of decision-making within departments and within Government had changed. Earlier generations of civil servants and politicians had considerable leisure time to handle files and deal with specific cases. That was part of a genteel world which was lost forever.

The handling of Church-State relations had been conducted at a very deliberate and a very slow pace up to the 1960s. So much had depended upon the informality and the friendly relationship between minister and bishop. So much had depended upon the willingness of a minister to attach a very high priority to issues of Church and State. If the pace of decision-making had accelerated and all government business was now overshadowed by the security concerns brought about by the spillover of Northern-related violence into the South — bank raids, robberies of guns and explosives and a general increase in the incidence of subversive activity — then were Church-State relations perceived to have been relegated to a lower priority level.

The impact of the Northern violence on the decision-making capacity of the Catholic Church has also to be examined. To what extent did concern for the situation in the North deflect Cardinal William Conway's attention away from the management of Church-State relations in the South? As Archbishop of Armagh between 1963 and 1977, he had provided determined leadership for his community. The former Bishop of Derry, Edward Daly, described him after his death in the following terms:

> ... a Northerner through and through. He was born and grew up in the Falls Road in Belfast. He shared the feelings, the insights, the sensitivities that we all have as Northern Catholics. However, he went beyond the narrowness that sometimes hedges us in. He reached out to the Protestant community in the North in an exemplary manner. His relationship with the heads of the Churches was closer than that of any

of his predecessors. He gave us all example and leadership. He was a man who demanded justice for his people. He was an outspoken opponent of discrimination in any form. It is conveniently forgotten by some that it was primarily his firm statement of the facts that brought public credulity to the alleged torture of prisoners after Internment Day in August 1971.[169]

The Church in Northern Ireland lived in a state of continued crisis during the latter years of Cardinal Conway's life. It would be surprising if the archival evidence does not show that that was his major pastoral concern.

Reviewing those early years of the 1970s, the politics of Church and State must continue to be set in the context of the deteriorating situation in Northern Ireland. The violence appeared nightly on television screens. The South did not escape the direct effects of the violence. Two people were killed and eight injured in Dublin on 1 December 1972. Two years later, on 17 May 1974, twenty two people were killed in Dublin in no-warning car bombings in Dublin. In Monaghan town, the same day, five people were killed in explosions. (Three more people died later as a result of injuries received in the explosions.)[170] Senator Billy Fox (FG) was murdered in Monaghan in March 1974. The British Ambassador, Christopher Ewart-Biggs, and a senior British civil servant, Judith Cooke, were killed in an IRA explosion on 21 July 1976. A number of gardaí also lost their lives in violence related to Northern Ireland.

The ferocity of the Northern conflict posed serious new pastoral problems for all Churches. But those problems could be much more effectively addressed if the Churches sought to transcend their various differences and find ground for common action. Vatican II had encouraged ecumenism. The establishment of the Irish School of Ecumenics in Dublin in 1970 was a significant step forward in the development of cooperation between the different Churches.[171] The Jesuit, Fr Michael Hurley, was appointed as its first director.[172]

The new Archbishop of Dublin, Dermot Ryan, held an inter-denominational service in the Pro-Cathedral in Dublin during Christian Unity week in 1973. Representatives from the Catholic Church were sent for the first time to the General Synod of the Church of Ireland in 1974. There had been a proposal from the Irish Council of Churches, which represented a number of the Christian Churches, that a system of high level meetings be instituted to discuss the question of inter-Church marriages and other practical matters. Cardinal William Conway responded positively by requesting the meetings to include discussion on a range of scriptural, doctrinal and pastoral issues.[173] Ballymascanlon, County Louth, became the annual venue from 1974 for meetings which proved to be of historical importance.[174] Perhaps future historians will be able to show from the archives that this was a period of great openness between the Churches on the island?[175]

There was also the broader question which emerged in the early 1970s of how the South appeared to the non-Catholic Churches in Northern Ireland? Would there be need for change in the South if an end to partition was to be seriously contemplated? That was a question which was answered in very different ways by Catholic Church leaders in the 1970s.

John Whyte concluded, in his review of the 1970s, that it was important not to 'exaggerate' the significance of the moves for change mentioned above. He wrote:

By the standards of advanced industrial societies, Ireland in the seventies remained a conservative country. Abortion and divorce were prohibited; laws against contraception, although increasingly a dead letter, remained on the statute book. Education remained preponderantly in the control of the Churches. Almost the whole active population continued to go to Church on Sundays. But traditional standards were being increasingly questioned.[176]

The agreement between Church and State to amend Article 44 of the Constitution appeared to indicate that legislative changes in the 1970s would be relatively painless. On 7 December 1977, 51 per cent of the electorate went to the polls, 81 per cent voting for change. The Bishop of Cork, Cornelius Lucey, was the only bishop in the country to encourage a 'no' vote.[177] Thus 'the special position' of the Catholic Church was removed from the Constitution, but so, too, was recognition of the other Churches — including the Jewish community.

But if the leadership of the hierarchy had accepted the removal of 'the special position' clause from the Constitution, it did not follow that a similar attitude would be adopted in the area of sexual morality. A year before the referendum, a statement was issued on 11 March 1971 following a meeting of the hierarchy in Maynooth:

The bishops fully share the disquiet, which is widespread among the people at the present time, regarding pressures being exerted on public opinion on the questions concerning the civil law on divorce, contraception and abortion.

These questions involve issues of grave import for society as a whole, which go far beyond purely private morality or private religious belief. Civil law on these matters should respect the wishes of the people who elected the legislators and the bishops confidently hope that the legislators themselves will respect this important principle.[178]

The enunciation of that particular principle by the bishops was problematical. That was to assume that a majority of the electorate would — in the perception of the hierarchy — continue to oppose the legalization of the sale of contraceptives. Would that argument also hold true if a majority of the electorate wanted a change in the law?

The statement of the hierarchy had been prompted by the decision of three independent senators, Mary Robinson, Trevor West and John Horgan, to have the law on contraception relaxed. It failed. Mr Tommy Mullins, the Fianna Fáil leader of the Senate said: 'There is no great overwhelming public demand that we should take any immediate action.'[179] A year later, another private members Bill was introduced by two Labour Party backbenchers, Dr Noel Browne and Dr John O'Connell. It, too, was defeated and there the matter rested until 1973.

It fell to the Fine Gael-Labour coalition Government, led by Liam Cosgrave, to guide the country between 1973 and 1977. The preoccupation of that Government with security questions was significant. Confronted by certain social questions, that heterodox group of coalition ministers was divided in a very public fashion in a manner which would never have been allowed to manifest itself in a single-party Government.

The issues of abortion, divorce and contraception were highly contentious. The Catholic Church was opposed to any change in the law in all three areas.

Writing in 1980, John Whyte said: 'Abortion need not detain us long'.[180] The bishops devoted the first section of their joint pastoral, *Human Life is Sacred*, to an extensive and detailed attack on abortion. Whyte argues:

Indeed, far from there being much support for legalised abortion, the issue was most often raised by those who resisted change elsewhere. They would use the unpopularity of abortion as a weapon, arguing that it would be the natural consequence of change in other respects. In *Human Life is Sacred*, for instance, the bishops claimed: 'it is significant that many of those who have been most prominent in campaigns for contraception are also found among the leading advocates of abortion'.[181]

The question of divorce had become very problematical in the 1970s. A rise in broken marriages meant that both Church and State were confronted with growing difficulties. The Church annulment procedure provided no solution to the wider social problem and neither did the nullity jurisdiction of the civil courts. It still remained possible in Ireland to be valid in the eyes of the Church but not in the eyes of the State. The reverse also held true. While the Catholic Church remained opposed to divorce, opinion polls seem to show a significant shift in the attitudes of people from the beginning to the latter part of the 1970s. In 1977, a poll found 65 per cent in favour of legalizing divorce with 26 per cent against. The figure in 1971 had been seventy three against and twenty two in favour.[182] Experience in 1995 continued to show the volatility of Irish public opinion on divorce — and the high level of opposition at the polls.

In parenthesis, it might be mentioned here that the Northern bishops had strongly objected to the implementation of the Draft Matrimonial Causes (Northern Ireland) Order 1978 which 'would bring divorce law here substantially into line with that already in force in England and Wales.' Signed by the six bishops who had jurisdiction in Northern Ireland, the statement said that the Order was 'causing widespread concern in the Catholic community, as well as in many sections of the community as a whole. The Catholic bishops share this concern.'[183]

The statement vigorously opposed the proposal to 'make civil divorce easier to obtain in Northern Ireland'. It stated:

> The Catholic Church teaches that marriage is indissoluble; that is, that people who are validly married are never free to abandon their marriage and contract a new one. Sacramental marriage, once consummated, can only be ended by the death of one of the partners.
>
> We do not accept that the State can either make or dissolve a marriage where members of our faith are concerned; all it can do is to regulate the civil aspect of marriage.[184]

That position was adopted by the entire hierarchy in 1986 and in 1995 when the question of the removal of the constitutional ban on divorce was raised.

The bishops maintained a strong and unified opposition to a change in the law on the sale of contraceptives in the South throughout the 1970s. In 1973, they issued a statement which provoked great interest. It stated:

> The question at issue is not whether artificial contraception is morally right or wrong. The clear teaching of the Catholic Church is that it is morally wrong. No change in State law can make the use of contraceptives morally right since what is wrong in itself remains wrong, regardless of what State law says.

The hierarchy then went on to state a position which was reiterated in other statements during the 1970s and affirmed at the New Ireland Forum in 1984. In 1973, the bishops wrote:

> It does not follow, of course, that the State is bound to prohibit the importation and sale of contraceptives. There are many things which the Catholic Church holds to be morally wrong and no one has ever suggested, least of all the Church herself, that they should be prohibited by the State.
>
> Those who insist on seeing the issue purely in terms of the State enforcing, or not enforcing Catholic moral teaching, are therefore missing the point.
>
> The real question facing the legislators is: What effect would the increased availability of contraceptives have on the quality of life in the Republic of Ireland?[185]

The bishops stated that the legalization of contraception was a question of public, not private morality: 'What the legislators have to decide is whether a change in the law would, on balance, do more harm than good, by damaging the character of the society for which they are responsible.' [186]

However, in 1973, there were legal developments which placed the introduction of enabling legislation to permit the sale of contraceptives beyond discussion. The Supreme Court decision in favour of Mrs Mary McGee had transformed the situation.[187] In this context, it is relevant to refer to the remaining part of the hierarchy's 1973 statement which sought to argue that legalization of contraception would do more harm

than good. There was evidence to show, the statement said, that where
the sale of contraceptives was legalized:

> ...marital infidelity increases, the birth of children outside of wedlock
> (surprising as it may seem) increases, abortions increase, there is a marked
> increase in the incidence of venereal disease and the use of contraceptives
> tends to spread rapidly among unmarried young people.

Turning to the danger to the morals of young people, the bishops
advised the legislators to 'think very carefully before making the
environment for moral living more difficult for them'.

The statement then described the 'link' between legislation on
contraception and abortion as being 'significant'. It continued:

> Increasingly abortion is being seen as the ultimate method of birth
> control. There seems to be a chain-reaction in these matters by which
> the first piece of legislation tends to set in motion a process of change
> which no one can control.

The bishops then addressed what they termed as being 'the most
serious consideration of all', and that was 'the effect which the
contraceptive mentality has on the very way marriage and the family are
looked upon in society.' But the bishops again emphasized that 'it is not
a matter for bishops to decide whether the law should be changed or
not. That is a matter for the legislators, after a conscientious
consideration of all the factors involved.' [188]

The issue was politically very divisive. Two years previously the
Archbishop of Dublin, John Charles McQuaid, had said:

> Any ... contraceptive act is always wrong in itself. To speak, then, in this
> context, of a right to contraception, on the part of an individual, be he
> Christian or non-Christian or atheist, or on the part of a minority or of a
> majority, is to speak of a right that cannot ever exist.[189]

Two bishops, Bishop Jeremiah Newman of Limerick and Bishop
Cornelius Lucey of Cork, spoke out strongly against any change in the
legislation. But the debate in Dáil Éireann showed how truly divisive an
issue this was in political circles. All three major political parties were
divided on the issue. When the vote was finally taken, the Taoiseach
Liam Cosgrave, and the Minister for Education, Richard Burke, voted
with five other Fine Gael TDs against a Bill sponsored by their own
Government. It was defeated by sixty one to seventy five.

Fianna Fáil returned to power in 1977 with a large majority. The new Minister for Health, Charles Haughey, published a Bill at the end of 1978. This sought to introduce a very restrictive measure — the selling of contraceptives on prescription by chemists to a person seeking the contraceptive, '*bona fide*, for family planning purposes or for adequate medical reasons and in appropriate circumstances'.[190] The hierarchy issued another statement reasserting the moral teaching of the Church and stating: 'The teaching is binding on the consciences of Catholics.' The good which a law may do must be set against the harm which it can do. It stated: 'It may be said that conscience is a sufficient safeguard of moral standards. But conscience itself can become confused and weakened by society's attitudes.' A change in the law, the hierarchy wrote, could deceive people into thinking that morality had changed also.

The statement also said that to have the distribution of contraceptives classed as a medical service could create problems in conscience for doctors, for nurses and other health board personnel, and for chemists. 'The conscientious rights of such persons must not be infringed', it added.[191] The Haughey Bill became law in July 1979.

Before the Act came into effect at the end of the year, the hierarchy issued another statement which welcomed certain aspects of the new legislation, in particular, the recognition of the natural methods of regulating birth. But the statement also pointed out that:

> The passing of the Family Planning Act, however, does not alter the morality of contraception. Contraceptive intercourse is contrary to God's design for the expression of married love and the transmission of human life. No State can alter this moral teaching.

The statement made particular reference to the conscience clause in the legislation: 'Everyone — and this includes Health Board personnel — has a legal as well as a moral right to withhold co-operation.' Anyone who felt that he or she was being subjected, even indirectly, to pressure in that matter had a right to appeal to that clause.[192]

The change in the legislation on contraception was, it would appear, viewed as a defeat for the institutional Church. It was a battle lost even more decisively in the 1980s. The outcome was viewed by many people, including very many Catholics, as a step forward for civil liberties. Although many Catholics supported the change in legislation, that did not mean that they were not concerned about serious moral issues raised in the hierarchy's statements concerning the role of commercial interest groups and the exploitation of young people. In their 1978 statement, the bishops had referred to the power of the 'multi-national contraceptive industry' which had 'set aside large sums for advertising' which exerted 'a constant pressure on people to use contraceptives'. The bishops expressed further concern that some of that advertising was 'beamed explicitly on the young, even from their earliest teens'.[193] Professor Joe Lee also echoed the concern of many in the country when he wrote the following about the change in sexual attitudes in the late 1970s and early 1980s:

> Some of the change in popular attitudes was probably due to genuine humanitarianism, but it seems clear that much of the general drift in terms of sexual morality was based on mere hedonism. No self-respecting church could compromise with this mentality.[194]

Neither could the other Churches.

Reviewing the 1970s, one is struck by the capacity for Church and State to reach consensus in many areas. The historian faces one major problem when writing on the area of Church and State in Ireland: there is a tendency to highlight the crises. But the Catholic Church continued to deal with government departments on a range of different levels in the 1970s, as it had done during previous decades without too many apparent difficulties. The system of arriving at consensus continued even when it was not always possible to resolve every issue. The legalization of contraception was one area where Church and State parted company.

The hierarchy had mixed results when negotiating the management structure of the new community schools and a dispute over the deeds of trust continued through the decade. But this was not a matter of significant Church-State conflict. The question of multidenomin-ational education also arose in the 1970s; but this seemed to cause more anxiety to the then Minister for Education, Richard Burke. His successor, the Fine Gael TD, Peter Barry, was more supportive of the two pilot projects in Dalkey and Marley Grange. The Dalkey school was opened in 1978 under the Fianna Fáil Minister, John Wilson.[195]

Reviewing the attitude of the Catholic Church towards education, it may be worth putting forward the argument that that is the area where, perhaps, the Church has done most strategic planning. The educational sub-committee of the national episcopal conference had been very active and far-sighted in its planning proposals.[196]

The Adoption Acts of 1974 and 1976 were two related pieces of legislation which might have provoked conflict between Church and State. John Whyte has pointed out that Section 12(2) of the Adoption Act 1952 required that the adopting parents were to be 'of the same religion as the child and his parents or, if the child is illegitimate, his mother.' But that had two significant consequences — it prevented orphan children of mixed marriage from being adopted and it prevented a married couple of mixed religion from being able to adopt. The coalition Government, taking up from the earlier efforts of Fianna Fáil, repealed Section 12 in 1974.[197]

Meanwhile, the relationship between the Catholic Church and the other Churches on the island had improved significantly since pre-conciliar days. However, the Catholic hierarchy were quite unmoved by arguments which suggested that changes in social legislation in the South should be made with a view to helping to ameliorate Northern non-Catholic views of the South. The Catholic Church was fortunate in the late 1970s to have as Cardinal Archbishop of Armagh a person who brought his own considerable virtues as an academic, an Irish-language scholar, an ecumenist and a pastor to a position which proved to be so demanding in the early 1980s.

CARDINAL TOMÁS Ó FIAICH
PLURALISM AND THE 1980S

Tomás Ó Fiaich, who was ordained Archbishop of Armagh on 18 August 1977, told a news conference the same day that he looked forward to the day when Ireland would be united though he did not feel that it would happen in his lifetime.[198] A former President and Professor of History at St Patrick's College, Maynooth, he was forced to confront the growing complexities of the Church-State relationship in the South and in the North. The historian, Oliver Rafferty, has written that it was Ó Fiaich's:

...warm personal charm and exuberance ... which most captured the imagination of northern Catholics in the 1970s and 1980s. A serious scholar, who wore his learning lightly, he was a committed ecumenist and yet passionately concerned with matters of justice and equality. For all that, he inspired distrust in many northern Protestants and sections of the British establishment for his unrepentant nationalism.[199]

As a Northerner, Ó Fiaich lived in a State where the Catholic minority had been obliged to live their lives under laws which permitted the sale of contraceptives and provided for the availability of divorce. There is little doubt that, had he lived, he would have agreed with the conclusion of Dr Patrick Hannon, Professor of Moral Theology at Maynooth, that:

> ...the Catholic theological inheritance leaves us with a principle which ... may be extended to say that in moral as in religious matters people should be free to follow their lights within the requirements of a common good. And a signal mark of this freedom is immunity from coercion by the law.[200]

The development of a pastoral approach in the South, based on such an attitude, might have changed the temper of certain Church-State exchanges during the 1980s and 1990s. At the time of his death in 1990, the Cardinal had witnessed a decade of unprecedented conflict between Church and State. More specifically, it was a decade when a number of stridently neo-conservative lay Catholic groups came to the fore. He regarded this as a very negative development.[201]

The absence of archival material makes the task of interpreting trends in the 1970s very difficult for the historian. An examination of the 1980s and early 1990s is even more problematical. Future historians might wish to isolate the following areas as being worthy of evaluation:

INTERNATIONAL FACTORS

- The growth of neo-conservative ideas during the 1970s and 1980s.
- Papal teaching on contraception and conservative trends during the last years of the pontificate of Pope Paul VI.
- The predominant papal orientation influencing episcopal appointments in the Church internationally during the 1970s and early 1980s.

INTERNAL FACTORS

- The relative strength of conservatism in the Irish society.
- The degree to which the ideas of Vatican II were implemented; the question of clericalism in the Church; the crisis of authority in the Church.

- The relative lack of a long-term strategic pastoral plan.
- The failure to provide a theological education for the laity in the constituent colleges of the National University of Ireland and in other third level institutions.
- And, of great importance, the failure to permit women to play a significant role in the leadership of the Church, and at all levels of decision-making within the Church.

Another generation of historians will be in a position to read the archives relating to many of the areas identified above. What will the sources reveal about the shifting balance of power between the local Church and the Holy See? What influence have the later policies of Pope Paul VI and the policies of Pope John Paul II had on Ireland? Here the historian has to work without access to archives. Pope Paul VI knew the history of Ireland very well.[202] He had significant experience of the country and its politics. During the war years, Éamon de Valera had helped save Rome from Allied bombing raids. In 1948, John A. Costello's inter-party Government had come to the assistance of the Holy See-supported Italian Christian Democratic party by helping provide funds for a critical general election campaign. Giovanni Montini knew Ireland to be a strong supporter of the positions of the Holy See in various international *fora*.[203] Why was it necessary, it might have been asked at the Holy See in the 1970s, for such a strong, 'Catholic' country to move away from its traditional roots? [204]

This interpretation is supported by certain passages in Dr Garret FitzGerald's memoirs. When Dr FitzGerald was Minister for Foreign Affairs, he met the papal Secretary of State, Cardinal Agostino Casaroli, in Helsinki in 1973. He explained in an informal meeting the concern of the Irish Government to establish good relations with unionists as well as nationalists in Northern Ireland. He mentioned the areas of mixed marriages and integrated education as being most problematical. Returning home, FitzGerald prepared a memorandum which he had agreed he would send to Casaroli. He sent it first to the Taoiseach, Mr Liam Cosgrave, whose views, according to Dr FitzGerald's memoirs, 'on these issues I knew to be much more conservative than mine'. There were no negative comments from the Taoiseach. Before finalizing and sending the document, Dr FitzGerald incorporated comments sent to Iveagh House by the Irish Ambassador to the Holy

See. FitzGerald had also spoken about the matter to the nuncio, Archbishop Gaetano Alibrandi who had advised Rome that unity would not come soon.[205]

When FitzGerald met Casaroli in Rome some weeks later (the memorandum had been sent on 14 August 1973), the latter said that certain points relating to doctrinal questions had been sent to the Sacred Congregation for the Doctrine of the Faith for comment. Casaroli inquired that since the proposed changes would not bring about unity, 'should we be upsetting people in our State by making such changes now?' FitzGerald agreed that unity would not be achieved 'soon'. However, he stressed the need for an interim stage of reform which might help shift unionist opinion in order to bring about a majority in Northern Ireland in favour of unity. The legalization of contraception was raised. FitzGerald also spoke about integrated education and laid great stress on the need for a change in Church law regarding mixed marriages where the Catholic partner had to promise orally to do his or her best to have the children brought up as Catholics.[206]

Casaroli 'kicked for touch at this point', according to FitzGerald, and he added:

> Casaroli did, however, go so far as to say that he was now of the
> opinion, having heard my case, that the Nuncio had given him the
> wrong slant; his — Casaroli's — comprehension of the complexities of
> the problem had been changed by our discussion. I wondered — not for
> the last time — just what the Nuncio had said to him.[207]

On a visit to Strasbourg in February 1977, FitzGerald was encouraged by Archbishop Benelli (later Cardinal Archbishop of Florence)[208] to see Pope Paul VI about Northern Ireland. FitzGerald saw Pope Paul VI at the end of March. The Pope read a text in French which lasted for about six minutes:

> The theme was uncompromising. Ireland was a Catholic country —
> perhaps the only one left. It should stay that way. Laws should not be
> changed in a way that would make it less Catholic. ... [Dr FitzGerald spoke
> about the tragedy in Northern Ireland to which the Irish State was trying to
> respond in a Christian way.] Before I could go any further he intervened.
> He knew how tragic the situation was there, he said, but it could not be a
> reason to change any of the laws that kept us a Catholic State. At that I
> more or less gave up. I left the audience somewhat shell-shocked.[209]

Pope John Paul II visited Ireland in autumn 1979. It had been part of the original plan to include a visit to Northern Ireland. The grounds of St Patrick's, Armagh, had been chosen as the venue for an open-air ecumenical service of reconciliation. The attendance would have included many of the people maimed by bomb blasts and victims of the violence. However, his trip to Northern Ireland had to be cancelled due to the volatile security situation which existed following the killing on 27 August of eighteen British soldiers near Warrenpoint, County Down. On the same day, Lord Mountbatten of Burma, Dowager Lady Brabourne, his fourteen year old nephew and a fourteen year old crew member were blown up in their boat off Mullaghmore, County Sligo. On security advice, the Holy See reluctantly agreed to cancel the trip.[210] However, the Pope did deliver a speech on the violence in Northern Ireland near Drogheda in the archdioceses of Armagh. The visit of Pope John Paul II had the same magnetic impact on many Irish people as the visits of Presidents Kennedy and Clinton. He delivered a series of important sermons, not least one on family values when he visited Limerick:

> It is true that the stability and the sanctity of marriage are being threatened by new ideas and by the aspirations of some. Divorce, for whatever reason it is introduced, inevitably becomes easier and easier to obtain and it gradually comes to be accepted as a normal part of life. The very possibility of divorce in the sphere of civil law makes stable and permanent marriages more difficult for everyone.
>
> ...And so I say to all, have an absolute and holy respect for the sacredness of human life from the first moment of its conception. Abortion, as the Vatican Council stated, is one of the 'abominable crimes'.[211]

The hierarchy quoted another passage from that sermon in their statement prior to coming into force of the Health (Family Planning) Act at the end of 1979:

> Dear fathers and mothers of Ireland, believe in your vocation, that beautiful vocation of marriage and parenthood which God has given to you. Believe that God is with you — for all parenthood in heaven and on earth takes its name from him.[212]

Different lessons were taken by different people from this highly successful papal visit.

In attempting to provide an historical context in which to evaluate the events of the following fifteen years, it is best to look to the

interpretations of theologians who can evaluate change in the universal
Church at different levels. I would like to quote here the reflections of
Bill Cosgrave, the parish priest of Monageer and a former lecturer in
Moral Theology at St Peter's College, Wexford. He argues that in the
pontificate of John Paul II there has been a:

> ... definite rowing back from the Vatican II perspective ... and we are in
> the midst of a 'restoration' of pre-Vatican II emphases and attitudes,
> something that is quite evident in the Vatican's relation to local Churches
> around the world. The appointment of bishops is, perhaps, the most
> widely known and debated example. Numerous very conservative
> bishops have in recent years been appointed, especially to crucial
> positions in the hierarchy. These bishops place loyalty to the Holy See at
> the head of their ministerial priorities and are chosen because they are
> 'safe' men who are judged by Rome to be 'sound', especially on the
> controversial issues of our day — contraception, the ordination of
> women and the law of celibacy. These bishops tend to adopt an earlier
> other-worldly perspective, and to de-emphasise social justice, the option
> for the poor and the Church's ministry in the political, social and
> economic areas. All this raises the issue of whether and why individual
> dioceses should not have a major say in appointing their own bishop, as
> in the early church, with Rome having, perhaps, a veto.[213]

Fr Cosgrave writes on the growing conservatism of the college of
cardinals, the synod of bishops which 'is now little more than tokenism
as far as collegiality is concerned', the weakening of episcopal
conferences and on the silencing of theologians.[214] This historian,
unable to discuss these questions because of a lack of archives, presents
Fr Cosgrave's arguments as a professional comment by a theologian on
the changing intellectual climate within the Catholic Church over the
past fifteen years.

The diversity of opinion on the status of national conferences of
bishops, a topic of central importance to a study of Church and State, is
discussed by Fr Avery Dulles SJ. Reviewing the distinction between the
munus docendi (teaching office) and the *potestas magisterii authentici*
(authoritative teaching power), he writes:

> While granting that the bishops of a territory can teach conjointly
> through their conference, they deny that the conferences have a power
> to teach authoritatively unless this is conferred by special mandate from
> the Holy See.

A position strongly favourable to the teaching authority of episcopal conferences is also quoted by Avery Dulles:

When the conference teaches, it teaches as such, and not the individual bishops in so far as they adhere to the opinions contained in the declaration. For this reason religious submission *(obsequium religiosum)* is due to the opinions proposed by the conference both on the part of the bishops themselves and on the part of the faithful of their churches.[215]

This somewhat technical area is germane to an examination of the decision-making process of the Irish hierarchy. The resolution of this balance of power debate within the Church is also of great significance for the future of Church-State relations in contemporary Ireland.

It may be the judgement of another generation of historians that the resilience and independence of the Irish Church did much to mitigate the full impact of such a radical shift away from Vatican II. Ó Fiaich was a good helmsman and the local Church he presided over was resilient, even hostile to pastoral direction from outside. Perhaps, left to themselves, the good sense of Irish people will allow them to view with justifiable scepticism the superficial fashions in 'restoration' theology.

In the light of Fr Cosgrave's judgements, developments in Ireland in the 1980s and 1990s must be set in the context of a changing papal policy. How vigorously was that policy applied to the Irish situation? Reflecting again on what the subtle-minded and most politically nuanced of popes, Paul VI, said to Dr FitzGerald in 1977, the Irish file was left open for Pope John Paul II. Therefore, in the absence of archival material, this historian is obliged to rely upon authoritative secondary sources to propose that Pope Paul VI's words to FitzGerald remained the position of the Holy See under his successors: the tragic situation in Northern Ireland could not be a reason to change any of the laws 'that kept us a Catholic State'.

However, changes within the Catholic Church internationally were also influenced by the growing phenomenon of neo-conservatism which was manifest, in particular, in the United States, in Latin America and in Britain. The rise of religious fundamentalism in the United States, in particular, further coloured attitudes. It is too soon to establish comprehensively the nature of the relationship between neo-conservative and 'single issue' religious groups in the United States and in Ireland. This historian merely offers the above observations in the expectation that another generation of academics, with access to primary sources, will be in a position to determine the nature of those relationships.[216] Professor Enda McDonagh has commented:

> There have been religious fundamentalists in Ireland and there are. Separated from political causes, they have not been so threatening. The present rise of fundamentalism in the wider world and the movement toward more closed and conservative views among many church leaders, Protestant, Catholic, and Orthodox, might make our situation more serious.[218]

It did.

Between 1980 and 1983, the country experienced unprecedented volatility in national politics. A short-lived Fine Gael-Labour coalition was followed by an equally brief Fianna Fáil Government. Hunger strikes, the Falklands' war, turmoil in Anglo-Irish relations, the weak state of the economy, made 1982 a very difficult year to be in government. A Labour-Fine Gael coalition returned to power in November 1982 and remained in office until 1987. An analysis of the reasons for the emergence of the Society for the Protection of the Unborn Child (SPUC) and the launching of the Pro-Life Amendment Campaign (PLAC) present a challenge.[218] This was very much a lay-led movement. It is not possible to evaluate, on the basis of the available evidence, the degree of authority the Irish bishops exercised over SPUC and PLAC. Very little, it might be stated tentatively. The difference between the 1950s and the 1980s, I would argue, was significant. In the 1950, the Archbishop of Dublin, John Charles McQuaid was in a position to determine the very existence of Maria Duce. In the 1980s, the hierarchy — if they had wanted to — were not in a position to exercise the same degree of authority over these new groups. What the years 1980-1983 did reveal was a strong level of alienation on the part of a large group within the State. They were very much opposed to the 'crusade' which Dr Garret FitzGerald had announced as Taoiseach in September 1981 to change the confessional and nationalist aspects of the Constitution.[219] The announcement took many people by surprise, even many of those who were sympathetic to his traditional line of argument. The use of the term 'crusade' was singularly ill-judged. A crusade for pluralism might be said to be a contradiction in terms. The absence of a blueprint for reform only increased the levels of suspicion within quarters already hostile to FitzGerald and his idea of 'pluralism'. Mistrustful of the State, and of the courts, SPUC and PLAC had sought to amend the Constitution to include an explicit prohibition on abortion.[220]

From the perspective of many people living in Northern Ireland, where there is strong opposition to abortion, the events of 1980-1983 prompted many questions about the nature of Irish democracy and the power of lobbies. Many citizens in the South were equally confused about the manner in which an issue of such great moral importance could have emerged as a subject for a referendum in the clandestine manner that it did do so. Some well-informed citizens, not seeing the necessity for this constitutional amendment, worried about the looseness and ambiguity of the wording which read:

> The State acknowledges the right to life of the unborn and, with due regard to the equal right to life of the mother, gurantees in its laws to respect, and as far as practicable, by its laws to defend and vindicate that right.[221]

How? And who drafted the wording? These questions are worthy of scholarly investigation as is the question of why it was considered necessary during the referendum on Maastricht in 1992 to add a protocol to that treaty.[222]

Despite the best professional advice available to the Government of the day, the wording was put to the people following a campaign which reached levels of unedifying acrimony, probably not witnessed in Ireland since the post-Treaty campaigning by rival sides in 1922.[223] The amendment, purporting to prevent abortion, was approved in the referendum by a two-to-one majority in a turnout of 53.7 per cent.[224] The 'X' case decision in 1992 might have taught many activists in the 1983 campaign a lesson in humility.[225] There is no evidence to show that was in fact the case.

Did the hierarchy undertake a review of those events and the implications for the future of the Church in Ireland? The events of the 1980s had produced a new phenomenon in Irish society, the emergence of organized groups at a national level which operated completely outside the the control of Church authorities and of the parish structures. It might well have profited from such an exercise. Such an examination might have revealed the level of theological illiteracy in many of the exchanges, not to mention, on occasions, the complete lack of charity. Professor Joe Lee commented:

> Public debate on the issues of moral principles were so under-developed in the political culture that neither side was able to relate to the assumptions of the other. It was a dialogue of the deaf, though not of the mute! It exposed not only the continuing hollowness of the symbolic universe of traditional thought, but also the shallowness of much liberal thought, fashionable in the media, and reeking with condescension towards the 'peasantry', defined to include virtually anyone who dared query their assumptions.[226]

Northern unionists, many belonging to Churches with very democratic structures, may have viewed the manifest deficiencies of Irish popular democracy in the South with well-founded apprehension.[227]

However, the vote in the referendum showed that the divisions in Irish society were not between a strong anti-abortion majority and a weaker pro-abortion minority. There were many who did not favour the inclusion of that Article in the Constitution on the grounds that it was quite unnecessary, not to say dangerous. It was a source of continuing regret that three different Governments could have allowed themselves to be forced, if not intimidated, into the holding of a referendum. What the holding of the referendum did demonstrate was the power exercised by lobbies in Irish society at a time when governmental majorities were slender. It had a negative impact on the credibility of political parties, on Church leadership and on relations between the Churches.

At a time when the Catholic Church might have felt it vital to develop a long-term strategic pastoral plan for Irish society, it remained in a reactive frame of mind. Some of the leadership appeared to be overwhelmed by the fear that the Church was on the defensive against the rise of liberalism and secularism. Certain dangers were far from being imaginary. But the Church allowed itself to be stereotyped as conservative if not reactionary — which was certainly not the case in a number of areas.

The Catholic Church, therefore, had a unique opportunity to present its ideas, vision might be a better word, for the development of Irish society, North and South, at the New Ireland Forum, established by the

Garret FitzGerald-led Fine Gael-Labour coalition, to consult on the manner in which lasting peace and stability could be achieved in a new Ireland through the democratic process.

When the Catholic Church delegation appeared before an oral hearing of the Forum on 9 February 1984, the members had an opportunity to outline the thinking of the Catholic Church in the context of a debate on the new Ireland. A written submission had been received from the hierarchy in January 1984. It consisted of five papers [the word used by Cardinal Ó Fiaich who wrote the introduction to the submission] covering ecumenism; the family; pluralism; alienation of Catholics in Northern Ireland; and the Catholic school system in Northern Ireland. This was not so much an integrated submission as papers prepared on central topics. Each of the papers appeared to have been written by a different person. The submission, apart from the Cardinal's comprehensive introduction, did not present a synthesis.[228] There was no integrated 'vision' of the role of the Catholic Church in a new Ireland. Here was at best a partially grasped and at worst a missed opportunity.

The paper on 'pluralism' contained the following interesting passage on 'the views of the majority':

> To require in the name of pluralism that public policy tolerate or even facilitate forms of public morality of which the majority of the citizens could not approve may sometimes be reasonable in the interests of the common good of harmony between all the citizens; but where the offence to the moral principles of the majority of the citizens would be disproportionately serious it is not unreasonable to require sacrifice of minorities in the interests of the common good. Britain, for example, does not allow polygamy even though certain of its citizens accept it from their religious convictions.[229]

Before attending the Forum, it is not clear whether the hierarchy sought to consult widely members of the laity on what they ought to emphasize in their oral submission. That would have been the practice in other Churches. As may be judged from the passage quoted above, this document lacked the gravitas, the focus and the coherence necessary to demonstrate that the Catholic Church had a unique contribution to make to the development of the new Ireland.

A Catholic Church delegation, made up of bishops, senior clergy and lay people, appeared at a public session of the Forum on 9 February

1984. Their performance, although somewhat uneven, was much more convincing than the written submission. To the discerning eye, too, there was a diversity of approach in the group. The Bishop of Down and Connor, Cahal Daly (Cardinal Archbishop of Armagh in 1990), told the Forum:

> The Catholic Church in Ireland totally rejects the concept of a confessional State. We have not sought and we do not seek a Catholic State for a Catholic people. We believe that the alliance of Church and State is harmful for the Church and harmful for the State. We rejoiced when that ambiguous formula regarding the special position of the Catholic Church was struck out of the Constitution by the electorate of the Republic. The Catholic Church in Ireland has no power and seeks no power except the power of the gospel it preaches and the consciences and convictions of those who freely accept that teaching. The Catholic Church seeks only the freedom to proclaim the gospel. It proclaims the same doctrinal and moral message under whatever constitutional or political regime operates in this island. The Catholic Church has always carried on its mission on the basis of a Thirty-two County Ireland.
>
> ... So far as the Catholic Church and questions of public morality are concerned the position of the Church over recent decades has been clear and consistent. We have repeatedly declared that we in no way seek to have the moral teaching of the Catholic Church become the criterion of constitutional change or to have the principles of Catholic faith enshrined in civil law. What we have claimed, and what we must claim, is the right to fulfil our pastoral duty and our pastoral duty is to alert the consciences of Catholics to the moral consequences of any proposed piece of legislation.....[230]

This passage is frequently quoted.

But the contributions by other members of the delegation — in particular, the Bishop of Clonfert, Joseph Cassidy, the Auxiliary Bishop of Dublin, Dermot O'Mahony and of Edward Daly of Derry were significant. While the perceptive questioning of the Forum members revealed an impasse on a range of issues, the forensic skills of the late John Kelly evoked what he termed 'an extremely frank and revealing statement' from Bishop Joseph Cassidy on the vexed question of mixed marriages. Cassidy's reply on this topic was a model answer, representing the best tradition in the Catholic Church for openness and transparency. While the full text of the answer is too extensive to reproduce here, it is worth highlighting certain points. John Kelly asked whether there would be a case for seeking a special regime tailored to the Irish conditions which would leave Protestant [his word] partners in mixed marriages feeling in a condition of absolute equality with the Catholic partner so far as making decisions about children's upbringing is concerned. Cassidy replied:

> I appreciate the point that you are making. It is something to which the Irish Episcopal Conference gave consideration and we did consider, in view of the attention given to and the sense of injustice that is sometimes felt due to this particular promise, we did consider that we might appeal to Rome for a derogation. I think we should only have appealed to Rome if we felt that there was some chance, even a slight chance that Rome would accede to that particular appeal. We did not feel that.[231]

Bishop Cassidy then went on to explain in detail why they had not followed that course. He further explained that in publishing their guidelines for mixed marriages 'we went really to the outer limits of generosity that the universal law of the Church would allow.'

Here was a perfect example of the Irish Church, and this is my interpretation of what Bishop Cassidy said, using its room to manoeuvre. He had also said earlier that if they [the bishops] had thought that there had been the slightest chance of a change in Church law, they would have appealed in the interests of reconciliation:

> Let me say that is not necessarily the end of the story. This kind of irritant is a consequence of disunity. The Churches are divided. This is a fact. It is a sad and tragic fact. As the document on ecumenism makes clear, we are trying to work towards unity and the closer we come to unity the closer we come to a full resolution of that kind of difficulty. I do not think that there can be a complete resolution as long as the Churches are divided. It is a challenge really to a more active ecumenism.[232]

Bishop Cassidy also said that in relation to the promise asking the Catholic partner in a mixed marriage to do his or her best to raise the child as a Catholic '...but you can take it if there is anything in this area that we can do to further reconciliation we will do it.'[233]

Dr Garret FitzGerald picks up this intervention in his memoirs. He wrote the following passage which may hold part of a clue to the reason why his name provokes expressions of impatience from some bishops:

A decade later I smiled to myself when I heard Bishop Cassidy at the
New Ireland Forum kicking that ball back to Rome, saying that the Irish
bishops had considered appealing to the Holy See for a derogation from
the requirement that the Catholic partner promise orally to do his or her
best to have the children brought up as Catholics, but that they had not
gone ahead with this, as they felt there was not even a slight chance that
Rome would accede to such an appeal. Two Government departments
seeking to shift the bureaucratic onus to each other could not have been
more skilful.[234]

An Irish bishop, sympathetic to the cause of reconciliation, might not
have felt that it was quite fair to compare the 'buck-passing' that goes
on between Government departments to the relationship between the
Holy See and the Irish Episcopal Conference. The 'point of equality',
to use John Kelly's phrase, was quite distinct. An appeal in the early
1980s might have resulted in the Irish bishops being told by the relevant
Congregation of the Holy See to retreat radically from the position
Bishop Cassidy said the hierarchy occupied — 'the outer limits of
generosity that the universal law of the Church would allow.'[235] The
'outer limits of generosity' was not so much in favour at the Holy See,
then or now.[236] But there are also those who argue that, in the cause of
natural justice, the hierarchy might have at least tried even if the answer
was to be a rotund 'no'.

The response of Bishop Cassidy was an example of a Catholic bishop
who understood that he was working in a democratic culture of
openness and transparency. This might have been a point of departure
for a major discussion within the Catholic Church — that is, taking the
wider Vatican II definition of Church to mean 'the People of God'. But
after appearing at the Forum and the publication of the transcript, it
would not appear that the document became a subject of structured
discussion within the parishes in the country. Vatican II had
recommended the establishment of structures in which the laity could
participate at a local level. An exercise of that kind — together with
widescale consultation with lay Church members before attending the
Forum — might have resulted in a range of new proposals coming
forward from the People of God. But the 1980s proved to be very weak
in dialogue between hierarchy and laity in many dioceses. That criticism
was more true for some dioceses than others. While the debate in the
Catholic Church on pluralism in the 1980s was quite extensive in

magazines and journals many of the laity — in ever diminishing numbers — sat and listened in Church.

In September 1985 — over a year after that statement was made at the Forum — the Minister for Foreign Affairs, Peter Barry, spoke after a lunch in Iveagh House.[237] His guest was the Cardinal Secretary of State for the Holy See, Agostino Casaroli.[238] A number of bishops were present including the Cardinal. The Minister paid tribute to the role of the Churches in Irish society and to their fine missionary records through the centuries. But then he continued:

> It cannot seriously be denied that during the fifty years which followed the establishment of an independent Irish State, there was a considerable intimacy between the State and the Catholic Church. The extent of this intimacy has been greatly exaggerated in some quarters, and, in many ways the close relationship which marked that period was quite understandable, given the prevailing historical factors and the overwhelming proportion of Catholics in the population. Nevertheless, in retrospect, it has been argued — most notably by the Catholic Bishops at the Public Session of the New Ireland Forum on 9 February 1984 — that the alliance of Church and State was harmful for both parties. That is why the Catholic Bishops, to quote one member of the Hierarchy 'rejoiced' when the provision concerning the special position of the Catholic Church was removed from the Constitution, following the referendum of 1972.

The Minister then spoke about the change in the relationship between the State and the various Churches since 1972. That had sometimes led to instances of misunderstanding: 'Measured against international standards, the causes of these difficulties have been minor, but in an Irish context they have occasionally been allowed to assume major proportions.' That was a source of regret to the Government not least because little or no benefit is derived by Church or State when they are seen to be at loggerheads: 'The Government accepts, however, that these episodes are the price that has to be paid for a relationship with the Churches that is based on equality and mutual respect.'

That was based on two principles which the Church had accepted at the Forum:

1   Every Church and religious denomination had, subject to the provisions of the Constitution, the right to speak out on any issue they wish.

2   The members of the Oireachtas have the right to legislate according to their conscience and in what they consider to be the best interests of the Irish people.[239]

The pursuit of actions based on those principles has placed Church and State on a number of collision courses in the latter part of the 1980s and again in the mid-1990s. What interpetation did Casaroli, who may not have been expecting to hear a speech on that occasion, put on the content of the speech? It very much reinforced the line of thought in the memorandum submitted by Dr FitzGerald to the Cardinal Secretary of State in 1973. The bishops present on that occasion may have felt that they were a captive audience. Oral sources confirm that at least some of the bishops present, if not the papal party, remained somewhat underwhelmed.[240]

The volume of discussions which took place between Church and State in the mid-1980s is difficult to catalogue. But arising out of a public exchange of letters between Cardinal Ó Fiaich and Dr FitzGerald in 1990, it is possible to demonstrate that discussions took place between a delegation of bishops and representatives of the coalition Government on 7 April 1986 on the question of marriage and the law. Writing in *Alpha* on 21 December, Dr FitzGerald stated:

> Indeed, there was even a suggestion by the Hierarchy delegation that we 'bend' our civil marriage laws so as to accommodate these bigamous marriages, a suggestion that was, in my view, quite improper.[241]

The Cardinal replied: 'No such suggestion was made by the delegation or by any member of it.' [242] There followed a long explanation by the Cardinal which also revealed that the draft report of the meeting had never been agreed.[243] Dr FitzGerald replied, in an equally detailed fashion, on 13 March 1990.[244]

It is to be hoped that the passage of the Freedom of Information Act will make access available to Government files on that and other Church-State discussions during the 1980s and 1990s. In the absence of such access, we must remain grateful to Dr FitzGerald for writing about his experience in Government. His public contributions reveal something of the exchanges which went on between Church and State immediately prior to the announcement on 24 April that a referendum on divorce would be held in the country on 26 June 1986.

The sudden decision to hold such a referendum again produced a swift and well-organized reaction from various groups which had anticipated such an eventuality. Unlike the 1983 referendum where a new section was added to the Constitution, the proposal in 1986 required the removal of the constitutional ban on divorce and its replacement with a wording which permitted divorce in specific circumstances. The proposition was rejected by the electorate on 26 June 1986 by 63.1 per cent to 36.3 per cent. The turnout was 60.8 per cent Analysing the results, Brian Girvin found that:

In only six constituencies was there a 'yes' vote, and within Dublin (where all these pro-divorce constituencies are located) the difference between 'yes' and 'no' is only 0.20%. Outside of Dublin, the rejection of the proposal was much clearer. The further away from Dublin the constituency, the more likely it was to return a 'no' vote, while closeness to Dublin or an other urban centre increased the relative size of the 'yes' vote. In predominantly rural constituencies and in the west of Ireland, the 'yes' vote rarely exceeded 30% .[245]

Nine years later that situation was reversed when the electorate voted by a very narrow majority in favour of the inclusion of a clause permitting divorce to be placed in the Constitution. At the time of writing, the result is under legal appeal.

By focusing on the areas of abortion, divorce and sexual morality, one reveals Church-State relations in Ireland at their most adversarial. As has been mentioned previously, the Catholic Church relates to the State at a range of different levels virtually on a day to day basis. The education area may yet appear to be potentially a most divisive area. Yet, the response of Catholic educators to the challenge to transform structures — in the light of considerations regarding ecumenism and reconciliation — has been quite positive. Education is one of the areas where, given the changing needs in Irish society and the critical personnel shortages within the religious orders, the Catholic Church has engaged in planning.

The debate provoked by the Green Paper on education revealed the diversity of views within the Church. But it also showed that clergy, religious and Catholic lay teachers were not prepared to serve as the mere agents of an enterprise culture.[246] The proceedings of the Report on the National Education Convention are relevant to mention in this regard. Presentations by the Catholic Schools Managers' Association (11 October 1993), the Catholic Episcopal Commission for Education (12 October 1993), and the Conference of Religious in Ireland (CORI) (also 12 October) revealed the richness and the diversity of Catholic thought on educational issues. It is important to examine very carefully the different colours in Joseph's cloak.

It is not accurate, therefore, generally to depict the Catholic Church in Ireland, using that term in the Vatican II context, as a *conservative* force. Members of the Catholic Church — women and men, lay, clerical and religious — will continue to play a central role in the struggle for establishment of a more just, a more equal and a more democratic society, together with the other Churches and religious groups. Despite institutional crises, and swings to the right, the Catholic Church in Ireland has sought to remain loyal to the teachings of Vatican II, and that source — according to Fr Enda McDonagh will empower:

> ...Catholics, lay and clerical, to contribute to a society that is genuinely free and tolerant, just and egalitarian, fraternal (sororal) and peaceful. For biblical Christians the promotion of such a society would correspond to the partial and temporal promotion of the Kingdom of God. The ecumenical movement in which Catholics became active partners through the Vatican Council provides a similar impetus for other Christians.
>
> How dynamic is all this in Britain, Ireland, and Northern Ireland? Not as dynamic as it needs to be, but with considerable energy still.[247]

The weakening of the value system which underpins the work of that movement may be a source of celebration for some forces in Irish society. The Catholic Church may be viewed by some as a bastion of reaction. Many Catholics do not view with equanimity 'reactionary' features of their Church. Change is enthusiastically welcomed. But there are core values which, if lost to Irish society — even as ideals — may exacerbate social tensions and conflicts. Professor Joe Lee writes:

> The church's dilemma, to which there is no easy answer, should deeply concern civil leaders. The church is a bulwark, perhaps now the main bulwark, of the civic culture. It is the very opportunism of the traditional value system that leaves religion as the main barrier between a reasonably civilised society and the untrammelled predatory instincts of individual and pressure-group selfishness, curbed only by the power of rival

predators. Evidence of a sharp decline in formal religious observance among the young urbanised generation has deeply disturbed some observers who detect 'shallow' religious roots and a church suffering from 'spiritual malnutrition'. The more comforting conclusion that 'what the church is experiencing is less a crisis of faith than a crisis of culture' may be optimistic in a society where faith and culture are so intimately intertwined. It is precisely this close connection that leaves the civic culture so vulnerable to a rapid decline in the role of institutional religion. If religion were to no longer fulfil its historic civilising mission as a substitute for internalised values of civil responsibility, the consequences for the country no less than for the church could be lethal.[248]

Using even more trenchant language, Professor Patrick Corish makes a similar argument:

> I have suggested that the Irish national inheritance, those shared values for which people are prepared to make the necessary sacrifices, is a complex thing and may well be a fragile thing. I have also suggested that the strongest element in it may well be the religious inheritance. The Irish have only slender traditions of a philosophical humanism, much less of a secularist humanism. What humanism they are capable of is rather rooted in religion. It is in some ways a daunting thought that the real elements of pluralism in Ireland may well be the confessional churches; but if this is so, there is nothing gained by refusing to face it.[250]

Within the span of time when the two divorce referenda took place — from 1986 to 1995 — the institutional, clerical Catholic Church was beset by a range of internal problems, unprecedented in the twentieth century. Professor Enda McDonagh referred to this period as the 'The Winter name of Church' — the title of an article in *The Furrow*. He spoke of the great need for thought, prayer and experimentation:

> It's the need for thought that is worrying. Irish church energy is more available for any other activity. Without a serious commitment to scholarship and hard-headed intellectual analysis and debate, the church will remain captive to superficial diagnosis of its crisis and to shallow, quick-fix solutions. Like other institutions the church might consider establishing a national 'think tank' with the resources and freedom to explore the true dimensions of the crisis and develop long-term strategies. In any event a much more open and vigorous intellectual and theological life is a top priority for the church in Ireland.[250]

The reactive quality of Church actions had been one of the great weaknesses of the hierarchy in the latter half of the twentieth century. A lack of strategic planning has been most obvious at times of crisis. It will not be easy to change this pattern of action. But the following proposal might be worth exploring. In order to enable Church leaders to break away from the cycle of reactive decision-making, some thought might be given to the establishment of an ecumenical centre for the study of religion and society which would harness the creative intellectual energies of the different Churches and religious denominations.

The setting up of an interdisciplinary institute of higher learning might prove to be of enormous benefit to members of the different churches. Ironically, the Irish School of Ecumenics which, since its foundation on 9 November 1970 has done so much to deepen thinking on inter-Church matters, was experiencing grave financial difficulties in 1995. A 'Brookings style' unit might be added to that school — supported by the Churches — to provide a joint intellectual response to the crises confronting Irish society at the end of the twentieth century.

What might be termed the 'democratic deficit' is a second area of weakness which needs to be addressed. The Bishop of Cork, Michael Murphy, has been to the fore in proposing the holding of a synod to deal with 'emerging divisions in the Irish Church'.

Professor Enda McDonagh has developed this idea further in an article which was published in October 1995.[251] A synod, in itself, will not redress the 'democratic deficit' in the Church. But it will focus attention on structures which appear all the more incongruous in the light of the radical changes which have taken place in Irish democratic institutions. While the Irish State espoused a commitment to 'closed government', the manifest defects of the Catholic Church did not appear to be so obvious. Nowadays, that culture of secrecy is not merely anomalous. Many Church members would see it as a scandal.

The need for a freedom of information charter for the Church is also necessary at a time when State institutions are increasingly more open, more transparent and more accountable.

That might also necessitate giving some thought to the opening of the deliberations of the National Conference of Bishops to the public and to the press. The commitment to transparency at the national level will ultimately help transform the local Church.

An openness to public scrutiny of the affairs of the Church coupled with a strong commitment to the building of the intellectual resources of the Church, would help stem the growth of what Fr Joseph S. O'Leary, a theologian from the Cork diocese, has called *une religiosité sauvage*.[253]

That same combination of openness and intellectual endeavour would also enable people to rediscover the richness of the local Church and regain confidence in the identity of Irish Catholicism.

Professor Andrew M. Greeley has argued recently against the simplistic application of the term 'secularization' to the process of change in Ireland today when in fact 'they [certain Irish theologians] mean a rapid change in attitude on certain issues of sexual morality.'[253] He proposes a model with which to approach the subject of religion in Ireland:

...is one that assumes that the Irish have an ancient and powerful heritage which is deeply rooted in their culture and tradition, a heritage that is unique and fascinating, and a heritage that will, as it has in the past, both change and survive. I also suggest that the 'retrieval' of the richness of this heritage will not take place either in the universities or the episcopal offices unless teachers and leaders are more willing to listen to the religious experience of their own people than they seem today.

From ... the extraordinary current literary, artistic, cinematic and musical productivity of Ireland, one might learn much about the Irish religious imagination and its fascinating mix of simplicity and complexity, fatalism, and hope, worldliness and mysticism. ...

I recommend that future research on religion in Ireland (and among Irish Americans) go beyond such matters as the ebb and flow of Mass attendance or the alleged decline of religion or the question of how prejudiced the Irish are and focus on the experiential, imaginative, metaphorical and narrative content of Irish religion — which is both unique and important to the rest of the Catholic world.[254]

Professor Greeley has presented a serious challenge to academics who may find it difficult to work with such a model. Despite the sense of disillusionment with aspects of the institutional Church, there remains in this country a strong analogical or religious imagination.

At the height of the crisis in the Catholic Church in the mid-1990s, a new journal was launched by the Dominicans under the editorship of Fr Tom Jordan. Entitled *Spirituality*, it sold out its first two issues.[255]

Seán Dunne's *The Road to Silence* has enjoyed a wide circulation as have many other works dealing with the religious imagination.[256] Professor Greeley's model indeed presents a challenge.

The appraisal of the situation confronting the Irish Church in the mid-1990s by Bishop Willie Walsh of Killaloe has much in common with the Greeley approach:

> Yes, the Church in Ireland is undergoing a crisis. Any reading of history
> will show that it has survived greater crises before and it will survive
> this one. Maybe we will have less power, less authority over people,
> but I don't see that as a bad thing. Christ announced that he came
> not to be served but to serve. We are about service and not about
> power.[257]

With those thoughts as the guiding principles of the Catholic Church, the door on this island is open to reconciliation with the other Churches and religious denominations. The very depth of the crisis in the Catholic Church ought to make it more open to dialogue and cooperation with other Churches on the island.

That process is already far advanced. As Fethard-on-Sea has been mentioned earlier in this paper, it is appropriate to end with another episode which has been recorded by Colm Tóibín about relations in Wexford between the Catholic Church and the Church of Ireland:

> On Saturday, 16 April 1994, then, evening Mass was said to a packed
> congregation in the Protestant church in Enniscorthy [the Catholic
> cathedral was under repair]. On the way into the church groups of
> people were photographed to mark what the priest called 'this historic
> occasion'. ... My eye wandered to the plaque on the wall to my left. It
> was to the memory of Archibald Hamilton Jacob, Late Captain of the
> Loyal Vinegar Hill Rangers, Who Departed This Life, December 1836,
> Aged 66 Years: 'As a Magistrate, He Was Impartial, As a Subject Loyal,
> As A Soldier Generous and Brave'.
>
> He must have been up there on Vinegar Hill during the battle in
> 1798, and he must have been around for the slaughter afterwards,
> which I heard so much about when I was a child. We were in his
> church now; we had been invited. Protestant service as well as Mass
> would be said here in the morning. No one else was very interested in
> this plaque, or the sectarian legacy. The plaque was a memorial to a past
> which we would not repeat. History had come to an end in
> Enniscorthy.[258]

Now, let me here openly declare a bias. Reviewing the reasons why that form of tolerance and ecumenism — now the norm in relations between Churches in Ireland today — has come about, the answer will not be found in the tracts, pamphlets, leaflets and posters of Ireland's Catholic new right.

A much more fruitful source for reflection on the contribution of Catholicism to the development of Irish society in the twentieth century will be found in the pages of the Irish Dominican publication, *Doctrine and Life*, and in the Maynooth-based journal, *The Furrow*. The first editor of the *The Furrow*, Fr J. G. McGarry, who was also Professor of Pastoral Theology at Maynooth from 1939 until 1969, was a force for renewal in the Catholic Church. A colleague, writing about his contribution, stated:

> In Irish terms *The Furrow* played a providential role in preparing for the Second Vatican Council before that council was even conceived. The theological, liturgical, ecumenical and pastoral concerns of the council had already surfaced in *The Furrow* in the 'fifties and were to receive fuller and deeper consideration in its pages in the 'sixties and 'seventies.
>
> By a judicious combination of borrowing abroad and stimulating home production, Gerry McGarry, as editor, helped to enlarge the vision of the Irish Church and deepen its understanding to a greater degree than perhaps any other single individual in this generation.[259]

McGarry represented one strand of thought within the Irish Catholic Church — a Christian humanism which was receptive to the dynamic of permanent reform. That same approach has been articulated more recently by the theologian, Dermot Lane. Writing on the malaise in the Church with particular regard to women, he states:

> .... the practice of justice is a condition of the credibility of one's preaching about justice.
>
> There is a fundamental issue at stake here concerning the very meaing and heart of Christian faith. Christianity is primarily a religion of the way, that is a religion which focuses not just on knowing the truth or simply proclaiming the truth but ultimately on doing the truth in love. At present there is a serious credibility gap between the theory and practice of the Catholic Church in regard to women. Equally serious is the distinct absence of any particular strategy to change the existing situation of sexism and injustice in the Church. The visionary statements of the Church concerning equality, justice, and participation have not

always been followed up by a liberating praxis or indeed by much structural change or institutional conversion.

It is at this level of praxis that a stark contrast is beginning to exist between ecclesial statements and political statements.[260]

That 'stark contrast' has become even more accentuated in those areas since that statement was first made in December 1993. The sense of alienation felt by lay and clerical members of the Catholic Church has grown exponentially in the first half of the 1990s. But that, too, helps bring new Hope.

ACKNOWLEDGEMENTS

Many people, too numerous to mention, helped while I was researching in the area of Church and State in Ireland. I am very grateful to a number of people who helped me while I was researching this paper. My thanks to the following: Catriona Crowe, Dr David Craig and the staff of the National Archives, Bishop St., Dublin; Mr David Sheehy, archivist, Archdiocesan Archives, Dublin; the archivist, Archdiocesan Archives, Armagh; Fr Leo Layden, Holy Ghost Fathers, Dublin; the archivist, Jesuit Order, Dublin; and the archivist, Éamon de Valera papers, Franciscan House, Killiney. I also wish to record my thanks to Fr Gearóid Ó Suilleabháin, Dr Mary Harris, Ms Suzanne Buckley and to a number of senior ecclesiastical and political sources.

NOTES

1   Two other episodes in recent Irish history may be compared with the situation in the mid-1990s: the civil war between 1922 and 1923 and the Parnell divorce crisis 1890-1891. See Dermot Keogh, *The Vatican, the Bishops and Irish Politics, 1919-1939*, Cambridge: Cambridge University Press, 1985, pp. 77-122; See also Frank Callanan, *Parnell — The Split, 1890-1891*, Cork: Cork University Press, 1992.

2   The full details of the survey, which were to come out later in autumn 1995, were not published by the paper. The question, as cited by *The Sunday Tribune* does not appear to be very precise. The poll was conducted by Behaviour and Attitudes Limited on behalf of the Institute of Advertising Practitioners in Ireland and was carried out between March and April 1995. That meant that the findings were not coloured by stories which had 'broken' in the late summer and early autumn 1995.

3   *The Sunday Tribune*, 1 October 1995.

4   *Ibid.*

5   John Whyte, *Church and State in Modern Ireland 1923-1979*, Dublin: Gill and Macmillan, 1980; See also by the same author, *Catholics in Western Democracies*, Dublin: Gill and Macmillan, 1981.

6   Whyte, *Church and State in Modern Ireland*, p. 376

7   Noel Browne, *Against the Tide*, Dublin: Gill and Macmillan, 1986, p. 150

8   See James Deeny, *To Cure and to Care — Memoirs of a Chief Medical Officer*, Dublin: Glendale Press, 1989, pp. 177-178.

9   Tom Inglis, *Moral Monopoly — The Catholic Church in Modern Irish Society*, Dublin: Gill and Macmillan, 1987, p. 216

10   Tony Fahey, 'Catholicism and Industrial Society in Ireland', in J. J. Goldthorpe and C. T. Whelan, *The Development of Industrial Society in Ireland*, Oxford: The British Academy and Oxford University Press, 1994, pp. 241-263.

11   Patrick Corish, *The Irish Catholic Experience — a Historical Survey*, Dublin: Gill and Macmillan, 1985.

12   Keogh, *The Vatican, the Bishops and Irish Politics*, and *Ireland and the Vatican — The Politics and Diplomacy of Church State Relations 1922-1960*, Cork: Cork University Press, 1995.

13   See the essays of the philosopher Desmond M. Clarke, *Church and State*, Cork: Cork University Press, 1984.

14   Patrick Hannon, *Church State Morality and Law*, Dublin: Gill and Macmillan, 1992.
15   Joseph Dunn, *No Lions in the Hierarchy — An Anthology of Sorts*, Dublin: Columba Press, 1994.
16   Seán Mac Réamoinn (ed.), *Authority in the Church*, Dublin: Columba Press, 1995.
17   Mention here might be made of the following who have contributed over a long period to the debate on Church-State relations in Ireland. Among those who have either written or edited books are: Sean Freyne, Gabriel Daly, Enda McDonagh, Liam Ryan and Dermot Lane. Lay women and women religious have provided the most trenchant critiques of aspects of Church life in Ireland. Women theologians have come more and more to the fore in the general debate about Church and State.

    This latter development is a very positive contribution to the life of the Catholic Church.
18   I am also conscious of the fact that any issue of *The Furrow, Doctrine and Life, Studies* etc., contain high level reflection on topics which relate directly and indirectly to the study of Church and State. The topic is also covered on a regular basis by the staff and guest lecturers in St Patrick's College, Maynooth, in Milltown Park, Mater Dei, the Irish School of Ecumenics, in the diocesan seminaries, religious orders and in the universities. A lay group Pobal has organized conferences on the topic of Church-State relations. Such activities have given rise to a continued questioning of Church structures and the use of power in the Church.
19   The National Archives Act has introduced a thirty-year rule for governmental files. A large selection of material relevant to the study of Church-State relations is now available to scholars in the National Archives, Bishop St., Dublin. The personal papers of many leading politicians are now open to scholars. The best collection is held in the Archives Department, University College Dublin. Éamon de Valera's papers have been partially opened. The material on the framing of the Irish Constitution of 1937 is of particular importance.
20   The archives of many dioceses and archdioceses are also available to scholars. The holdings of Dublin and Armagh are of particular importance. Unfortunately, scholars have not seen files later than 1945 in Armagh and 1940 in Dublin. See my archival essay, 'Church and State in Modern Ireland', in Réamonn O Muirí (ed.) *Irish Church History Today*, Special issue of *Cumann Seanchais Ard Mhacha*, 1990, pp. 100-111
21   I refer here to the continued closure of the papers of Archbishop John Charles McQuaid (1940-1971) and the only partial opening of the papers of Éamon de Valera. McQuaid's archives have been catalogued. In the spirit of openness, so much talked about in Ireland in the mid-1990s, both sets of papers should be opened to scholars forthwith.
22   It is difficult to find neutral terms for a study of this kind. I use terms, 'the Catholic Church' or 'the Church', to refer to the Roman Catholic Church. This is used for convenience and is meant to convey no disrespect to other Churches.

    Very often 'the Catholic Church' refers to the hierarchical or clerical Church. This will be evident from the context. The concept 'Church', meaning 'People of God' and including the laity, is used in a post-Second Vatican Council context.

    Sometimes the terms, 'minority religions', 'minority Churches', and 'other denominations', are used. These are used as a form of shorthand and are not meant to be disrespectful in any sense.

23   Mary McAleese, 'Living with Authority', in Seán Mac Réamoinn, (ed.) *op.cit.*, p.17.

24   Quoted in Keogh, *The Vatican, the Bishops and Irish Politics*, p. 8

25   John A. Murphy, 'Priests and People in Modern Irish History', *Christus Rex*, Vol. XXIII, No 4, October 1969, p. 257.

26   Catholic thinking and teaching is used here in shorthand form; it is one of the central arguments of this paper that a multiplicity of sub-currents are covered by this phrase.

27   See Keogh, *The Vatican, the Bishops and Irish Politics*, chs 1-3.

28   *Ibid.*, p. 73 (quoted).

29   *Ibid.*, p. 73 (quoted).

30   Seán Cannon, C.S.S.R. *Irish Episcopal Meetings, 1788-1882 — a Juridico-historical study*, Rome: Pontificia Studiorum Universitas A S. Thoma AQ. in Urbe, 1979.

31   *Ibid.*, pp. 46-51

32   Keogh, *The Vatican the Bishops and Irish Politics*, pp. 233-235; I am grateful to Bishop Michael Smith of Meath who provided me with the information to compile this section.

33   In accordance with post-conciliar procedure, statutes were approved by Paul VI on 9 August 1969. New statutes were drafted in 1991.

34   Keogh, *The Vatican the Bishops and Irish Politics*, pp. 257

35   This resulted in the death of seventy seven anti-Treatyites, the bodies of many being buried in quicklime. See Keogh, *The Vatican, the Bishops and Irish Politics*, pp. 77-122; *Twentieth Century Ireland — Nation and State*, Dublin: Gill and Macmillan, 1994, pp. 15-18; and *Ireland and the Vatican — The Politics and Diplomacy of Church and State, 1922-1960*, Cork: Cork University Press, 1995, pp. 1-35.

36   See Denis Carroll, 'Fr Michael O'Flanagan, 1976-1942 — A Priest for the People', *The Furrow*, Vol. 43, No 10, October 1992, pp. 547-551

37   Peadar O'Donnell, 'The Clergy and me', October 1974, Vol. 24, *Doctrine and Life*, p. 543

38   Breifne Historical Society, one of the most active local history societies in the country, has chronicled the development of the Kilmore Diocese. See, in particular, Bishop Francis J. MacKiernan, *Diocese of Kilmore, Bishops and Priests, 1136-1988*, Cavan: Breifne Historical Society, 1990. For the history of the Archdiocese of Armagh, see the proceedings of Cumann Seanchais Ard Mhacha.

39   Quoted in Mary Harris, *The Catholic Church and the Foundation of the Northern Irish State*, Cork: Cork University Press, 1993, p. 134.

40   *Ibid.*, p. 134.

41   See also the work of Eamon Phoenix, *Northern Ireland — Nationalist Politics, Partition and the Catholic Minority in Northern Ireland 1890-1940*, Belfast: Ulster Historical Foundation, 1994.

42   *New Ireland Forum Report*, Dublin, 1984, para. 4.9.2, p. 21.

43   See Harris, *op.cit.*

44   See Michael O'Neill, '70 Years ago — Saint Columban's Society', *The Far East*, January 1988, p.3. I am also grateful to Fr O'Neill for showing part of his manuscript on the history of his order. See also Edmund M. Hogan, *The Irish Missionary Movement: A Historical Survey, 1830-1980*, Dublin: Gill and Macmillan, 1992

45   Keogh, *The Vatican, the Bishops and Irish Politics*, pp. 101-184

46   Séamus Ó Buachalla, *Education Policy in Twentieth Century Ireland*, Dublin: Wolfhound Press, 1988, pp. 60-61.

47   *Ibid.*, pp. 61-62.

48   *Ibid.*, p. 64.

49   Irish Catholic Directory, 1927, p. 581.

50   *Ibid.*, p. 597.

51   *Ibid.*, p. 597.

52   *Ibid.*, p. 583.

53   Quoted in Whyte, *Church and State*, p. 25.

54   Not every Irish bishop shared the preoccupations of the majority with the evils of dancing. One bishop used to organize a dance in his home after the end of the harvest on his farm outside Cavan town. The fiddle player was a priest on the staff of St Patrick's College. This piece of information was given to me by Bishop Francis MacKiernan of Kilmore, December 1991.

55   David Thomson, *Woodbrook*, London: Barrie and Jenkins, 1977, pp. 74-75; Earlier in the novel, Thomson refers to another incident to illustrate the capacity for tolerance between Catholic priest and Church of Ireland parson:

> Her father worked in the hay too. I was with him by the stacks one afternoon when a message came from Ardcarne vicarage, the Protestant one, and said that the parson wanted him. 'What about?'
>
> 'It is a matter of Colonel Kirkwood's grave, Major. Parson MacCormack and Father Martin are above in the graveyard now.'
>
> Charlie knew what it was about. He asked James to get the car out and went into the house for a bottle of whiskey. His uncle's foot was sticking out into the Catholic part of the graveyard. The bother of digging him up had been a threat for years. When he reached Ardcarne, he found the parson and the priest seated gloomily on the grave. They discussed 'the matter' there for some hours, all three, with the whiskey, and agreed by nightfall that old Uncle Tom's foot should remain where it was.

The parson and the priest consulted each other frequently. The Government of the Irish Free State had decreed religious toleration in 1921 and it seems to have succeeded. See p. 74.

56   See Keogh, *Twentieth Century Ireland*, pp. 71 ff. See the Report of the Committee on the Criminal Law Amendment Acts (1880-85) and on Juvenile Prostitution. This had been submitted to the Department of Justice on 20 August 1931. See Department of the Taoiseach, S 5998, National Archives, Bishop St., Dublin.

57   An Intoxicating Liquor Act reducing opening hours was passed in 1924 and in 1927 measures were taken to reduce the number of public houses.

58   Jack White, *Minority Report — The Anatomy of the Southern Irish Protestant*, Dublin: Gill and Macmillan, 1975, p. 116

59   Keogh, *The Vatican, the Bishops and Irish Politics*, pp. 128-129.

60   White, *op.cit.*, p. 116

61   Keogh, *The Vatican the Bishops and Irish Politics*, p. 129

62   See memorandum by Dan Costigan, 11 March 1952 file 102/323, Department of Justice, National Archives, Dublin; and quoted in Dermot Keogh (ed.), 'Irish Democracy and the Right to Freedom of Information', *Ireland — A Journal of History and Society*, Vol. 1, 1995, p. 41.

63   Michael Adams, *Censorship — the Irish Experience*, Alabama: University of Alabama Press, 1968, p. 48

64   Padraic O'Farrell, *The Burning of Brinsley MacNamara*, Dublin: Lilliput Press, 1990.

65   Seamus Deane, *A Short History of Irish Literature*, London: Hutchinson, 1986, p. 187

66   James Meenan, *George O'Brien — A Biographical Memoir*, Dublin: Gill and Macmillan, 1980, pp. 120-122

67   *Ibid.*, pp 117-118

68   Mainie Jellett exhibition guide, Irish Museum of Modern Art, 1992 p. 1

69   See Bruce Arnold, *Mainie Jellett and the Modern Movement in Ireland*, New Haven and London: Yale University Press, 1991 and S. B. Kennedy, *Irish Art and Modernism*, Belfast: Institute of Irish Studies, 1991

70   Kennedy, *op.cit.*, p. 40.

71   Tom Garvin covers this theme in a very original manner in his book: *Nationalist Revolutionaries in Ireland 1858-1928*, Oxford: Clarendon Press, 1987.

72   Keogh, *The Vatican, the Bishops and Irish Politics*, p.p 139 ff; and *Ireland and the Vatican*, ch. 2, pp. 36-159.

73   Quite how Paschal Robinson's arrival in Dublin was viewed by unionist opinion in Northern Ireland remains a matter for further research.

74   Bishop Collier report to June meeting of the hierarchy, Edward Byrne papers, Archdiocesan Archives, Drumcondra.

75   Whyte, *Church and State*, 37-43

76   This section is based on S2547A, National Archives, Bishop St., Dublin.

77   *Catholic Bulletin*, Vol. 21, no 1, p. 10

78   *Ibid.*, no 2, p. 143

79   Keogh, *The Vatican, the Bishops and Irish Politics*, p. 175

80   I am grateful to Cardinal Cahal B. Daly for sending me the text of this letter. See Joseph MacRory papers, Armagh Archdiocesan Archives, Armagh; Cosgrave also requested the hierarchy to look to the attitude of certain periodicals which, by their title, led the general public to believe that they were authorized exponents of Catholic doctrine. Those journals often carried inaccurate comments on government policy, according to Cosgrave. Those comments were often not merely inaccurate but 'so intemperate as to be violently abusive' and they had done considerable damage not just to the governing party but to the State as a whole. Cosgrave felt that those articles had resulted in 'weakening the respect for authority'. These journals operated in the absence of a directive from the hierarchy, wrote Cosgrave.

81   Keogh, *The Vatican, the Bishops and Irish Politics*, p. 177

82   See White, *op.cit.*, pp. 101-102.

83   Keogh, *The Vatican, the Bishops and Irish Politics*, p. 178.

84   See Keogh, 'De Valera, the Catholic Church and the Red Scare, in J. P. O'Carroll and John A. Murphy, *De Valera and his Times*, Cork: Cork University Press, 1983, p. 140.

85   White, *op.cit.*, p. 102.

86   See Seán P. Farragher, *Dev and his Alma Mater — Éamon de Valera's Lifelong association with Blackrock College 1898-1975*, Dublin: Paraclete Press, 1984.

87   See John Feeney, *The Man and the Mask*, Dublin: Mercier Press, 1974 and Roland Burke Savage, 'A Study of the Episcopate of Most Rev. John Charles McQuaid, D.D.', *Studies*, Vol. LIV, No 216, Winter, 1965, pp. 297-338.

88   Keogh, *The Vatican, the Bishops and Irish Politics*, pp. 188 ff.

89   For a detailed examination of social Catholicism in Ireland, see Finín O Driscoll, 'The Search for the Christian State — an analysis of Irish Social Catholicism, 1913-1939', MA, University College Cork, 1994.

90   Maurice Manning, *The Blueshirts*, Dublin: Gill and Macmillan, 1970.

91   Keogh, 'An Eye Witness to History: Fr Alexander J. McCabe and the Spanish Civil War 1936-1939', in *Breifne — Journal of Cumann Seanchais Bhreifne*, 1994, pp. 445-488; See also Keogh, *Ireland and Europe, 1919-1989*, Dublin and Cork: Hibernian University Press, 1989, pp. 63-97.

92   *The Catholic Mind*, Vol. 4, no 4, April 1933, p. 69.[Quoted in Finín O Driscoll, *op.cit.*, p. 190.]

93   Quoted from Denis Fahey, *The Kingship of Christ*, Dublin: Browne and Nolan, 1936, pp. 96-97. Cited from Finín O Driscoll, *op.cit.*, p. 190.

94   O'Driscoll *op.cit.*, p. 191.

95   For background, see *Ibid.*, 136-177.

96   See Leon Ó Bróin, *Frank Duff — A Biography*, Dublin: Gill and Macmillan, 1982, p. 62 ff.

97   I have reviewed the role played by the Jesuits in the drafting of the Constitution in my article: 'The Irish Constitutional Revolution: An Analysis of the Making of the Constitution', *Administration*, Vol. 35, No 4, 1988, pp. 11-19.

98   *Ibid.*, pp. 19-25.

99   This text can be found in Cathal Condon, 'An analysis of the contribution by Dr John Charles McQuaid to the drafting of the 1937 Constitution of Ireland', MA thesis, University College Cork, 1995, pp. 93-94. This study is an original contribution to the drafting of the Irish Constitution. Based extensively on the private papers of McQuaid, this is an important piece of historical research. It argues that McQuaid was the main architect of many of the articles in the Constitution.

100   *Ibid.*, p. 98.

101   *Ibid.*, p. 105.

102   *Ibid.*, See chs 1, 2, 5, 6 and 7, p. 105.

103   Keogh 'The Irish Constitutional Revolution: An Analysis of the Making of the Constitution', pp. 4-85.

104   See manuscript of my forthcoming work on 'Ireland and the Jewish community since the foundation of the State'. In progress.

105   *The Irish Times*, 10 April 1937.

106   Keogh, *The Vatican, the Bishops and Irish Politics*, p. 239.

107   Quoted in White, *op.cit.*, pp. 108-109.

108   *Ibid.*, p. 108.

109   Keogh, *Twentieth Century Ireland*, pp. 96-104.

110   Ó Faoláin, *loc. cit.*, p. 23

111   See Keogh, *Twentieth Century Ireland*, pp. 143-146.

112   *Ibid.*, p. 187.

113   Keogh, *Ireland and the Vatican*, pp. 225-264.

114   *Ibid.*, pp. 265 ff.

115 This episode is discussed in my book, *Twentieth Century Ireland*, pp. 201-212.
116 For text, see Whyte, *op.cit.*, pp. 449-452.
117 Keogh, *Ireland and the Vatican*, pp. 338-339.
118 Keogh, *Twentieth Century Ireland*, p. 213.
119 This section will form part of my forthcoming study on the role of the Catholic Church in twentieth century Irish politics.
120 See Keogh, *Twentieth Century Ireland*, pp. 214-243.
121 Leaflet 'Fiat — Its History and Aims,' in Maria Duce 1, Denis Fahey papers, Archives of the Holy Ghost Fathers, Dublin.
122 Maria Duce leaflet, Maria Duce 2, Denis Fahey papers.
123 Unsigned article entitled 'Anti-semitism at Oberammargau', in *Fiat*, No 10.
124 Memorandum signed by leading officers of Maria Duce and sent to the Archbishop and to the editor of *The Standard*, Maria Duce 2, Denis Fahey papers. Archives of the Holy Ghost Fathers, Dublin.
125 Undated Fallon letter to the editor of *The Standard*, Peadar Curry, Gabriel Fallon file, Denis Fahey papers.
126 Thomas Roseingrave folder, Correspondence files, Denis Fahey papers.
127 Maria Duce memorandum, Denis Fahey papers.
128 Fr Christopher Mangan to Tom Agar, President of Maria Duce, 14 February 1951, Denis Fahey papers.
129 This North American anti-Catholic was in Dublin to research his book *The Irish and Catholic Power*, London: Derek Verschoyle, 1954.
130 Fr Liam Martin to Tom Agar, 8 December 1952, Denis Fahey papers.
131 Roseingrave folder, Correspondence files, Denis Fahey papers.
132 Stephen O'Keefe 'Maria Duce is Alive and Well and living in Dublin', *Hibernia*, 9 August 1974.
133 White, *op.cit.*, p. 112.
134 See Andrée Sheehy Skeffington, *Skeff — A Life of Owen Sheehy Skeffington 1909-1970*, Dublin: Lilliput Press, 1991.
135 *The Irish Times*, 27 May 1957.
136 *The Irish Independent*, 25 June 1957.
137 Department of the Taoiseach, S16247, National Archives, Bishop St., Dublin.
138 *Ibid.*
139 *The Irish Press*, 1 July 1957.
140 Quoted in Maurice Moynihan (ed.), *Speeches and Statements by Éamon de Valera, 1917-1973*, Dublin: Gill and Macmillan, 1980, p.580.
141 J. Monahan, Clontarf, Co. Dublin, 5 July 1957, Department of the Taoiseach, National Archives, Bishop St., Dublin.
142 McQuaid to de Valera, Rockwell College, 5 July 1957, Department of the Taoiseach, National Archives, Bishop St., Dublin.
143 *The Irish Times*, 8 July 1957.
144 *The Irish Press*, 8 July 1957.
145 *The Irish Times*, 15 July 1957.
146 Moynihan to T. J. Coyne, Secretary of the Department of Justice, 16 July 1957. Department of the Taoiseach, S16247, National Archives, Bishop St., Dublin.
147 *The Irish Press*, 24 February 1957.
148 Jean Blanchard, *The Church in Contemporary Ireland*, Dublin: Clonmore and Reynolds, 1963, trans. from the French *Le Droit Ecclésiastique Contemporain D'Irlande*, Paris: R. Pichon and R. Durand-Auzias, 86-87

149   *Ibid.*, p. 87

150   *Ibid.*, p. 89

151   See Gabriel Le Bras, *Introduction à l'Histoire de la Pratique religieuse en France* and *Études de Sociologie religieuse.*

152   Heinrich Böll, *Irish Journal*, London: Secker and Warburg, 1967, p. 10 [originally published in German under the title *Irisches Tagbuch* in 1957].

153   Michael Ryan (ed.), *Peter Birch — The Church and the Nation*, Dublin: Columba Press, 1993, p. 18.

154   *The Irish Times*, 10 March 1969.

155   *Ibid.*

156   Archbishop Derek Worlock, 'Whatever Happened to Holy Mother Church?', *Priests and People*, August-September 1995, p. 303.

157   For a good overview of American Catholicism, see Jay Dolan, *The American Catholic Experience*, New York: Image Books, 1985.

158   Quoted in Archbishop Derek Worlock, *op.cit.*, p. 302; see Avery Dulles, *Models of the Church*, Dublin: Gill and Macmillan, 1985; See also Avery Dulles, *The Reshaping of Catholicism*, New York: Harper and Row, 1988.

159   Quoted in Archbishop Derek Worlock, *op.cit.*, p. 305.

160   Keogh, *Twentieth Century Ireland*, p.262.

161   Whyte, *Catholics in Western Democracies*, Dublin: Gill and Macmillan, 1981, p. 142.

162   *Ibid.*, p. 143.

163   *Ibid.*, p. 138 ff.

164   See Joseph Dunn, *No Tigers in Africa — Recollections and Reflections on 25 years of Radharc*, Dublin: Columba Press, 1986.

165   Keogh, *Twentieth Century Ireland*, p. 285; see also Garret FitzGerald, *All in a Life — An Autobiography*, Dublin: Gill and Macmillan, 1991, pp. 63-111.

166   Keogh, *op.cit.*, p. 285; see also FitzGerald, p. 65.

167   Peter Hebblethwaite, 'The Vatican's Latin American Policy', in Keogh (ed.), *Church and Politics in Latin America*, London: Macmillan, 1990, p. 54

168   Keogh, *Twentieth Century Ireland*, pp. 308-311.

169   Bernard J. Canning, *Bishops of Ireland 1870-1987*, Ballyshannon: Donegal Democrat, 1987, p. 55.

170   W. D. Flackes and Sydney Elliott, *Northern Ireland — A Political Directory 1968 — 1993*, Belfast: The Blackstaff Press, 1994, p. 9.

171   Josiah Horton Beeman and Robert Mahony, 'The Institutional Churches and the Process of Reconciliation in Northern Ireland: recent progress in Presbyterian-Roman Catholic Relations', in Dermot Keogh and Michael Haltzel (eds.), *Northern Ireland and the Politics of Reconciliation*, Cambridge: Cambridge University Press, 1993, p. 151.

172   For a work which encapsulates the spirit of this ecumenical project, see Michael Hurley (ed.), *Reconciliation in Religion and Society*, Belfast: Institute of Irish Studies, Queen's University, 1994.

173   Josiah Horton Beeman and Robert Mahony, *op.cit.*, p. 151.

174   See Cahal B. Daly and A. S. Worrall, *Ballymascanlon: A Venture in Inter-Church Dialogue*, Belfast and Dublin, 1978, p. 152.

175   Whyte, *Church and State in Modern Ireland*, p. 385.

176   *Ibid.*, p. 386.

177   *Ibid.*, p. 386.

178 Statement issued by the Catholic Press Office on behalf of the hierarchy on 11 March 1971.

179 Whyte, *Church and State in Modern Ireland*, p. 405.

180 *Ibid.*, p. 400.

181 *Ibid.*, p. 400.

182 *Ibid.*, p. 403.

183 Statement on Draft Matrimonial Causes (Northern Ireland) Order 1978; This was signed by Archbishop Tomás Ó Fiaich of Armagh; Bishop Edward Daly of Derry; Bishop William Philbin of Down and Connor; Bishop Francis Brooks of Dromore; Bishop Patrick Mulligan of Clogher and Bishop Francis McKiernan of Kilmore.

184 *Ibid.*

185 Statement of the Irish Episcopal Conference, 1973.

186 *Ibid.*

187 Whyte, *Church and State in Modern Ireland*, p. 408. Mrs Mary McGill was a mother of four. Born in 1944, she had married in 1968. All of her four pregnancies had been very difficult. Her doctor advised her that another pregnancy might lead to her death or to paralysis. Unable to use the pill for medical reasons, her doctor prescribed a spermicidal jelly which had to be imported from England as it was not made within the State. Customs' officers seized her parcel containing the jelly under S.17(3) of the Criminal Law Amendment Act 1935. Supported financially by the Irish Family Planning Association, she took a case to show that that Section of the 1935 Act was unconstitutional. She won.

188 Statement of the Irish Episcopal Conference, 1973.

189 Whyte, *Church and State in Modern Ireland*, pp. 405-406.

190 *Ibid.*, pp. 415.

191 Statement from the Irish Bishops' Conference on proposed legislation dealing with family planning and contraception, 1978.

192 Statement by Catholic Hierarchy, 1979.

193 Statement from the Irish Bishops' Conference on proposed legislation dealing with family planning and contraception, 1978.

194 Joe Lee, *Ireland 1912-1989 — Politics and Society*, Cambridge: Cambridge University Press, 1990, p. 656.

195 Whyte, *Church and State in Modern Ireland*, pp. 395 ff.

196 Confidential clerical source.

197 Whyte, *Church and State in Modern Ireland*, pp. 398-399.

198 Bernard J. Canning, *Bishops of Ireland 1870 — 1987*, p. 57.

199 Oliver Rafferty, 'Catholicism in the North of Ireland since 1891', Eamon Phoenix (ed.), *A Century of Northern Life — The Irish News and 100 Years of Ulster History 1890s-1990s*, Belfast: Ulster Historical Foundation, 1995, p. 163.

200 Hannon, *op.cit.*, p. 125

201 I discussed this matter personally with him in 1990.

202 Paul VI had followed Irish affairs with the keenest of interest while a senior member of the Secretariat of State. But his interest in Ireland dated back to the War of Independence. As a member of a family that supported the Popular Party (Christian Democrats) he followed the activities of Sinn Féin and visited the Irish College in Rome, in 1920.

203 Keogh, *Ireland and the Vatican*, p. 357-69.

204   This question is framed for the Pontificate of Pope Paul VI on the basis of the evidence provided in the files of the Department of Foreign Affairs. See Dermot Keogh, *Ireland and the Vatican,* in particular, chs 5 and 6.

205   FitzGerald, *op.cit.,* pp. 184-185.

206   *Ibid.,* p.185.

207   *Ibid.,* p.185.

208   Benelli, who held the position of Prime Minister — according to FitzGerald's description — at the Vatican, had served in Ireland in the early 1950s. While serving at the Vatican, two Irish Medical Missionaries of Mary from Drogheda, had served as his administrative assistants. They both continued to work with him in Florence until his death.

209   FitzGerald, *op.cit.,* p.186.

210   This information was given to me by an Irish bishop. I was given further confirmation of the intended visit to Northern Ireland by the Pope at the Vatican in August 1979.

211   *The Visit — John Paul II in Ireland — A Historical Record,* Dublin: Veritas, 1979, pp. 87-88

212   Text of statement from the Irish Catholic Hierarchy on the Health (Family Planning) Act 1979.

213   Bill Cosgrave, 'Structures of Authority', in Seán Mac Réamoinn (ed.), *Authority in the Church,* Dublin: Columba Press, 1995, p. 39

214   *Ibid.,* p. 39

215   Avery Dulles, 'Doctrinal Authority of Epsicopal Conferences', in Thomas J. Reese (ed.), *Episcopal Conferences — Historical, Canonical and Theological Studies,* Washington DC: Georgetown University Press, 1989, p. 209

216   The following reference does not deal with the relations between fundamentalist groups in Ireland and in the United States. But for an excellent historical survey of the development of Protestant fundamentalism in the United States, see Professor R. Laurence Moore, *Selling God — American Religion in the Marketplace of Culture,* New York: Oxford University Press, 1994. Read, in particular, p. 239 ff.

217   Enda McDonagh, 'New Forces for Positive Change in Ireland', in Keogh and Haltzel (eds.), *op.cit.,* p. 148.

218   See Tom Hesketh, *The Second Partitioning of Ireland — The Abortion Referendum of 1983,* Dublin: Brandsma Books, 1990.

219   Richard Sinnott, *Irish Voters Decide — Voting Behaviour in Elections and Referendums since 1918,* Manchester: Manchester University Press, 1995, pp. 226-227.

220   See Emily O'Reilly, *Masterminds of the Right,* Dublin: Attic Press, 1988.

221   Sinnott, *op.cit.,* p. 227.

222   I have been informed, on good authority, that a draft of that protocol in 1992 included a reference to the constitutional ban on divorce. This was removed from the final draft after determined interventions by senior civil servants.

223   According to oral sources, the Attorney General, Peter Sutherland, is believed to have written a memorandum to Government of over 100 pages outlining his negative observations on the wording.

224   Joe Lee, 'Dynamics of change in the Irish Republic' , Keogh and Haltzel (eds.), *op.cit.,* p. 124.

225 The Attorney General had sought to prevent 'X', a fourteen-year-old girl and the victim of rape, from leaving the country with her parents to have an abortion in England. The Attorney General's request for an injunction was upheld by the High Court and then sensationally overturned by the Supreme Court.

226 Lee, *Ireland 1912-1985*, p. 655.

227 Here I am grateful to John Dunlop's *A Precarious Belonging — Presbyterians and the Conflict in Ireland*, Belfast: The Blackstaff Press, 1985, for the insights he has given me into his tradition. I also found the latter section of Seán Mac Réamoinn's *Authority in the Church* very useful. The writings of other authors, such as Terence McCaughey, have been very helpful.

228 *Submission to the New Ireland Forum from the Irish Episcopal Conference, January 1984*, Dublin: Veritas, 1984. The hierarchy also submitted a list of printed documents: *The Catholic Church in Ireland: Information and Documentation*, 1981; *Human Life is Sacred*, 1975; *In pursuit of an Ideal, Ireland Christianity and Europe*, 1979; *Conscience and Morality, a doctrinal statement*, 1980; *What God has Joined, a Study of Faithfulness in Marriage*, 1982; *Christian Faith in a time of Economic Depression*, 1983; *The Storm that Threatens — War and Peace in the Nuclear Age*, 1983; *Reconciliation and Penance in the Mission of the Church*, 1983; *Directory on Mixed Marriages and Preparing for a Mixed Marriage*, 1983.

229 *Submission to the New Ireleand Forum from the Irish Episcopal Conference, January 1984*.

230 *New Ireland Forum Report*, p. 2.

231 *Ibid.*, p. 48.

232 Irish Episcopal Conference Delegation, report of proceedings, 9 February 1984, p. 49.

233 *Ibid.*, p. 49.

234 FitzGerald, *op.cit.*, p. 185.

235 Irish Episcopal Conference Delegation, report of proceedings, 9 February 1984, p. 49.

236 It might also be worth reflecting upon the possibility that the way in which such a promise is viewed by Irish bishops might differ radically depending upon whether one is discussing Northern Ireland or the Republic of Ireland.

237 The Taoiseach, Dr Garret FitzGerald, had not been told in advance that the speech was going to be made.

238 Dr FitzGerald, it will be remembered, had met Cardinal Casaroli in 1973 in Helsinki and had had discussion with him later at the Vatican on the content of a memorandum which he had sent there.

239 See Keogh, *Ireland and the Vatican*, pp. 365-366.

240 It may be apocryphal but one of the comments passed after the speech on Church and State had been delivered before Casaroli was: 'It would not have happened in a banana republic.'

241 FitzGerald, *op.cit.*, p. 648 ff. The Cardinal wrote to Dr. FitzGerald on 9 January 1990; the latter replied on 13 March 1990.

242 *Ibid.*, p. 648.

243 *Ibid.*, p. 649.

244 *Ibid.*, p. 650-652.

245 Brian Girvin, 'The Divorce Referendum in the Republic: June 1986', in *Irish Political Studies*, Vol. 2, 1987, p. 96.

246   Government of Ireland, *Green Paper: Education for a Changing World*, Government Stationery Office, Dublin, 1992.

247   Enda McDonagh, 'New Forces for Postive Change in Ireland', in Keogh and Haltzel (eds.), *op.cit.*, p. 148.

248   Lee, *Ireland 1912-1985*, p. 657.
       Lee draws on M.P. Gallagher, 'What Hope for Irish Faith?', *The Furrow*, October 1978; Liam Ryan, 'The Church Now', *The Furrow*, February 1981; A. Falconer et al., *Freedom to Hope — The Catholic Church in Ireland Twenty Years after Vatican II*, Dublin: Columba Press, 1985.

249   Patrick Corish, *The Irish Catholic Experience*, p. 258.

250   McDonagh, 'The Winter Name of Church', *The Furrow*, p. 12.

251   McDonagh, 'Bruised Reeds and the Mystery of the Church — In Memory of Tommy Waldron', *The Furrow*, Vol. XLVI, No. 10, October 1995, pp. 543-553.

252   Joseph S. O'Leary, *La verité chrétienne à l'age du pluralisme religieux*, Paris: Les Éditions du Cerf, 1994.

253   Andrew M. Greeley, 'Are the Irish Really Losing their Faith?', in *Doctrine and Life*, Vol. 44, March 1994, p. 142.

254   *Ibid.*, pp. 141-142.

255   See *Spirituality*, Vol. 1, No 1, July-August 1995 and Vol. 1 No 2, September-October 1995.

256   Seán Dunne, *The Road to Silence — an Irish Spiritual Odyssey*, New Island Books, Dublin, 1994.

257   Bishop Willie Walsh, 'Strength in Weakness', *The Furrow*, Vol. XLVI, No 2, February, 1995, p. 74.

258   Colm Tóibín, *The Sign of the Cross — Travels in Catholic Europe*, London: Jonathan Cape, 1994, pp. 294-295.

259   Quoting Professor Enda McDonagh, see Ian Ellis, *Vision and Reality — A Survey of Twentieth Century Irish Inter-Church Relations*, Belfast: Institute of Irish Studies, 1992, pp. 108-109.

260   Dermot Lane, 'The Equality of all in Christ: Theological Reflections', in *Women in the Church in Ireland — Proceedings of a Study Day, 23 October 1993*, Dublin: The Irish Commission for Justice and Peace, 1993, pp. 12-13.

APPENDIX I

TEXT OF LETTER
FROM WILLIAM T COSGRAVE
TO CARDINAL JOSEPH MACRORY
28 MARCH 1931

Roinn An Uachtaráin
(DEPARTMENT OF THE PRESIDENT)

Baile Átha Cliath
(Dublin)

Your Eminence,

It is with much hesitation that I venture to trouble your Eminence with certain matters which have recently given rise to considerable anxiety in the minds of my Colleagues and myself because of their possible reactions upon State Institutions, and upon the happy relations which exist between the Church and the State in this country.

Any appearance of public disagreement between individual ecclesiastical authorities and the State is always deplorable; in a country so overwhelmingly Catholic as this it may have results of a very serious and far-reaching kind. The dangers which would normally be present in such a situation, where State Institutions command universal respect and recognition, are, in our case, enhanced by the unfortunate fact that there exists here, a considerable body of opinion which either openly by implication refuses to accept and recognise these institutions, and would only be too glad of any pretext for attacking them. I need not assure your eminence of the anxiety of those who are charged with the responsibility of Government to avoid any such situation, or of our sincere desire to ensure that no occasion of disagreement may arise.

We feel confident that Your Eminence and Their Lordships the Bishops appreciate the effective limits to the powers of Government which exist in relation to certain matters if some of the fundamental principles on which our State is founded are not to be repudiated. Such repudiation direct, or indirect, by any Irish Government would, we are convinced, entail consequences very detrimental to the country's welfare.

We feel confident too that Your Eminence and Their Lordships will be completely satisfied that any representation of ours are made in a spirit of the greatest reverence and respect, and it is in this spirit that we venture to put before Your Eminence the State point of view on certain specific matters, and to express the hope that you will see your way to bring these matters before Their Lordships. I do so, not by way of suggesting any public pronouncement but in the desire that Their Lordships might be pleased to give them their earnest consideration.

Of these matters that which seems most likely, in individual cases, to lead to the dangers we are anxious to avoid relates to the appointment of Medical Officers, especially of Dispensary Doctors. The system of appointment of Medical Officers now in operation was devised to prevent grave abuses which were, unfortunately, far from uncommon in the past. It has been recently conveyed to us that if a non-Catholic Doctor or indeed a doctor not qualified in the National University, is appointed as dispensary doctor some of the bishops may feel it to be their duty to denounce the appointment. There is little doubt that a denunciation of this kind would be regarded and represented as a denunciation, by implication at least, of the Government under whose agency the appointment was made.

In connection with this matter Statutes 256 and 257 of the Maynooth Synod (1927) have been adduced in support of the contention that action of this nature is a duty incumbent on the Bishops. It is, of course not for me to express an opinion as to the interpretation of the Statutes in question. My concern is rather with the general principal raised and now brought, for the first time to our notice, as well as with the reactions which may be reasonably expected to follow on a course of action of the kind suggested. It would clearly be impossible for us, having regard to fundamental principles upon which the State is based, and which are enunciated in the Treaty, to discriminate by the way of religious test in these appointments either against non-Catholics as such or against graduates of Trinity College, or the Queen's University, Belfast. Indeed, it is open to serious doubt whether a demand for information as to the religious belief of a candidate would be sustainable.

The same principles are also operative in regard to the position of County Librarians, which has become acute in one portion of the country

There are other questions, which, fortunately, have not hitherto arisen in any acute form, but which it is, nevertheless, possible may be brought forward by persons or incidents outside Governmental control. One of these, for instance relates to Dispensations on the ground of non-consummation granted by the Church of which the Civil Authorities receive no notification, and for the judicial civil cognisance of which no machinery exists. There is also the possibility of difficulty arising out of marriages which are regarded as valid by the Civil, and not by the Ecclesiastical Law.

That these and other difficulties exist is not open to question. That in the present circumstances they are capable of a solution which could be regarded as satisfying, at once, the requirements of the Church and the State is, I fear, open to grave doubt. Any failure following an attempt to solve these problems would only add to the difficulty and once it came to public knowledge might prove a source of unrest, if not of scandal.

These considerations render us all the more fearful of the danger that incidents, which with the good will that exists, might be avoided, may be precipitated if the attention of the public is unduly focussed [sic] on these questions in an unauthorised way. It is for this reason that I venture to mention to Your Eminence the attitude of certain periodicals which, by their titles, lead the general public to believe that they are authorised exponents of Catholic doctrine. Though we are aware that these papers have no official sanction, we are also aware that many pious Catholics are misled by the titles of these publications whose comments on Government policy and on Government departments, often inaccurate and at times so intemperate as to be violently abusive, have done considerable damage not merely to the political party associated with the Government, but to the State as a whole, and have resulted in weakening the respect for authority. Other papers, whilst their comments are more temperate, purport to lay down Catholic principles and their application to various aspects of governmental activity and notwithstanding the absence of any authoritative pronouncement by the Hierarchy, criticise Government for failure to follow the interpretation of those journals in these matters. The danger and injustice of these comments and criticisms come from the fact that the general public sees only that a charge is made against the Government of acting contrary to Catholic principles. The result is a weakening of the authority of the Civil Government in a country where such a weakening is so undesirable.

I realise that it is not possible in the limits of a letter to cover all the points which arise out of the matters which I have ventured to mention — nor indeed, is it possible exactly to convey, without elaboration and explanation in personal discussion, the views which I have attempted to set forth on these difficult subjects. I should esteem it a great favour, therefore, if Your Eminence before entering upon consideration of this letter would favour me with an opportunity of an interview when you are next in Dublin and when I could explain and elaborate any points that may not be quite clear. I should like, if Your Eminence has no objection, to have the Minister for Education with me.

In conclusion, may I assure Your Eminence that in bringing these considerations to your notice I do so solemnly with the desire that Your Eminence and their Lordships may be seized of all the difficulties of the situation.

[Liam Cosgrave]

His eminence Joseph Cardinal MacRory,
Archbishop of Armagh,
Ara Coeli,
Armagh.

APPENDIX II

IRISH RELIGIOUS PERIODICALS

AFRICA
Editor: Rev Gary Howley SPS
Nine issues per year. A family mission magazine.
Published by St Patrick's Missionary Society, Kiltegan,
Co. Wicklow.
Tel : 0508 732 33 Fax : 0508 732 81.

African Missionary (SMA)
Editor: Rev. Peter McCawille SMA
Five issues per year (including calendar issue).
Published by the Society of African Missions, Blackrock Road,
Cork.
Tel : 021 292 871

Bulletin of St. Vincent De Paul
Editor : Mr Tom McSweeney
Quarterly
Published by the Society of St Vincent de Paul in Ireland,
8 New Cabra Road, Dublin 7.
Tel: 01 838 1161 / 838 1167 Fax: 838 7355.

Carmel
Editor: Rev. Philip McPartland ODC
A bi-monthly magazine on prayer and Christian living.
Published by the disabled Carmelites,
55 Marlborough Road,
Donnybrook,
Dublin 4
Tel : 01- 6601 832

The Church Directory Cork and Ross
Editor: Rev. Tom Hayes
Annual
Published by the dioceses of Cork and Ross,
Diocesan Communications, St Maries of Isle, Cork.
Tel: 021 312 330 Fax: 021 965 209

Church of Ireland Gazette
Editor : Rev Cannon C.W.M. Cooper
Published by Church of Ireland Publishing Company,
36 Bachelors Walk,
Lisburn, Co. Antrim B128 FAN
Tel: 0 181 6 676 748

Daystar
Editor: Sr Hyacintha Hudson OSF
Biannual
Published by the Franciscan Missionary Sisters for Africa,
Mount Oliver, Dundalk, Co.Louth.
Tel : 021 711 21 / 713 21 Fax : 021 711 59.

Doctrine and Life
Editor: Rev. Bernard Treacy OP
Ten issues per year.
Published by the Dominican Publications,
42 Parnell Square,
Dublin 1.
Tel: 01 872 1611 Fax: 01 873 1760.

The Far East
Editor Rev. Alo Connaughton SSC
Nine issues per year.
Published by the Missionary Society of St Columban,
St Columban's,
Navan, Co. Meath.
Tel: 01 6 872 215 25 ext. 276

The Fold
Editor: Rev. Bernard Cotter
Monthly (except for single summer issue)
Published by the dioceses of Cork and Ross,
Diocesan Communications Office, St Marie's of the Isle, Cork.
Tel: 021 312 330 Fax: 021 965 209

The Furrow
Editor: Rev. Ronan Drury
Monthly
Published by the Furrow Trust,
St Patrick's College, Maynooth, Co. Kildare.
Tel: 01 628 6215

Impact Journal
Editor: Mr Brian McCarthy
Journal on the mentally handicapped.
Published by the Brothers of Charity,
10 Victoria Terrace, Dundrum, Dublin 14
Tel: 01 298 0310 Fax: 01 298 6237

Intercom
Editor : Rev. Kevin Donlon (CSSR)
Tel and fax: 097 82270
Monthly
A pastoral magazine for priests and religious.
Published by the Catholic Communications Institute of Ireand,
7-8 Lower Abbey Street, Dublin 1.
Tel: 01 878 8177 Fax: 01 878 6507

Irish Catholic
Editor: Mr David Quinn
Weekly
Published by the Irish Catholic,
55 Lower Gardiner Street Dublin 1
Tel: 01 874 7538 / 874 2795 Fax: 01 836 1805

Irish Theological Quarterly
Editors: Rev. Patrick Hannon, Rev. Patrick McGoldrick
Published by the Faculty of Theology,
St Patrick's College, Maynooth, Co. Kildare.
Tel: 01-628 6007

Kairos
Editor: Rev. Michael Melvin SVD
Bi-monthly
Published by the Divine Word Missionaries,
Maynooth, Co. Kildare.
Tel: 01 628 6007

Maria Legionis
Quarterly
Published by the Legion of Mary,
49 North Great George's Street
Dublin 1.
Tel: 01 874 2527

Medical Missionaries of Mary
Editor: Sr Isabel Smyth (MMM)
Quarterly
Published by the Medical Missionaries of Mary,
Rosemount, Booterstown, Co. Dublin
Tel: 288 7180 Fax: 01 283 4626

Milltown Studies
Editor: Rev. Gervase Corcoran (OSA)
Published by Milltown Institute of Theology and Philosophy,
Milltown Park, Dublin 6.
Tel: 01 269 8802 / 269 8186 Fax: 269 2528

New Creation
Contact: Ms Anne Gibney
Monthly. Serves the charismatic renewal in Ireland.
Published by Charismatic
Renewal Services and the National Service Committee,
Emmanuel, 3 Pembroke Park, Dublin 4
Tel: 01 668 5551

New Liturgy
Editor: Rev. Patrick Jones
Quarterly.
Bulletin of the National Secretariat, Irish Episcopal Commission for Liturgy
Published by the Irish Institute of Pastoral Liturgy, College Street,
Carlow.
Tel: 0503 129 42 Fax: 0503 428 00

Oblate Missionary Record and Lourdes Messenger
Editor: Rev. John Archibold OMI
Five issues per year.
Published by Oblate Fathers Inchicore, Dublin 8.
Tel: 01 451 2417

Outlook (Mission Outlook)
Editor: Rev Brian Gogan CSSp
Bi-monthly
Published by Holy Ghost Missions,
169 Booterstown Avenue,
Blackrock, Co. Dublin.
Tel 01 288 1789 Fax: 01 283 4307

Pioneer
Editor: Ms Maureen Manning
Monthly
Published by Pioneer Total Abstinence Association,
27 Upper Sherrard Street, Dublin 1
Tel: 01 874 9161 Fax: 01 283 4307

Presbyterian Herald
Editor: Rev. Arthur Clarke
Monthly
Published by Presbyterian Church in Ireland,
Church House,
Fisherwick Place, Belfast B1 6DW
Tel: 1 232 322 284 Fax: 1 232 248 377

Proceedings of Irish Biblical Association
Editor: Rev. Wilfrid Harrington OP
St Mary's Tallaght, Dublin 24
Tel: 01 151 5244

Reality
Editor : Rev Gerard Maloney CSSR
Monthly
Published by Redemporist Publications,
75 Orwell Road,
Rathgar, Dublin 6
Tel: 01 492 2688 / 492 2488 Fax: 01 492 2654

Recover
Editor: Rev. Greg Price OSCam
Quarterly
Published by the Cammillion Fathers and Brothers,
Killucan, Co. Westmeath
Tel: 044 741 15

Religious Life Review
Editor: Rev. Austin Flannery OP
Bi-monthly
Published by the Dominican Publications,
42 Parnell Square, Dublin 1
Tel: 01 873 1855 Fax : 873 1760

Sacred Heart Messenger
Editor: Rev. Brendan Murray SJ
Monthly
Official publication of the Apostleship of Prayer,
37 Lower Leeson Street, Dublin 2
Tel : 01 676 7491

An Sagart
Eagarthóir: an Canonach Pádraig Ó Fiannachta
Folisitear ceithre uair sa bhliainn
Cumann na sagart,
An Daingean, Co. Chiarraí
Tel: 066 511 04

The Salesian Bulletin
Editor: Rev. Eddie Fitzgerald SDB
Quarterly
Published for the Salesians of Don Bosco by
SDB MEDIA,
St Teresa's Road, Dublin 12.
Tel: 01 455 5605 Fax: 01 455 8781

Scripture In Church
Editor in Chief: Rev. Martin McNamara (MSC)
Quarterly
Published by Dominican Publications,
42 Parnell Square, Dublin 1
Tel: 01 677 7651 Fax: 01 873 1760

The St.Anthony Brief
Editor: Rev. John Hanley OFM
Bi-monthly
Published by the Franciscan Missionary Unit,
Merchant's Quay
Dublin 8
Tel: 677 7651 Fax: 01 677 7293

St Joseph's Advocate
Editor: Rev. Larry English MHM
Quarterly
Published by Mill Hill Missionaries,
St. Joseph's,
Waterford Road, Kilkenny
Tel: 056 2482 Fax: 056 51490

St. Martin Magazine
Editor: Rev Francis Macnamara OP
Monthly
Published by St. Martin De Porres Apostolate,
42 Parnell Square, Dublin 1
Tel: 01 873 0147 Fax: 01 - 873 1989

Timire an Chroí Naofa
Eagarthóir: An tAt Diarmaid Ó Laoghaire SJ
Pairc Bhaile an Mhuilinn, Baile Atha Claith 6
Tel: 01 269 8411

Studies
Editor: Rev. Noel Barber SJ
Published by the Irish Jesuits,
35 Lower Leeson Street, Dublin 2
Tel: 01 676 6785 Fax: 01 676 2981

The Word
Editor: Rev. Thomas Cahill SVD
Monthly
Published by the Divine Word Missionaries,
Maynooth, Co. Kildare
Tel: 01 628 5961 Fax: 628 9184

RELIGIOUS MINORITIES
IN THE IRISH FREE STATE
AND THE
REPUBLIC OF IRELAND
1922 – 1995

TERENCE BROWN

TRINITY COLLEGE, DUBLIN

PREFACE

THIS SURVEY CONSIDERS THE TWO MAIN RELIGIOUS MINORITIES in
the State — the Protestant and the Jewish — and assesses their
experience since independence. It makes no pretence to in-depth
research or to scientific inclusiveness. Rather it is an attempt to employ
existing literature to supply a sense of what it has been like to be a
member of these minorities in the period and to consider how that
experience has been shaped by the political and social context of
independent Ireland. The problems confronting the two minorities are
raised and some tentative speculations are entertained.

Throughout, it should be noted, the term Protestant is used to refer
to those members of the Church of Ireland who profess the Anglican
faith, for, as the very considerable majority of the Protestant minority,
their experience has been the most studied and reflected upon.
Furthermore, since the Protestant population is such a small proportion
of the total, Church of Ireland experience has tended to be normative
for the whole minority. Presbyterians and Methodists accordingly do
not feel as distinct from their Anglican fellow-citizens as they do from
their Catholic fellow-citizens (inter-Protestant-Church marriage is
scarcely considered a 'mixed marriage', for example, and Presbyterians
and Methodists often send their children to Church of Ireland schools
where schools under the management of their own clergy or within
their tradition do not exist). Valuable research could be done, however,

on how both Presbyterianism and Methodism with their strong connections to Northern Ireland, where members of their Churches are very much more numerous, have understood their position as distinct Protestant Churches since independence. In this regional factors would certainly be significant since, for example, Presbyterianism in the border counties of Ulster has strong ties of kin and custom with Northern Ireland (Presbyterian ministers are usually 'called' from Northern Ireland and they often serve for a time in the South before returning to the Presbyterian heartland in Counties Antrim and Down). It should also be noted in this regard that the training of Presbyterian ministers has, since the foundation of the New University of Ulster (now the University of Ulster) which ended a link between Magee University College, Derry and Trinity College, Dublin, been almost entirely conducted north of the border.

Members of other Churches and religious groups have made striking contributions to Irish life in the period — members of the religious Society of Friends, for example, of the Baptist Church or of the Brethren who have sustained the tradition of evangelicalism which was from the early nineteenth century to the early years of Irish independence so marked a feature of Protestantism in the South of Ireland, as it is now in the North. Some of these groups have experienced in an extreme form the problems that have confronted Protestantism as a whole in the State. These, as we shall see, are largely due to demographic changes and to the disappearance of a large working class Protestant population in Dublin. Indeed, the fact that Merrion Hall in central Dublin (Bloom in *Ulysses* observes it in 1904 when it was in its hey-day) which at the end of the nineteenth century drew hundreds of worshippers to evangelical services conducted by members of the Plymouth Brethen (a religious movement founded in the nineteenth century in County Wicklow by an Irishman) has recently been refurbished as a hotel, might serve as one kind of depressing symbol for Irish Protestantism in the period. As we shall see the picture is by no means so comprehensively bleak.

INTRODUCTION

CONTROVERSIES ABOUT MAJORITY AND MINORITY rights in Ireland are not of recent vintage in this century. Indeed questions about rights and opportunities for the religious majority as against those of religious minorities were addressed vigorously in the public domain before and during the Home Rule Crisis of 1912–13. For example in 1913 Edward Haviland Burke asserted, as reported in the *Leinster Leader*:

> The record of the Catholic County Councils—the National County Councils—throughout the Catholic provinces and districts of Ireland was an honour and glory to them. They did not boycott and exclude non-Catholics from employment by the County Councils and he remembered well staggering an English meeting where a Tory got up to heckle him and cross-examine him on this question when he told him that he Mr Burke in common with his friend and colleague, Mr Reddy, represented the King's County in which 7/9 of the people were Catholic and in which 40% of the employees of the County Council were non-Catholic.[1]

Not all non-Catholics in 1913 could have afforded to feel as sanguine as did Mr Burke about their situation, for without doubt there were significant voices raised in pre-independence Ireland to press the issue of long established injustices which must be put right as soon as possible. Writing in the *Irish Rosary* in 1903 about the recently formed Catholic Association the Reverend Jeremiah O'Donovan (later to win a modest

fame as the author of a fictional study of priestly life, *Father Ralph*) stated
a case against Irish Protestantism with exacting, unapologetic directness:

> A century ago Protestantism ruled this land. A minority held a majority
> in thrall. Catholicity was the under dog. Catholics lived under sufferance.
> They held no offices of trust or emolument, they exercised no power.
> Education was denied them. They bore the burden and heat of the day
> for their Protestant masters, and were expected to thank God daily for
> being allowed to live as slaves. Protestants looked upon themselves as a
> chosen people with God-given rights. The law of life in Ireland was
> Protestant to rule, Catholic to obey; Catholic to till the land by the sweat
> of his brow, that his Protestant master might live in ease and luxury.[2]

O'Donovan does it is true admit 'the laws which produced this
condition of things have almost disappeared from the Statute Book'
though 'not a few still remain to give sanction to inequalities to which
Catholics are subjected'. What he finds more insidious however, even
than these vestiges of statutory discrimination is the instinctive bigotry
which such a past has bequeathed to many Irish Protestants:

> It is not the legal disabilities which Catholics suffer most under, or feel
> most keenly. A prejudice against Catholics has impressed itself on the
> minds of many Protestants. It is the growth and heritage of centuries. To
> the average Protestant a Catholic is never equal.[3]

The consequences of this are clear to the writer. In Ireland:

> ...the great majority of high office holders are Protestants.
> Their patronage is extended mainly to Protestants. The larger businesses,
> the railways, the banks, the steamship companies are as a rule directed
> and manned by Protestants. Here and there a Catholic enjoys office, but
> it is always because of some very special reason. [4]

Determined that this situation should be remedied O'Donovan
nevertheless sought to assure Protestants that they had no reason to 'fear
unjust treatment at the hands of the Catholic majority' [5] and of public
appointments he unequivocally stated:

> Equal justice all round should be the principle upon which all public
> boards should act. The fittest man should always get the job...I should be
> sorry to think that the labours of a great lay Catholic organization would
> be confined to mere office-seeking for Catholics. [6]

Protestants who may have been made aware of Father O'Donovan's views could perhaps have been reassured by such unexceptionable sentiments. Though they may have wondered whether an analysis of their social role in Ireland past and present so stark as the one supplied by O'Donovan, if widely shared by his co-religionists, would always result in such essentially liberal intentions. Be that as it may the Catholic Association did not manage to gain a secure hold on the nationalist community as a spokesperson of its interests. In consequence the movement to reverse what Protestant hegemony had effected in Ireland was carried forward by other, less conscientious agencies than the Association as envisaged by Father O'Donovan. The Ancient Order of Hibernians (AOH) in the period just before the Home Rule Crisis significantly increased its membership and as Paul Bew has argued 'Where AOH influence was strong, the implications for employment practices tended to be substantial. In Monaghan for example, all thirty-seven jobs in the gift of the council went to nationalists; this, in a county with a substantial unionist majority.'[7] And he further notes that by 1912, despite John Redmond's assurance that the democratization of Irish local government would pose no threat to Protestants:

> In fact by 1912 only fifteen out of 703 Irish county councillors outside
> Ulster were unionist. More to the point was the record of these councils
> in salaried appointments: Fourteen of them had not made one single
> Protestant appointment, it was claimed, while five others had made only
> one each.[8]

THE NEW STATE

After partition and the founding of the Irish Free State there were those ready to see the new political order as one in which Catholics would specifically thrive. The Catholic Truth Society in 1927, for example was unabashed in its celebration of Catholic opportunity and in its impatience with continued Protestant power and social prestige:

> Once again in the 26 Counties the Catholic is substantially in control
> of the government. The Civil Service and the judiciary, the Army and
> the Police force are at his disposal. The opportunity of education is

again within his reach. The learned professions boast of many
distinguished Catholic members. And yet in two important aspects
the Catholic still suffers as a result of the penal laws—in the industrial
and commercial life, from the handicap of poverty under which he
started a century ago; the Protestant continues to maintain an ascendancy
in social life. The cultivated pose of superiority of the Protestant
oppresses us. Until these blemishes are removed from Irish life the
work of emancipation, gloriously initiated a hundred years ago, will
not be completed. [9]

And it is undoubtedly true that Protestants in the new State felt
themselves under pressure as the national minority which they felt
themselves to be and as they were viewed by the majority (if not always
in the aggressively confessional terms of the Catholic Truth Society
pamphlet). Writing in 1944 W. B. Stanford (Professor of Greek in
Trinity College, Dublin and subsequently Senator and Chancellor of
his university) was explicit enough about what he felt were the
difficulties experienced by his co-religionists in the Church of Ireland.
In his pamphlet *A Recognised Church: The Church of Ireland in Éire* (his
title refers to the 1937 Constitution which 'recognises' the Church of
Ireland) he acknowledges his Church's difficult role ('a Church of the
governing class had become the Church of a politically discredited
minority'[10]) but is anxious that its members should now play their part
in a new Ireland. As members of a minority, however, they have
problems:

> The pressures against the Church of Ireland began soon after the treaty—
> despite, I repeat, efforts by governments and fair-minded citizens to
> prevent it. It took, it takes, two forms: politico-economic and religious.
> The first works by excluding Irish Churchmen from public and private
> appointments (this is more evident in the provinces than under the
> government's eye in Dublin; by obstructing purchase of sites, houses,
> land, shops; by preventing Protestants from sharing in the control of
> public works and charitable organisations; by emphasising their social
> fewness and loneliness; by arguing that to be a true Irishman one must be
> a Roman Catholic; by banning all literature which criticises the Roman
> Catholic Church and encouraging that which criticises any form of
> Protestantism (this is more easily achieved by local libraries and
> booksellers than by the Censorship Board). These, and a host of
> other matters ranging from impositions to inconveniences, are steadily

pressing on those who do not belong to the Church of the majority in Ireland. [11]

In a further pamphlet published in 1946, *Faith and Faction in Ireland* Stanford identified 'jobbery' as one of the peculiarly baneful pressures with which the members of his Church had to contend in the new Ireland. He acknowledges 'the present government of Éire has done all in its power to prevent...discrimination in matters under their control. But the same cannot be said for some of the local government bodies and semi-public firms.' [12] Stanford knows that Irish discrimination is a limited affair compared with 'the excesses of discrimination that have been shown in other countries of Europe' but reckons that 'there is enough to harm public confidence and public efficiency, and enough to give the Northern Unionists some grounds to repeat their cry that *Home Rule Means Rome Rule.*'[13]

It should not surprise that it was jobs and 'jobbery' that focused attention on relationships between the religious majority and the minority. The tradition of the 'Protestant firm' was long-established, particularly in Dublin, and it was scarcely surprising that such exclusivism was emulated by Catholic employers. What of course gave the matter its sharp edges was the depressed state of the Irish economy in the thirties, forties and fifties, when as the emigration figures demonstrate, jobs in Ireland were unavailable for many thousands of Irish men and women. In fact the marked decline in the Protestant population in the period meant that young members of that community did not face the kind of intense competition their Catholic peers did, as they moved fairly readily into posts in family firms and businesses that had close links with Protestant schools. This gave to middle class Protestant life in the first decades of Irish independence a kind of stability and sense of continuity which allowed for eventual acceptance of the new political and social order.

NUMERICAL DECLINE
AND ITS EFFECTS

If such comfortable social structures made middle class Protestant life a comparatively secure experience in this period, it was made so in part because the Protestant community was in marked numerical decline. The community as a whole accordingly required steadily fewer opportunities and resources and was not in the kind of invidious position it would have been if it had been increasing numerically in a context of limited social and economic opportunities generally. Its position was paradoxically made easier by virtue of the demographic decline it suffered, especially when one analyses the nature of that decline.

The figures are simple and stark enough. Between 1911 and 1926 (the inter-censal period) in the Protestant community the number of Irish Anglicans declined by 34 per cent. Deaths in the Great War certainly played their part in this but the founding of the Irish State and the withdrawal of the Imperial power were principal agents of this change. It has been estimated that the departure of the British army accounted for a quarter of the decline in Irish Anglicans between 1911 and 1926. And 65 per cent of the minority in the police forces left the country.[15]

This Protestant diaspora significantly affected the social composition of Southern Irish Protestantism. As Martin Maguire has shown: 'In spite of the imagery of hunting and shooting and "big house" gentility, Protestants in Ireland have been primarily an urban rather than a rural population and have embodied a full spectrum of urban social classes, including the working class.'[16] Before independence indeed Dublin had a considerable Protestant working class composed of about 10,000 men and their dependents. Maguire concludes of this defining period for Irish Protestantism, while admitting that acts of terrorism did play a part in the Protestant haemorrhage:

> Not only had the numbers of Protestants changed but the nature of
> Protestant society in independent Ireland had also changed. A lot has
> been said about the impact of partition on Catholic Ireland, not enough
> has been said about the impact on Protestant Ireland. The changes from
> being a 25 per cent minority to being either a 66 per cent majority or a
> 5 per cent minority demanded profound adjustments. The decline in the
> Protestant population in the twenty-six counties was predominately a
> decline in its urban population. A population that was an urban
> population in the main in 1911 was by 1961 about evenly balanced
> between urban and rural.What appears to be a loss of Protestants in
> general was in fact a loss of mostly urban working-class Protestants. The
> Protestant population has been eroded by socio-economic trends

(especially exogenous marriage) which have had the greatest effect on the
urban working-class, leaving Protestantism in independent Ireland a
predominately middle-class phenomenon. This is especially true of
Dublin. If we need a catastrophic event to explain this decline in
population it lies in the impact of the 1914–1918 war. As rural Ireland
prospered, Dublin became an industrial graveyard as war-time controls
strangled non-essential industries.[17]

There were socio-cultural consequences of this change for Irish
Protestantism as a whole. The Protestantism of the Dublin working class
before independence had been to a large extent of the robust, often
evangelical variety. Anti-Catholicism and a tradition of Orangeism (the
headquarters of the Orange Order were in Dublin) made it a cousin of
the kind of vigorous evangelical Protestantism now associated with the
North of the country. The disappearance of this class has accordingly
made Southern and Northern Protestantism seem distinct phenomena,
with aggressive, anti-Catholic fundamentalist expressions of faith
reserved to the Northern part of the country. Protestants in Ireland have
therefore grown apart since partition and independence with Northern
Protestants viewing their Southern co-religionists as constitutionally
genteel and cautious while Southern Protestants deprecate the
'sectarianism' of the Northerners, forgetting how much loyalism and
evangelicalism characterized some of the Dublin Protestant working
class before partition.[18] The loss of this sector of the population in the
country's capital also made it difficult for Protestantism in the new State
to establish for itself a sense of geographic location as a functioning
community[19] (the ecclesiastical capital for Irish Anglicans was across the
new border in Armagh) while inner city Protestantism in Dublin, with
its two national Anglican cathedrals and well-known parish churches
(most famously St George's in Hardwicke Place whose bell tolling the
hours Leopold Bloom hears in *Ulysses*), went into almost terminal
decline. As the sociologist of Southern Irish Protestantism, Kurt Bowen,
has put it:

> In general it would be fair to say that the small and scattered Church of
> Ireland community rarely possessed the unconscious insularity of
> residential and geographic segregation which was so characteristic of the
> North. This, in turn, implies that Irish Anglicans have long been forced
> to rely upon essentially social means of maintaining their separateness. [20]

DEMOGRAPHIC CHANGE
CAUSES AND EFFECTS

The history of Protestantism in independent Ireland from 1922 to the late 1960s is a history of decline and isolation. Demographers and social scientists are agreed that the decline was in no way the result of a deliberate policy of a State intent on achieving religious homogeneity. In broad terms as Brendan Walsh demonstrated in 1970 the decline in the numbers of non-Catholics in the jurisdiction of the Irish State between 1946 and 1961 (the main period of his analysis) was the result of a natural decrease which reflected a:

> ... low marriage rate, moderately low marriage fertility, an abnormally old population age structure (the consequence of a falling population in previous decades), and the impact of mixed marriages in which all the offspring are raised as Catholics (the Catholic Church's Ne Temere Decree particularly affected this).[21]

A draft paper issued by the Central Statistics office in 1992 makes a similar case about the lengthier period 1911–1981 when it concludes 'the Protestant denominations, in particular the Church of Ireland and Methodist, have experienced a natural decline in population over the whole period.' It observes that 'significantly higher rates of emigration [higher than those prevailing in the majority community]' played a part but notes 'with the exception of the Presbyterians, the migration rates have moved closer to one another in recent decades.'[22]

Accordingly the Protestant minority as a scattered and largely middle class and farming (Walsh notes 'the almost complete absence of an OD [Other Denomination] "working class" '[23] in the Republic of Ireland) population in the first four decades of independence sought to maintain itself, in the absence of a geographic, regional locus of social existence through a series of distinct social institutions. Among these most obviously were the Churches themselves which were required to offer through their bishops, priests and ministers the kind of leadership in the community that had hitherto been provided by the landed gentry and substantial businessmen. The disintegration of Anglo-Ireland as a distinct political caste (pro-Union and property, led by an aristocratic gentry)[24] placed therefore a peculiar onus on the clergy in a community which had only limited political representation and saw itself as in

danger of extinction as emigration, old age and mixed marriages all
made inroads on numbers. Church life, Church schooling, both at
primary and secondary level, an ancient university with a Protestant
tradition which was forbidden to Catholics by hierarchical edict,
Protestant hospitals, a plethora of religious and semi-religious youth
organizations, (Scouts, the Boys Brigade, the Young Men's Christian
Association), a round of dances, dinners, tennis and golf clubs, rugby
teams, the Masonic Lodges, all operated to allow Irish Protestants to
maintain their social distinctiveness. A kind of unofficial, almost
unspoken apartheid existed in Irish life, which made Protestantism a
primary mark of social and cultural identification for Protestants and
Catholics alike.[25] In the years between 1922 and the late sixties most
Protestants would have understood instinctively that 'we' were not
'them'. Indeed as Jack White reflects in his book *Minority Report: the
Protestant Community in the Republic of Ireland*: 'the system of dual
institutions — school, university, hospital — enabled some Protestants
to live in a kind of mental reservation, secure from any real contact with
Catholics.' [26]

CAUSES OF ALIENATION
AND ITS DIMINUTION

Although the State was scrupulous in its dealings with the minority (as
many have attested) [27] and went to considerable lengths to ensure that
non-Catholic institutions would be viable (in a social order where the
Churches still played the major role in the provision of education and
social services) and although the property rights in a conservative
property-owning democracy were never put in question, there were
things in the new order other than the natural decline in their numbers
and the serious difficulty of the Ne Temere Decree,[28] that certainly
increased the minority's sense of isolation and marginality. Among these
were the State's policy of language revival and a general tendency to
equate Irish identity with the majority religious expression. It is I
believe without question that many in the Protestant minority felt that
the language revival policy as it was developed by the Department of
Education was an assault upon their English language cultural identity.
Indeed the policy was one of the few things about which Church

representatives as leaders of their community made strenuous objection in the early years of independence. In 1928 the opportunity arose to debate the issue of compulsory Irish when a private member's Bill was introduced in Parliament to make Irish compulsory in the legal profession. Kurt Bowen concludes of the debate:

> ... appeals on the basis of tolerance, the pragmatic value of cultural uniformity with Britain, and the possibility of discrimination against the already privileged fell on deaf ears. The response of T. Mullins, a Fianna Fáil TD, well expressed the majority sentiment: 'The garrison must give place to the nation.' [29]

In the early decades of independence most members of the minority saw the State's language policy as an unwelcome imposition on them. They felt their culture and social reality were mediated most intimately in the English language and, with notable individual exceptions, they had few nationalist imperatives to make them enthusiasts for the revival of Irish. Furthermore, the more personally religious they were the more likely they were to have difficulty with the ideals of the language revivalists that Ireland become universally Irish-speaking. For much that characterized the culture of Protestantism in Ireland was bound up with the English language. The Church of Ireland rejoiced in the Anglican Prayer Book, the Presbyterian Church in the Metrical Psalms in English, the Methodist Church in the hymns of Charles Wesley. They shared too in liturgy, worship and private devotion, a profound involvement with the the prose of the Authorized Version of the Bible and an emotional attachment to the inheritance of English language hymnology.

Now it is certainly possible to envisage how over time the religious life of the minority could have come to be expressed in a language other than English, but to the devout Protestant the State's avowed policy in the early years of independence could well have been felt as an assault on his or her religious identity in its cultural expression

As it became clear that the revival policy could not succeed in the absolute terms in which it was first attempted and as it became evident that the best that could be hoped for by the supporters of that policy was the creation of a bilingual society, the minority and its spokespersons became much less antagonistic to the State's insistence that Irish be an integral part of the educational system. The adjustment of the Protestant community to the new linguistic context was aided also by the firm commitment to cooperation given by Dr John A. F. Gregg, Archbishop of Dublin and by the fact that the Department of Education, appreciative of that commitment, was cognizant of the difficulties faced by the Church of Ireland Training College in Dublin in its training of teachers for Church of Ireland National Schools. A preparatory college, Coláiste Moibhí, was established in 1926, which was 'served by a group of talented and dedicated teachers and soon became renowned for the high standard of its achievement'. And, as the historian of the Church of Ireland Training College concludes 'Coláiste Moibhí came to be seen as a successful pioneer venture, making a marked contribution to the life of the Church of Ireland.'[31] The same historian cites a 1938 editorial in *The Irish Times* which had earlier opposed the State's language policy and had attacked the Church of Ireland for its acquiescence to it. The editorial recognizes that the pupils in this Irish-speaking school are ' "Reconcilers of the Past and Present" and as such are called to play an unusual part...a part of heroic responsibility and inspired courage. They defend and uphold the faith of their forefathers in a new spirit.'[32]

If Irish Protestants had difficulties with the concept of a Gaelic identity which was to find expression in the new State's linguistic policy in the schools they were not insurmountable, as the history of the Church of Ireland Training College shows. Rather more troublesome for the minority in the first three or four decades of independence was the close identification of Irish identity with the religion of the majority in the twenty six county State. However scrupulous the State might be in recognizing and vindicating the rights of all in law there was no great sensitivity to the fact that the new State was multi-religious in social complexion. This became marked after the accession to power of Mr de Valera who made it his business as the leader of a party which had its origins in a movement which had suffered hierarchical disfavour in the 1920s to act with what seemed to many like deference to Roman authority. Indeed as historian and political scientist John Whyte records: 'some of the published statements of Mr de Valera and his colleagues imply, that to them, the only true Irishmen were Catholics.' Whyte writes as follows:

In his St Patrick's day broadcast to the United States in 1935, Mr de Valera said: 'Since the coming of St Patrick, fifteen hundred years ago,

Ireland has been a Christian and a Catholic nation. All the ruthless attempts made down through the centuries to force her from this allegiance have not shaken her faith. She remains a Catholic nation.' The same attitude can be detected, perhaps, in the preamble to the 1937 constitution: 'We, the people of Eire, humbly acknowledging all our obligations to our Divine Lord, Jesus Christ, who sustained our fathers through centuries of trial....' These are moving words, but one might ask: *whose* fathers were sustained through centuries of trial? The words fit the situation of Irish Catholics, whose ancestors endured the penal laws, but they might not be felt as appropriate by Irish Protestants.[33]

Nor indeed, one might add, by Irish Jews. It should also perhaps be noted that the Constitution affirms a Trinitarian theology in its preamble.

The identification of Irish identity with Catholicism was rendered more precise in this period since Roman Catholic Church discipline forbade the attendance of the faithful at Protestant religious services. This meant that the State was represented by senior Government ministers at all kinds of Catholic occasions but rarely at those of the Protestant minority. The absurdity of this situation was demonstrated in 1949 when at the funeral of Douglas Hyde, first President of Ireland, in St Patrick's, the only Catholics to kneel at the obsequies were the poet Austin Clarke and the French ambassador ('Outside./The hush of Dublin town, /Professors of cap and gown, /Costello, his Cabinet, /In Government cars....').

It was not only the identification of Irishness with Catholicism and the consequences of the Roman discipline of the faithful which gave Protestants a feeling of being marginalized in the new State however fully their rights to residence, property and practice of religion were honoured and protected. The new State quickly ensured that such things as divorce, contraception and literary works which dealt in anything other than the most regular of sexual lives would be proscribed in Ireland. Many Protestants of course would have shared their Catholic fellow citizens' abhorrence of most of these things but some of them would have preferred that they be left to the individual's conscience rather than being entered definitively on the statute book and in the case of divorce, in the 1937 Constitution. Their experience in relation to more broadly based political issues, however, would not have given them much hope that their distinctive attitudes to issues of the above kind would have been likely to meet with anything but disregard.

The Protestant minority in the settlement of 1922 had reason to feel that some of what it esteemed in the Union of Britain and Ireland remained secure or had been fairly satisfactorily reformulated. Its political experience over the next twenty six years was one of systematic attrition of its political desiderata. In general terms anything in which they put their political faith was to disappear over two and a half decades: the Oath of Allegiance to the Crown, the right of appeal by Irish men and women to the Privy Council, representation as of right in the Upper House of the Irish Parliament, which had been guaranteed in the settlement of 1922, Irish membership of the British Common-wealth of nations. Indeed it must have seemed an ironical blow that it was a Fine Gael Taoiseach, whose party as Cumann na nGaedheal had distinguished itself in the politics of the 1920s as 'the Commonwealth Party', should have set in motion the steps which took the twenty six county State out of the Commonwealth to declare a republic in 1949. As Kurt Bowen succinctly states it:

> ...by the end of the Coalition's short reign, there was little left in Irish politics to interest Protestants. Their divergent religious interests were clearly of no account to either party, and there were now no public issues or symbols around which they could focus their fading British allegiance.[34]

The 1950s accordingly saw the final stage of a process whereby a stance of 'indignant marginality' at the foundation of the State had 'rapidly evolved into one of indifference, estrangement and apathy'[35] and then became the entrenched political disengagement of Protestants as Protestants, even if a few of their number joined in the political life of the country as individuals. Accordingly, while individual Protestants play a part in public life today in various political parties they do so, not as Protestants, but as party members under party discipline even in areas such as Donegal, Monaghan, Cavan and parts of Wicklow where the Protestant population probably does favour a co-religionist in a general election. Even in these areas they do not seek to advance specifically Protestant concerns.

ASSIMILATION OR INTEGRATION?

Kurt Bowen in his study *Protestants in a Catholic State* judges that the main minority in the independent Irish State entered on a new phase of its life after 1945 so that by the end of the 1970s as many as 40 per cent of those entering marriage may have been doing so with a Catholic partner. He writes as follows:

> This dominant and growing trend might be described as either assimilation or integration. If assimilation is the more appropriate description, it suggests that Protestants will eventually disappear by being absorbed into the larger Catholic community. Integration, on the other hand, implies that Protestants will survive as their differences with Catholics decline in social importance and become matters of personal and private choice. Since the old differences have only recently started to crumble, it is still far from certain whether assimilation or integration best describes the Protestant experience after 1922. [36]

Much of Bowen's book is an analysis of the social and economic forces with their concomitant cultural changes which have been responsible for breaking down the differences between Protestant and Catholics in the Irish State since about the mid 1960s. A key area is that of employment (so fraught an issue earlier in the century as we have seen) where the old segregation of the minority in Protestant firms had by the 1980s given way to much a more meritocratic general ethos. There were several reasons for this. At the most basic level there were simply too few Protestant workers coming into the labour force. Furthermore, employing some Catholics was reckoned to be good for business. More decisively, amalgamations of companies were sometimes with companies owned and staffed by Catholics so that continued segregation became impossible to justify or effect. In such reorganizations indeed Protestants sometimes lost managerial control of recruitment. Overall Bowen sees this change as 'a product of the rapidly industrialising economy of the 1960s and 1970s.' [37] Bowen offers the following assessment of the economic processes of the sixties and seventies and of their direct effects on the Protestant minority. Concluding that 'the economy was transformed by rapid growth' in the period and that with this change there occurred a huge increase in the size of the upper middle classes in which, with a dwindling population, Protestants 'were barely able to hold their own', he writes:

> In the process, Protestant influence at the higher levels of the economy was reduced; the visibility and hence the social significance of their remaining influence was further obscured by the demise of the segregated

Protestant firm; and their competitive edge over Catholics of similar
class backgrounds was weakened by the decline of preferential
employment practices among Protestant employers. Faced with an
increasingly powerful, established, and well-educated Catholic
community, the minority's sense of superiority and social exclusivity
inevitably declined; and Catholics had less and less reason to feel either
resentful or subservient. Many older Protestants regretted the passing of
the old days, but neither they nor the younger generation appeared to
feel embittered or personally threatened by the transformation. In fact
there was little reason for such feelings since economic growth enabled
the rising Catholic majority to engulf—rather than to displace—the
minority. [38]

One effect of this process seems to have been that such anti-Protestant
feeling as may have existed among the Catholic majority, which had in
the past had a focus for grievance in the issue of employment, was
apparently reduced to a trivial level. Evidence of this was supplied in
1977 when Micheál Mac Gréil, reported on his research findings on
prejudice and tolerance in Ireland which showed that in Dublin 73.4
per cent of the sample group surveyed were ready to admit a Protestant
to the family by marriage.[39]

Bowen reckons that three less direct effects of the social changes
of recent decades can be identified. First, in the context of the
ecumenism of the post Vatican II era and in a society displaying signs of
secularization, Protestants have been less inclined to emphasize their
adversarial stance in relation to Catholic claims and have sought to
establish relations marked by courteous and fruitful coexistence. The
Northern conflict was certainly a factor in this development. Protestants
in this State would have found it difficult to express open sympathy for
their Northern co-religionists without risking their hard-won
acceptance as members of the Irish national community. But they were
in truth often appalled at and embarrassed by the intensity of anti-
Catholic feeling expressed by some Northern Protestants and wished to
disassociate themselves from it and to do so by exploring their
relationship with their Catholic fellow-citizens. This shift in attitude
towards Catholicism was aided not only by the eirenic spirit encouraged
by Vatican II's Decree on Religious Freedom but by the development
of secularism in Ireland. By this term is meant not a decline in religious
practice, which has only occurred to a limited degree, but a process

whereby religion is increasingly regarded by many as a matter of private conviction, personal preference and choice, where individual con-science is guide. Religion operates accordingly more in the private sphere than in the public. This has meant that Protestants have found themselves in recent years sharing publicly expressed, politically-sponsored attitudes with Catholics on such issues as contraception and divorce which hitherto would have been almost uniquely Protestant. This has allowed them to feel more relaxed about their role in Irish society than in the past when their views on such things, which they did not press with great vigour, were simply ignored by the State. There are of course dangers for the Protestant minority in this situation when their demographic weakness is factored into the equation. Bowen astutely suggests that the possibility of integration rather than assimilation for the Protestant minority depends significantly, given its numerical fragility, on the continued existence of a degree of secularization among Catholics. He writes:

> As a useful though somewhat crude general rule, integration might now be said to depend on the growth of secularization among *both* Protestants and Catholics. Assimilation. on the other hand, would seem to be the likely result if secularization was primarily confined to one of the two parties—and to the minority in particular.[40]

Of this it can be said that there is every sign that the process of secularization which Bowen reported on in 1983 has continued into the mid-nineties, with the concomitant possibility that the integration of the Protestant minority into Irish life is on the way to becoming an achieved fact.

Secondly, Bowen sees that changed attitudes in both the Protestant and Catholic communities about schooling and education have broken down the barriers of the past and allow Protestants and their educational institutions a crucial role in influential sectors of society. As Protestant schools and colleges have adopted less doctrinal programmes of instruction and emphasized an ecumenical understanding of a shared faith, Catholic parents have sought to enrol their offspring in what effectively become religiously mixed schools. Put bluntly, a significant number of Catholics want Protestant institutions to continue to exist as alternatives to Catholic schools and are prepared to disregard their Church's view on the matter of enrolling their children in such schools.

By the late 1970s, as Bowen reports it, approximately 20 per cent were Catholics in Protestant schools. He reflects:

> Without discounting the class-based attraction of Protestant schools, which has always existed, I would argue that the recent growth in the number of Catholic applicants reflected their desire for a more secular education than that available in their own schools. With their diminished emphasis on denominational instruction and their religious mixture among teachers and pupils, Protestant secondary schools went a long way to meet this demand. In turn the schools reflected and fostered an integrationist and secular outlook within their community. However, it was integration — and not assimilation — which Protestants sought, and hence most schools continued to give priority to Protestants by putting a quota on the admission of Catholic applicants.[41]

This process has continued into the current decade and is perhaps the aspect of current social practice which gives most valency to the integrationist model of relations between the Catholic majority and the Protestant minority. The continued success of the Protestant comprehensive schools in Dublin, Newpark and Mount Temple, which function in this fashion are evidence to support the view that what Bowen observed at a relatively early stage has become an accepted practice.

Thirdly, Bowen noted in the 1970s how the social isolation of the Protestant minority was giving way, both in urban and rural settings, to cooperative activity in a wide variety of civil institutions which had once been 'almost exclusively Catholic in make-up'. Once again the impulse was integrationist:

> In short, in both rural as well as urban areas, there seemed to be emerging among both Catholics and Protestants a new secular conviction that religious affiliation should not be a consideration in recreational and special interest activities not directly connected to their parish churches. At the same time, Protestants continued to mix primarily with one another in more intimate areas of close friendship, visiting, dinner parties and the like. Taken together, this combination of greater public intermingling and persisting segregation in the more private areas of social life again suggests the growth of integration rather than assimilation. [42]

What made Bowen hopeful in 1983 that Protestantism in the Republic of Ireland would be defined in the future by integration rather than assimilation was the fact that the minority's small size paradoxically was now its best defence. For it only required a small proportion of the large Catholic majority to adopt and sustain the kind of secular understanding of religious profession identified above, for the social conditions to exist whereby cooperative relations between distinct religious communities could develop in Church, educational and civic life. Twelve years after the publication of Bowen's book all the signs are that his analysis is a sound one. Indeed the fact that relations of the kind he identified at an early stage in the 1970s and early eighties are now the norm in a society marked by an increasingly secular spirit might suggest that the concept of integration is now, more than a model of possibility, a description of established social practice. However, the evidence for such an assertion is anecdotal and impressionistic since no up-to-date research of the kind Bowen's book records and analyses has been done.

THE LITERARY RECORD

Insight into the experience of the Protestant minority in independent Ireland is not only to be derived from historical treaties and sociological surveys. Memoirs, autobiographies, works of literature supply a means of access to the felt life of a community which has undergone profound change since 1922. Most instructive about the segregated world of post-independence Protestantism in the early years of independence is Brian Inglis's amused account (*West Briton*, 1962) of a comfortably vestigial bourgeois world in North County Dublin where an exclusive golf club and habits of assumed social superiority kept a way of life intact, as we have seen above, until quite recent times. Significantly, this is one of the few works of record, recollection or literature which deals in the ways of life of the Protestant middle class, which as we have also seen was the predominant social category in Protestantism in the period in the twenty six counties. In fact, Protestantism in twentieth century Irish writing from the South of Ireland makes itself present most obviously in what is termed 'Big House' fiction (the work of Elizabeth Bowen is a distinguished instance). The sources of this image are to be found in nineteenth century Ireland but it was given compelling contemporary life by the poetry of W. B. Yeats who in the 1920s and thirties made the idea of a great Irish house in ruination, or claimed by the fires of revolution, a metaphor for ancient courtesy and order overwhelmed by the levelling forces of modernity. It was as if Yeats made the idea of such a house and its fate a metaphor for the caste whose power went into eclipse in 1922. Many writers have been in thrall to this conception since, whether the demise of Anglo-Ireland is welcomed or regretted. They have used it to explore aspects of the Protestant community's experience (its sense of insecurity, its isolation, its ambiguous relationship with the majority population, its demographic imperilment) but more generally one might speculate that the purchase this conception has on the Irish sense of things in this century reflects an awareness that a seismic shift took place in the years leading to independence. A house that had stood since the Act of Union, since the Williamite settlement indeed, was now at the end of its life. Accordingly 'Big House' fiction and a good deal of writing by Protestants has been marked by a sense of terminal states, infertility, dead ends, uncertainty about the future and nostalgia.

The fact that this image of Protestantism in Southern Irish life has proved so perennial a literary preoccupation may of course be not simply due to the fact that it represents a truth about the proportions of the British démarche of 1922. In the English-speaking world in general a fascination for *anciens régimes* has provoked since the 1970s a spate of novels, films and television series in which works like, for example, J. G. Farrell's *Troubles*, or William Trevor's *The Silence in the Garden* (1970 and 1988 respectively, both tales of the troubles with 'Big House' settings) find a place. What this has meant however is that the actual experience of the Protestant minority in its middle class reality has received little literary or artistic expression either in works by members of that community or by writers and artists external to it. Among the few who have written from and of its experience is, pre-eminently Samuel Beckett, whose exploration of terminal states of being, of alienation and inexorable self-scrutiny can be seen to have sources in the Protestant religious ethos of his youth in Foxrock, County Dublin. In general terms too, Beckett's work may be said to reflect the Protestantism of his origins in the pervasive allusiveness of his text to the Authorized Version of the Bible.[43] In his radio play *All that Fall* (1957), which takes its title from one of the Psalms of David, though it would be wrong to restrict its import to the merely sociological, something of the isolation and demographic insecurity of a small Protestant community is represented. The world evoked in this work is one of neurosis, infertility, death, in which even language possesses a bizarre or chilly conventionality, which makes the word on the tongue part of the issueless predicament of the protagonist (she is tragically childless). The play might indeed be read as a kind of comic elegy for a dying community. Another radio play of exactly ten years later, though lacking the imaginative force of Beckett's small masterpiece, offered by contrast a more hopeful portrait of the community which Beckett had so remorselessly associated with decline and decay. Jack White's *The Last Eleven*, broadcast by RTÉ, offered to a diminishing community as something to be considered in the ecumenical atmosphere of the times, the possibility of cooperation with their Catholic neighbours. What makes this play of social and cultural interest (as a play it has its own dramatic impact) is that it anticipates in a markedly hopeful way the possibility of the process of integration that Kurt Bowen was to posit sixteen years later in the study adverted to above.

The play concerns a small rural parish, which has declined to its last eleven regulars. A modernizing, cost-conscious bishop proposes an amalgamation with a neighbouring parish and the closure of the church itself. This provokes varied reactions in a community that perceives itself as embattled. For the elderly incumbent Canon Sheridan, this is betrayal of tradition and another nail in the coffin of the Protestant minority. The following is a telling exchange in which the Canon speaks his mind to a prosperous businessman who knows how the world wags:

> Your bishop is making an effort to come to terms with the society he lives in. He recognises that as Protestants we are a minority of five per cent: and we are dependent for our future on the tolerance and goodwill of the ninety-five per cent.

> So we must humour them? Even if it means turning our backs on all our own tradition?

> Canon, you're living in the past. The whole tide of feeling in the world is running in favour of Christian unity.

> You are falling into a vulgar error; you confuse what is modern with what is right.

> I am delighted to see our church being dragged, kicking and screaming, into the twentieth century. We're not an ascendancy anymore, Canon. We're just a minority who are different, like the Jews.

And how do you think the Jews have survived? How have they retained
their own identity over the past two thousand years? Because,
throughout all their wanderings, all their tribulations, they have held
together their own community; they have clung to their own faith; they
have preserved their essential sense of difference. [44]

The play's dénouement involves an apparent act of sacrilege against
the church in which two eccentric elderly unmarried sisters, two of the
last eleven, worship. They had been distributing poppies (the flowers
which the Canon calls 'the badge of all our tribe') in memory of the
fallen and especially of their father who was shot dead in British uniform
on his own doorstep during the troubles. It transpires, however, that the
defacers of the church are a couple of delinquent lads and the Catholic
parish priest gets the local young people to make good the damage. This
is the beginning of cooperation between them which allows the old
Canon to accept his Bishop's suggestion that they donate their church
building to the Catholic community, since they do not have a church
in the immediate vicinity. The Canon is moved to make the ecumenical
gesture, though he himself feels defeated at the play's end. However, his
bishop is more hopeful. He envisages a future in which it will be
possible for Protestants to act cooperatively with their Catholic fellow
citizens but to remain a distinct, unassimilated but integrated
community. On being asked does he not feel like the Dutch boy with
his finger in the dyke with more and more holes appearing, he replies:

I don't feel as pessimistic as that. We have three Swedish families arriving
here for the factory within the next few months. There's a nice
American just arrived to manage the paperboard factory at Killaglen—
his family are joining him soon. The same sort of thing is happening all
over the country. Ireland is involved in a new phase of voluntary
plantation. I expect us to form a kind of rallying point for a lot of these
new elements...Our people have always had a tradition of looking
beyond Ireland. They used to look to Britain and the outposts of
Empire. But in future perhaps they'll look to Europe.

Not all recent literary representations of the experience of Protestants
in this State are as benign as White's play, marked as it was by immediate
post-Vatican II hopes for religious tolerance and a new eirenic spirit in
the Churches generally. Some telling writings suggest in fact that while
the resolution of ancient enmities and communal tensions has taken

place on the macro-level of social process (which a sociologist like Bowen can observe), on the micro-level of actual individuals' lives they remain active. Such writing suggests that in personal memory, psychology and experience, residual fears continue to operate and not, sometimes, without reason. Many Protestant families in the State, while perfectly at ease in times of social and political stability, would have their own folk memories of the departures of many Protestants, sometimes under threat of violence or in consequence of actual violence in the 1920s and would recall how insecure their community felt at that time. Crises such as Bloody Sunday in 1972 and the hunger strikes in 1980-81, when it seemed as if the Republic of Ireland could be drawn into a direct involvement with the Northern *imbroglio* made the Protestant community, aware of its own history, distinctly uneasy, even where individual members of it were in complete sympathy with the outrage at British policy expressed by many of their Catholic fellow citizens. Two powerful, disturbing stories by William Trevor explore this troubled hinterland of Protestant feeling, the artist daring to articulate what cannot easily be spoken of and what is in all probability only an experience of certain moments of national crisis and not a settled state of mind and feeling.

'The Distant Past' tells the story of two elderly Protestants, a brother and sister who eke out a vestigial existence in a decaying Georgian house with 12 acres of land to sustain them. Although they do not in the early years of the State believe that the new regime will last, through drink they manage to establish 'convivial relationships with the people of the town' [45] — even with the men who had once stood in their house with shotguns waiting for the arrival of expected British soldiers. They survive through the 'Emergency', the post war economic resurgence and it seems that they had been integrated into the community:

> The visitors who came to the town heard about the Middletons and
> were impressed. It was a pleasant wonder, more than one of them
> remarked, that old wounds could heal so completely, that the Middletons
> could continue in their loyalty to the past and that, in spite of it, they
> were respected in the town. [46]

It is the outbreak of violence in the North which suggests that scar tissue can reopen those old wounds. The atmosphere changes:

On Fridays, only sometimes at first, there was a silence when the
Middletons appeared. It was as though, going back nearly twenty years,
people remembered the Union Jack in the window of their car and saw it
now in a different light. It wasn't something to laugh at any more, nor
were certain words that the Middletons had gently spoken, nor were they
themselves just an old peculiar couple. Slowly the change crept about, all
around them in the town, until fat Cranley didn't wish it to be
remembered that he had ever given them mince for their dog. He had
stood with a gun in the enemy's house, waiting for soldiers so that soldiers
might be killed: it was better that people should remember that.[47]

They are ostracized in the town after fifty years of a 'tolerance that
never again in the years that were left to them would they know'.[48] The
tale ends chillingly as it touches on an insecure minority's most visceral,
atavistic fear 'Because of the distant past they would die friendless. It was
worse than being murdered in their beds.'[49]

Now of course this is a work of fiction with no claim to be based on
an actual occurrence. However, in a country which has known
notorious boycotts with a sectarian and political agenda[50] it has its own
disturbing authenticity. As does another of Trevor's intense stories about
the impact of the Northern violence on a Southern Protestant. 'Attracta'
explores how the horrors of the past in the South have their contemporary equivalents north of the border and implies that the understandable desire of most people in the South to maintain a distance from that
contemporary reality may inhibit the processes of forgiveness and
healing that the story invokes. Attracta is an elderly Protestant school
teacher in a small Southern town. She is single-handedly responsible for
the average of sixteen pupils who present themselves annually for
instruction. The narrative concerns her horror at the news of a
particularly sickening Northern atrocity and this is linked to her own
experience as the child of violence (her parents were killed accidentally
by an IRA flying column in the War of Independence, by one of her
co-religionists and his Catholic former lover who now acts as his
housekeeper). Attracta came to know of their involvement in her
parents' deaths only after she had been befriended by them and treated
almost as if they were related. For Attracta, her story is a lesson in the
powers of healing. She seeks to explain to her charges what she has
come to understand only to be asked to retire, over sixty as she is, since
she has upset the consensus that would wish such raw reality to be

suppressed in childrens' schoolrooms (though in the story it is implied that it is the parents rather than the children who are outraged). By contrast Attracta feels 'Every day in my schoolroom I should have honoured the small, remarkable thing that happened in this town.'[51] She recognizes that the past in the South and what is happening in the Northern present are not as easily distinguishable as some in her community would wish. A violent act of hatred and revenge brings that home to her most painfully.

It may be worth noting, however, that in recent years the experience of the Protestant minority has begun to be articulated with more force and frequency than in the first five decades of independence. The publication of the essays of Hubert Butler, for example, is one sign of an interest in the voice of the minority. Until the Lilliput Press made them widely available in 1985 these lucid, rational, passionately argued, sometimes gentle, sometimes angry reflections on Kilkenny, Ireland and the world were known by only a limited number of readers who had access to the small magazines and journals in which he had originally published them. Dervla Murphy writes of their past and present reception: 'The road he chose was rough and unpredictable; the toll-fees had to be paid in the coinage of courage; the destination was uncertain but bound to demand difficult adjustments when/if the traveller arrived. Happily there is by now a bolder generation eager to explore the unknown.'[52] Roy Foster has described what that courage involved in respect of his community:

> An Irish Protestant friend recently recalled to me the atmosphere of that curious sub-culture, complacent and insecure all at once, in the Republic of the 1950s. Any expressed ambition to criticize aspects of Irish life, he remembered, caused your co-religionists to round on you with one over-riding injunction: *Don't rock the boat!* Hubert Butler has made a lifetime's habit of administering graceful but vigorous rocks. [53]

And Foster reports that the 'irony was not lost to him' that by his ninetieth year he 'become widely accepted in Ireland as an inspirational figure: almost an institution'. That such success and respect were granted to a man who had in the 1950s endured obloquy and social opprobrium because of an inferred insult to the papal nuncio at a public meeting over the issue of Croatian Catholic behaviour towards Orthodox Serbs in Yugoslavia, is certainly an indicator of a markedly changed Irish social atmosphere. Further evidence that a community that once found little public expression for its traditions is now accepted as a cultural presence is the success of such plays as Frank McGuinness's *Observe the Sons of Ulster marching towards the Somme* (1985) and Sebastian Barry's *The Steward of Christendom* (1995) which both address the complex traditions of Irish loyalism. So while the Northern conflict may have induced insecurity at moments of particular crisis and its implications for a minority with its own history of political conflict and violence could not be ignored, there is evidence that the distinctive, Protestant voice of a Hubert Butler can now find a significant Irish audience and that plays about minority or anomalous experience gain appreciative reception.

At the symbolic level the State has in recent years given due acknowledgement to the variegated traditions of the communities that compose the Irish population. Among these acts of imaginative inclusiveness most notably have been the refurbishment of the war memorial to the dead in British wars at Islandbridge and the inauguration of an annual memorial ceremony, attended by State representatives, for all Irish men and women who have died in combat. A current postage stamp commemorates the Royal Dublin Fusiliers of 1914, many of whose members perished in the terrible European conflict which broke out in that year.

THE JEWISH COMMUNITY

One historian of Irish Jewry, Bernard Shillman, finds evidence for a Jewish presence in Ireland as early as 1062 and there certainly seem to have been some Jews in Ireland in the thirteenth century. In the year 1583–84 it also seems that the mayor of Youghal was a Jew. It was in the seventeenth century that some Portuguese Jews established the country's first synagogue in Dublin. From that date, numbers of Jews in Ireland remained extremely low until the late nineteenth and early twentieth centuries when pogroms in Eastern Europe (primarily in Lithuania and in parts of what now is Russia) provoked a wave of Jewish migration, some of which broke on Irish shores. Accordingly, where the Jewish population in all of Ireland stood at 258 in 1871, in 1891 it had risen to 1,779. By 1901 it stood at 3,771 and by 1946 it had risen once more to 3,907 in the Southern state alone. This was the high-water mark.[54]

Most of these immigrants in the South settled in Dublin in one specific area of the city on the South Circular Road which became known as 'Little Jerusalem' giving Jewishness in the State a geographic centre. From the 1940s this new Jewish community began to shift its centre of gravity to Rathgar and Terenure. From this area subsequent moves were more on the basis of individual relocations as families moved to the south eastern suburbs and were less visibly associated with a distinct community with a recognized geographic locus.

From the early stages of this Jewish settlement steps were taken to ensure that the community's distinctive religious practice could be sustained. Jewish shops catered for the Jewish diet and in time a new synagogue was built in Terenure and a sports centre in Kimmage. Jewish national schools were established and a secondary school was founded in 1952 and moved to its current Rathgar site in 1983.

The Jewish community in Ireland might be seen to mirror in a more extreme form the problems confronting a numerically small religious group in a predominantly Catholic country. It too has experienced serious demographic decline from the high point of over almost 4,000 in 1946. Since then the community has experienced significant numerical diminution so that in the 1981 census the number of Jews resident in Ireland had dropped to 2,128. The key factor in this decline has probably been emigration rather than the combination of emigration in the early years of independence, assimilation and and low fertility which accounts for the decline in the number of Protestants in the State. One researcher in 1983 estimated Jewish emigration at the rate of twenty families a year.[55] Another researcher commented that this was 'removing the young-marrieds and single people of child-bearing age. So the Jewish community is not experiencing the under-25 bulge found in the age-distribution of the population at large.'[56]

Certainly a factor in this pattern of emigration must be the existence of the State of Israel (an embassy of Israel was established in Dublin in 1994, marking a new phase in Irish-Israeli relations). It can be pointed out in this context that the multinational company Intel which has a significant role in the Irish economic future also has among its multinational sites of operation a plant in Israel which because of its precise activities has links with the Intel company in Ireland. A major player in the company's plans for development in this country is an Israeli citizen who will settle his family in Ireland for the duration of his posting. Equally a stimulus of emigration from the Jewish community here must be the desire of Jewish young men and women to move to larger Jewish communities abroad in search of Jewish marriage partners. What such emigration does, however, is set in question the future of the Jewish community in Ireland, for it is difficult see how a such a small number of families can survive as a distinct community.

The Jewish wish to sustain that religious distinctiveness is reflected in the fact that even so small a community is willing to help finance a Jewish secondary school in Dublin. However, not all Jewish parents send their children to that school. Many choose to enrol their children in Dublin's well-known Protestant secondary schools, particularly Wesley College (Methodist), Alexandra and High School (Church of Ireland), and St Andrew's (Presbyterian). This is a well-established practice in Dublin's Jewish community and has not been noticeably affected by 'the dictum of successive Chief Rabbis that the only defence of their Jewishness lay in going to a Jewish school.'[57] As a result, the Jewish secondary school has in practice admitted significant numbers of non-Jewish students and employs non-Jews on its teaching staff. In 1985, only about 40 per cent of the 108 pupils enrolled for the year 1984-5 were Jewish and the majority of the staff were Catholic.[58]

Mac Gréil in his survey, published in 1977, reported on some evidence that the Jewish community in Dublin was not viewed with the same degree of tolerance as the Protestant. Only 57 per cent of the total sample expressed a willingness to welcome a Jew into the family by marriage (though this should be set against the lower figures of 40.9 per cent for Agnostics and 37.7 per cent for Atheists).[59] Perhaps this may be due to lack of knowledge about a community that observes different feast days from both Catholics and Protestants and which in the early years of Jewish settlement inhabited its own specific area of the city and was understandably jealous of its own traditions. It might also be attributed to a perception among the religious majority that the Jewish faith is clearly more different from Catholicism than that professed by

Protestants who play a role in Christendom. Be that as it may, Gerald Davis wrote informatively of Jewish religio-cultural distinctiveness in 1968:

> Rigid observance of the Sabbath and Holy Days often interferes with social activities because the Jewish religious calendar is different from its civil counterpart. Most Jewish employees are also embarrassed by the amount of time they have to take off from their jobs when High Holy days coincide with the working week. Fear of intermarriage makes most parents anxious about their children becoming too involved with others who are not of the Jewish faith. Up to a few years ago, it was a brave Jewish girl indeed who would venture unaccompanied to a 'non-Jewish' dance. In fact it would still be rather frowned upon.[60]

Despite such a tendency to inhabit a segregated world, Jews have played a significant role in Irish public life. This was perhaps best symbolized by the fact that Dr Robert Briscoe was twice elected Lord Mayor of Dublin, in 1956-7 and 1961-2 (in its own way as significant a demonstration of Irish tolerance as the fact that two Irish Presidents since 1937 have been Protestant) and by the presence of Jews in the major political parties. Gerald Davis's reflections on the place Jews have played in Irish life are sensitive and sensible:

> The desire for the security of the professions and the strong streak of practicality in the Jewish make-up are probably the reason for a lack of creative expression in a community like Dublin. To a family man—and most Jews are family people—first things come first; a comfortable home with a wife and children is basically more important than taking to the Arts as a career or a way of life....But this applies only to the majority— and there are many Jewish names to remember in the creative field in this country. Academically, the contribution has been even greater and there are prominent names in the fields of Medicine and Law. Possibly the best known of these was that of Michael Noyk. When he died last year he was honoured by the State with a military funeral for his part in defending Irish patriots during the Troubles.
>
> That there are not more Jews in public life is probably due to the natural reluctance of minority groups to push themselves into the public eye. There is also much inter-communal organisation to be done and this takes up a lot of time which might otherwise be channelled outwards into the community at large.[61]

JEWISHNESS AND LITERATURE

Davis has himself made a notable contribution to the artistic life of his native city since he wrote this article. This was recognized and honoured by the President of Ireland, Mary Robinson this year when she opened an exhibition in the Davis Gallery, Dublin which celebrated the twenty five years of its existence. Among Davis' various activities has been a genial, theatrical identification with the hero of Joyce's *Ulysses* each Bloomsday. There is of course a serious point in this — about which Davis in his humourous way is right to remind us. For Joyce may have chosen a Jewish hero for his epic of Dublin life (Bloom's paternal ancestors were Hungarian Jews) since as a Jew in Dublin he was something of an outsider and as such was a suitable figure in whom to express the alienation of modern man in the universal city. It is Bloom too who offers in the face of xenophobia a serviceable definition of Irishness when he replies to an aggressive enquiry about his nation: 'Ireland, says Bloom. I was born here. Ireland.' That such an inclusive understanding of citizenship was a necessity in Edwardian Ireland is evidenced by Bloom's insistence 'And I belong to a race too, says Bloom, that is hated and persecuted. Also now. This very moment. This very instant.' This is reckoned by some critics to be a reference not only to European anti-Semitism but to events unfolding in 1904 in Limerick City. For in January that year, a priest of the Redemptorist Order had preached a sermon indicting Jewish business methods in the city, even including in his sermon the classic anti-Semitic charge of child-slaughter. A second sermon provoked a boycott of Jewish business which by the end of two years had driven forty members of the Jewish community from the city, leaving a bare forty behind. Influential Irish Catholics spoke against this boycott and the Jewish historian of the Limerick attack on the Jewish community does reckon it 'a sad but uncharacteristic and atypical episode'.[62] A recent story by an Irish Jewish writer suggests that we cannot perhaps be quite so sanguine.

Who Ever heard of an Irish Jew? (1988)[63] is a collection of short stories by David Marcus, one of Ireland's most significant literary figures. As the editor of the quarterly *Irish Writing* and subsequently for many years of 'New Irish Writing' in *The Irish Press* newspaper he was responsible for first publishing many of the Irish poets and prose-writers who are now household names. Himself Jewish, he writes with an insider's knowledge of and affection for the Dublin Jewish inner city community which had formed a partial backdrop for Joyce's text. Mostly pitched to a droll and humourous note, the stories do suggest some of the poignancy of a small and diminishing community poised between a European past of persecution and barbarism (one character is a pauperized misfit who has never recovered from his experience of the camps) and difficulties of assimilation and integration. One story is much more disturbing in its implications.

Larry Levin is the son of a father who is convinced, in a way his son finds almost racialist, of the superiority of Jews as performing musicians. Larry has been educated at a Catholic school, and dissatisfied with his job in the family tailoring firm, spends his nights drinking with ex-schoolmates 'with whose idiom he was familiar but to whose world he was alien'. After a particularly unsatisfactory conversation with his father about the recently-dead and Jewish singer Al Jolson, Larry finds himself in a most distressing altercation in the pub with his Irish Catholic companions. Marcus clearly intends the setting to remind us of *Ulysses* where Bloom encounters anti-Semitism in Barney Kiernan's pub. Indeed, one of Larry's companions makes explicit and mocking reference to that scene, as if to goad him to respond to heavily implied racial slurs. Where Bloom escapes from Barney Kiernan's pub in mock-heroic splendour, Larry can only barge out in futile rage: 'He didn't know who he was or what he was. As he looked around him, for a moment he didn't know even where he was. Had he lost all physical bearings along with any sense of identity?' [64] And the story ends in the doubt and confusion which makes one aware how insecurity can assail the minority consciousness in Ireland when confronted by the kind of ignorant prejudice represented by the anti-Semitism of Larry's companions. For to be a member of a minority is to be liable to the experience of vulnerability and estrangement, since one's well-being and sense of acceptance are to some extent dependent on the understanding and goodwill of the majority.

> Where was Jerusalem? Not in Ireland anyway, that was for sure. Bloom's words swam back into his mind. 'I was born in Ireland,' Bloom had said, 'I am an Irishman.' 'Are you now?' Larry asked. 'Are you indeed?'
> He entered his bedroom and as he sat on the bed an answer—an answer of sorts—came to him 'Go home, Leopold Bloom, all is forgiven.' It was

meaningless. Just words, words. Jerusalem, Irishman, Bloom, Jew, home. There was a song, wasn't there? 'Show me the way to go home.' Did Al Jolson ever record that? he wondered.

Such a story reminds us that it is often in the areas of feeling, personal identity and social endorsement that issues of minority status make their most exacting demands upon us as citizens of a republic, even as we may be inclined to congratulate ourselves on the generally successful way in which the State has handled such matters. That this awareness is stimulated by a story set amid a community whose demographic future seems so perilous, for whom assimilation or disappearance is a more likely prospect than integration, I believe, should further give us pause.

NOTES

1   Paul Bew, *Ideology and the Irish Question*, Oxford: Clarendon Press, 1994, p.74

2   Jeremiah O'Donovan, 'The Catholic Association', *The Irish Rosary*, (November, 1903), p.873. I am grateful to Mr J. Nolan who brought this article to my attention.

3   *Ibid.*

4   *Ibid.*, 874

5   *Ibid.*, p.877

6   *Ibid.*, pp.877-8

7   Bew, *op.cit.*, p.74

8   *Ibid.*, p.151

9   'The Catholic Truth Society and Emancipation', *Catholic Truth Society of Ireland Report*, 1927, p.13

10   W. B. Stanford, *A Recognised Church: The Church of Ireland in Éire*, Dublin and Belfast: A.P.C.K, 1944, p.16

11   *Ibid.*, p.17. This pamphlet drew from Seán Ó Faoláin in *The Bell* a markedly unfriendly and caustic riposte. He began his response to Stanford by asserting 'any Catholic knows more about grievances, ancient and modern, than all the Anglicans of Ireland and Great Britain put together', 'Toryism in Trinity, The Editor', *The Bell*, Vol. 8, No 3, (June, 1944), p.185. Indeed Ó Faoláin wrote to deplore Stanford's opinions 'because until I had read these things I never thought of myself, in relation to Ireland, as a Catholic at all and I strongly resent being compelled to think of myself as a Catholic.' *Ibid.*, p.18 In fact the severity of Ó Faoláin's judgement of Stanford and what he represents might be taken to indicate, since Ó Faoláin was a strongly liberal voice in the period, the difficulties which Protestants faced in articulating any sense that they had a point of view that should be heard. While Ó Faoláin had the grace to say 'I am glad that he has at least shown that Protestants are not all stone-dumb' (*Ibid.*, p.196) his overall view is characterized by the following passage: 'where a man's political attitude was sound his religion has never been anybody's concern. I am not sure that *as a religion* Irish Protestantism was ever as strong as it should have been, but I am quite certain that it will not even be as strong again until it is not merely above suspicion politically, but until it is strong politically, and that what keeps it weak is that it is sulking in a vestry. There is no reason why it should, for it has things to offer in the creation of a rich mode of Irish life.' (*Ibid.*, p.192). It does not take an especially acute ear to be disturbed by that phrase 'political attitude was sound'. However, Ó Faoláin sought further commentary on a section of Stanford's pamphlet (which he reprinted in *The Bell* from seven of the Professor's co-religionists, several of whom reckoned that there was some pressure on Protestants of the kind Stanford had addressed, while others were unaware of such.

12   W. B. Stanford, *Faith and Faction*, Dublin and Belfast: A.P.C.K., 1946, p.21

13   *Ibid.*

14   See Kurt Bowen, *Protestants in a Catholic State: Ireland's Privileged Minority*, Kingston and Montreal: McGill/Queen's University Press, 1983, p.20

15   *Ibid.*, p.22

16   Martin Maguire, 'The Church of Ireland and the problem of the Protestant working-class of Dublin', in *As by Law Established:The Church of Ireland Since the Reformation*, eds A. Ford, J. McGuire and K. Milne, Dublin: Lilliput Press, 1995, p.195

17. *Ibid.*, p.202. A sense of the violence of the War of Independence and the Civil war in which Protestants sometimes felt they were being targeted simply as Protestants is given in Robert Kee, *The Green Flag: A History of Irish Nationalism*, London: Weidenfield and Nicolson, 1972. See also Jack White, *Minority Report: The Protestant Community in the Irish Republic*, Dublin: Gill and Macmillan, 1975, pp.84–6

18   Sean O'Casey's play *Red Roses For Me* (1943) is set in the context of an ecclesiastical conflict between militant anti-Catholic Protestantism, which the playwright remembered from his Dublin youth, and more liberal Christianity and socialism.

19   Border county Presbyterianism would be an obvious exception here with communities sensing themselves to some extent on the periphery of the large Presbyterian communities in Northern Ireland. The General Assembly of the Presbyterian Church meets annually in Belfast, where the Church's theological college is also situated. This contrasts with the Church of Ireland, which meets in national synod in Dublin, the city where its ordinands are theologically trained.

20   Bowen, *op. cit.*, pp. 28–9

21   Brendan M. Walsh, *Religion and Demographic Behaviour in Ireland,* (Paper, No 55, May, 1970), The Economic and Social Research Institute, p.35

22   Draft Paper: *Religious Denominations In The Republic Of Ireland 1911-81*, (September, 1992), Dublin: Central Statistics Office.

23   Walsh *op. cit.*, p.25

24   For an excellent analysis of the rapid decline of Anglo-Ireland as a political and social force see L. P. Curtis, Jr, 'The Anglo-Irish Predicament', *Twentieth Century Studies*, (No 4, November, 1970), pp. 37–63

25   See Paul Durcan's witty but revelatory poem 'What's A Protestant, Daddy?' with its concluding lines: 'Protestants were Martians/Light years more weird/Than zoological creatures;/But soon they would all go away/For as a species they were dying out, /Soon there would be no more Protestants.../O Yea, O Lord, /I was a proper little Irish Catholic boy/Way back in the 1950s.' Paul Durcan, *Selected Poems*, ed. Edna Longley, Belfast: The Blackstaff Press, 1982, p.60

26   White, *op.cit.,* p.165

27   For example see Jack White's comment 'It is not easy to think of another case in which a defeated ascendancy has been treated with such exemplary generosity by a victorious people.' White *op.cit.*, p.92. That this is not simply a piece of polite flattery of the powers that had come to be, is evidenced by another comment by this writer: 'We've had fair play, certainly, but why not? By and large the protestants are an industrious group....We have a tradition of integrity and honour, and that's still relevant. We play our part in this country. I don't think we would ever feel anything but Irish.' White, *op.cit.*, p.30

28   The Ne Temere decree was promulgated in 1908. This 'laid down that any marriage to which a Roman Catholic was a party, if not solemnized according to the rites of the Church of Rome, should be regarded as invalid from a canonical point of view'.

Bew, *op. cit.*, p.31. The most contentious aspect of this decree was that it made the issue of mixed marriages between Catholics and Protestants very vexed indeed, for as it was given effect in Ireland in the Code of Canon Law, such marriages were only performed when the intending Protestant partner gave an undertaking (usually in writing) that any offspring of a union would be raised as Catholics. Undoubtedly this has been one of the most vexatious matters which Protestants have faced in Ireland in the period under assessment since it was perceived as a threat to their demographic survival. The State seemed to become implicated in the matter in the Tilson case in 1950 (which involved a Protestant father changing his mind about his pre-nuptial undertakings) when the Supreme Court upheld a judgement of the High Court that (although the Supreme Court judgement was couched in very circumspect terms), as Jack White has it, it gave the appearance 'that the State would back the ruling of the church'. White, *op.cit.*, p.127. And as John Whyte has stated: 'The judgement was followed by a crop of angry letters in *The Irish Times*, and has ever since remained a prime example for those who wish to argue that Ireland is a clerically-dominated State.' J. H. Whyte, *Church and State in Modern Ireland*, Dublin: Gill and Macmillan, 1971, p.171. However, in 1970, in the post-Vatican II climate, the apostolic letter *Motu Proprio* made more ecumenical arrangements possible. These are now applied with varying degrees of 'liberalism' in various parts of the country. Impressionistic evidence, drawing on newspaper reports and on personal conversations and observations, suggests that many young people today in mixed marriages make their own agreements with each other about the religious denomination and education of their offspring.

29   Bowen, *op.cit.*, pp.60-61
30   Susan M. Parkes, *Kildare Place: the History of the Church of Ireland Training College, 1811-1969*, Dublin: CICE, 1984, p.164
31   *Ibid.*, p.166
32   *Ibid.*
33   Whyte, *op.cit.*, pp.48-9
34   Bowen, *op.cit.*, p.66
35   *Ibid.*, p.58
36   *Ibid.*, p.3
37   *Ibid.*, p.202
38   *Ibid.*
39   Mícheál Mac Gréil, *Prejudice and Tolerance In Ireland*, Dublin: Research Section, College of Industrial Relations, 1977-78, p.242. This researcher also found that in Dublin only 3 per cent of the over 2,000 Catholics he polled felt that their religion was any impediment to their personal advancement.
40   Bowen, *op. cit.*, p.204
41   *Ibid.*, p.207
42   *Ibid.*, p.208
43   See Vivian Mercier, 'All that fall: Samuel Beckett and the Bible', in *Modern Irish Literature*, Oxford: Clarendon Press, 1994, pp.312-326
44   I am grateful to Mr Stephen White who made the script of this play available to me.
45   William Trevor, *Collected Stories*, London: Penguin Books, 1993, p.350

46   *Ibid.*, p.352

47   *Ibid.*, p.354

48   *Ibid.*, p.355

49   *Ibid.*, p.356

50   The most notorious of such events, of which there have only been a few, was the boycott of Protestant shops and businesses in Fethard-on-Sea in 1957 over a mixed marriage dispute. That issues of religion can still generate local friction is evidenced by the current dispute in County Mayo about whether an all-Irish national school should be Catholic or multi-denominational. It should also I think be said that although such incidents have been extremely rare, the size of the Protestant community as a whole gives such incidents their considerable symbolic power. In a small, rather scattered community they make an impact beyond their local ramifications. It is the size, I believe, of the Protestant community in the Republic of Ireland, that, analogously, makes such a matter as the final resolution of the Tallaght Hospital question so crucial for that community as a whole. Such an issue becomes more than a question of local politics but of social power and standing in general.

51   Trevor, *op.cit.*, p.690

52   Dervla Murphy, 'Foreword', *Grandmother and Wolfe Tone*, Dublin: Lilliput Press, 1990, p.IX

53   Roy Foster, 'Foreword', *The Children of Drancy*, Dublin: Lilliput Press, 1988, p.X

54   These statistics are taken from Bernard Shillman, *A Short History of the Jews in Ireland*, Dublin: Messrs Eason and Son, Ltd, 1945 and W. E. Vaughan and A. J. Fitzpatrick, *Irish Historical Statistics:Population 1821-1971*, Dublin: Royal Irish Academy, 1978

55   This figure is S. Waterman's, cited in Georgina Fitzpatrick, *The Story Of A Paradox: A Sociological Study Of Dublin Jewish Community's School, 'Aliya College'*, H. Dip. Ed. Dissertation, Trinity College, Dublin 1985. In this thesis Ms Fitzpatrick made use of a pseudonym. I am grateful to Ms Kate Bateman who brought this work to my attention and to Ms Fitzpatrick who made it available.

56   Fitzpatrick, *op.cit.*, p.31

57   *Ibid.*, p.23

58   *Ibid.*, p.6 and p.14

59   Mac Gréil, *op. cit.*, p.242

60   Gerald Davis, 'On Being Jewish In Ireland', *Everyman*, (No.1, 1968), pp.109-110. I am grateful to Mr Davis who made this article available to me and for his advice.

61   *Ibid.*, pp.110-11

62   Louis Hyman, *The Jews of Ireland from Earliest Times to the Year 1910*, Shannon: Irish University Press, 1972, p.217. It should be noted that this work has a sympathetic foreword by Mr Cearbhall Ó Dálaigh, then Chief Justice and subsequently President of Ireland.

63   Hyman cites a Dublin Jewish journalist and writer of 1906 as follows: 'You cannot get one native to remember that a Jew may be an Irishman. The term "Irish Jew" seems to have a contradictory ring upon the native ear....' Hyman, *op.cit.*, p.176.

64   David Marcus, *Who ever Heard of an Irish Jew and other stories*, London: Bantam Press, 1988, p. 89

65   *Ibid.*, p.91

FACTORS AFFECTING
POPULATION DECLINE IN
MINORITY RELIGIOUS COMMUNITIES
IN THE REPUBLIC OF IRELAND

J.J. SEXTON
AND
RICHARD O'LEARY

ACKNOWLEDGEMENT

The authors wish to express their appreciation of the assistance received from the staff of Central Statistics Office, Dublin (particularly Mr Aidan Punch and Mr Gerard Keogh) for the supply of special tabulations from past censuses of population.

CONTENTS

SUMMARY

Prior to considering the specific question of causation in relation to the decline in the size of the minority religious communities in Ireland it is appropriate first of all to provide some basic data regarding these communities. It is important to bear in mind that one cannot assess the position of the minority communities in isolation. Their situation has to be viewed in the context of the wider society within which these communities exist. Thus many of the analyses presented in this report embrace all religious groups, including the majority Catholic community.

Most of the statistical information used in this study is taken from censuses of population covering the period from 1881 to 1991. While this provides a valuable data source, the qualifications which apply to this information must be borne in mind. These are referred to in section 2 of this Report.

THE PRESENT POSITION

The most recent information is that available from the 1991 census. This shows that in that year of the total population of 3,525,700, over 3,228,300 were Roman Catholics, 89,200 were members of the Church of Ireland, 13,200 were Presbyterians, just over 5,000 were Methodists, nearly 1,600 were members of the Jewish community while 38,700 were recorded as being affiliated to 'other stated religions'. The majority of the last mentioned group consisted mainly of various Christian denominations. Nearly 66,300 persons at the 1991 census indicated that they had 'no religion' while 83,400 refused to respond to the census question on religion. These figures thus indicate that in 1991 there were over 147,700 persons, or 4.2 per cent of the total population, affiliated to specific stated religions other than Catholic. While this group encompassed a diversity of different creeds it is clear that it is predominantly Protestant in character — to the extent of some 80 per cent of the total, with the remainder consisting mainly of smaller unspecified Christian denominations.

Many of the analyses contained in this report are, for reasons of simplicity, presented in the form of comparisons between the aggregate group referred to as 'the minority religious communities' and the Catholic community. It would obviously have been more desirable to provide separate analyses for individual minority religious groups. However, this would have added greatly to the complexity of the presentation. We were, in any case, constrained by the availability of data from previous censuses in this regard.

OVERALL TRENDS

The minority religious communities have undergone a very substantial decline in numbers over the past hundred years or so. The total population for this group stood at 404,300 in 1881 but by 1991 it had fallen to 147,700, a decline of 257,000 or nearly 64 per cent. Over the same period, in tandem with the overall decline in the total population, the Catholic community also decreased in size by 237,000, but this represents a much smaller relative rate of decrease, about 7 per cent.

Between 1881 and 1911, the rate of decline for both Catholics and the minority communities was broadly similar, indicating that the decreases (which were primarily due to emigration) were mainly associated with socio-economic factors. However, between 1911 and 1926, a very significant period which covered the first world war and the transition to national independence in 1922, the minority communities decreased greatly in size, by over 106,000, or nearly a third in relative terms. In the following decades in the period up to 1961, even if the pace of decline diminished, numbers in those communities continued to fall at a rate significantly faster than that which applied to the total population.

During the 1960s the rate of decrease for the minority communities population began to diminish and throughout the 1970s the position

TABLE A: POPULATION TRENDS BY RELIGIOUS GROUPS, 1881-1991

No.

Year	Catholic	Other Denominations	No Religion	No Statement	Total
1881	3,465,332	404,294	–	–	3,869,626
1911	2,812,509	327,179	–	–	3,139,688
1926	2,751,269	220,723	–	–	2,971,992
1946	2,786,033	169,074	–	–	2,955,107
1961	2,673,473	138,136	1,107	5,625	2,818,341
1971	2,795,666	128,318	7,616	46,648	2,978,248
1981	3,204,476	128,381	39,572	70,976	3,443,405
1991	3,228,327	147,747	66,270	83,375	3,525,719

Annual Average Change (%)

Period	Catholic	Other Denominations	No Religion	No Statement	Total
1881-1911	-0.69	-0.71	–	–	-0.69
1991-1926	-0.15	-2.59	–	–	-0.37
1926-1946	+0.06	-1.32	–	–	-0.03
1946-1961	-0.27	-1.34	–	–	-0.32
1961-1971	+0.45	-0.73	+21.27	+23.56	+0.55
1971-1981	+1.37	0.00	+17.91	+4.29	+1.46
1981-1991	+0.07	+1.41	+5.29	+1.62	+0.24

Sources: Censuses of population.

stabilized in population terms. Between 1981 and 1991 these communities actually increased significantly in numbers, by some 20,000 or 15 per cent. This represents a much higher rate of increase than that which applied to the total population (or the Catholic community) which was less than 1 per cent. This increase related mainly to a variety of smaller Christian categories, some of which have undergone very substantial expansion in recent years. The actual size of this increase implies clearly that it must have occurred as a result of transfers from other religious groups, mainly it would appear from the Catholic community. As indicated in Table 1 of this report, the traditional Protestant denominations continued to decline during the 1980s, albeit at a relatively slow pace.

CAUSES UNDERLYING THE DECLINE

There are a number of demographic factors which can cause a population to decline, or increase. Principally these relate to births, mortality and migration. In the case of births, or the birth rate, the associated influences of fertility and nuptuality are of vital importance. However, where different religious denominations are being analysed it is also necessary to consider transfers between religious groups and inter-marriage (mixed marriages). In the case of the latter, the pattern of the religious denominations of the children of such marriages can play a significant role in influencing the numbers in different communities, especially smaller communities. We will now briefly summarize our findings in relation to each of these factors bearing in mind that they are interrelated, as outcomes and causations can be interactive in the particular context involved here, especially over time. We will begin with a consideration of external migration as this was the first influence to have a significant impact on the situation if it is viewed chronologically over the century long period under discussion.

MIGRATION

Even though no specific external migration data for different religious groups can be assembled for the period 1881–1911, the indications are that the attrition which applied to both communities in Ireland due to emigration was on much the same scale. In the subsequent period, however, between 1911 and 1926, the position was clearly quite different. Even allowing for the withdrawal of British security personnel (and their dependants) and the additional deaths within the minority communities due to the first world war the evidence suggests a net outflow from these communities of about 60,000. This represents a net annual outflow rate of over 15 per 1,000 of the average population for the minority communities, a high figure by any standards, and about twice the value of the contemporaneous rate for Catholics. There can be little doubt that the main causation underlying this exodus was a sense of apprehension in certain sections of these communities associated with the transition to national independence in 1922 and the upheavals which attended that event.

A still significant, if reduced, degree of emigration continued to apply to the minority religious communities in the period up to the end of the second world war. The relevant migration rates remained as high as 10 per 1,000 population, again markedly higher than the Catholic rates which were between 5 and 6 over this period. While these continuing high outflows may be partly explained by some residual effects attributable to the political transition of the early 1920s, new legal measures introduced in the immediate post independence period are also likely to have played a role. These measures, which reflected a strong nationalist and Catholic ethos, would have been viewed by many in the minority communities as restrictive and moving towards a form of society in which they would not be entirely at ease.

The situation changed in the post World War II era. The incidence of emigration for the minority communities decreased somewhat and Catholic emigration rose greatly, to a much higher level than that which existed for the minority communities. In this period, especially in the 1950s which involved periods of deep recession, the evidence suggests that economic considerations which applied to all sections of the population were the main influences which gave rise to very large migratory outflows. However, emigration persisted in the 1960s and with the advent of increased economic growth, overall emigration diminished. To the degree that it did exist, our analysis suggests that it applied equally to the Catholic and minority religious communities (with the exception of the Jewish community).

It is not possible to compile precise estimates of net external migration for different religious groups for the 1970s and the 1980s as the rising incidence of transfers between groups (including the 'no religion' category) greatly complicates the position. However, the earlier trends, and the limited insights into migration that can be gleaned from the data for these decades, would suggest that the migration patterns for Catholics and the minority religious communities were broadly the same, and dictated primarily by economic influences.

The large migratory outflows from the minority communities in the period between national independence and the end of the second world war were of considerable significance in a number of different ways. Not only did these losses directly reduce the size of the minority population, the majority of the emigrants were young and the depletion of the younger age groups had a subsequent knock-on effect in reducing the numbers of births for these communities in later decades.

FERTILITY

The question of relative fertility levels inevitably arises when population issues for different religious groups are considered, given the divergent views which are embodied in the ethos of different religions in relation to aspects such as birth control and contraception. It is a well established fact that the fertility levels associated with the minority religious communities in Ireland are lower than those for Catholics and that this position has prevailed for a very long time. This has been clearly indicated by fertility of marriage data available in previous censuses.

The method usually adopted to measure fertility, and the one which is used in this report, is to relate the number of births in a period (usually a year) to the number of women in the population in question in the fertile age band of between 15 and 44 years. Comparisons based on this ratio are usually confined to marital births. When applied to the Irish situation it reveals a significant excess in Catholic fertility over that for the minority religious communities — of the order of 50-60 per cent from the mid-1940s to the early 1980s, with some evidence of convergence thereafter (see Table 4 in section 4). However, for both communities in question, fertility levels decreased significantly over this period.

MIXED MARRIAGES

It is important to bear in mind, however, that in the particular context of identifying differences between religious groups, the above mentioned fertility indicator does not solely reflect fertility differences as such. It can be significantly affected by the incidence of religious intermarriage or mixed marriages because of the relative displacement of mothers and their children in these circumstances.[1] In this context most interest centres on the situation where one of the parents in a mixed marriage is Catholic, in view of the application by the Catholic Church of the Ne Temere decree, particularly its provisions regarding the upbringing of children.

This report reveals that mixed marriages have had a profound effect on the numbers of births and the birth rates associated with the minority religious communities, especially in more recent decades. This has arisen because the number of mixed marriages is quite sizeable in relation to the number of homogamous marriages where both spouses are from the minority communities, and because within these marriages the great majority of children are brought up as Catholics. Special tabulations taken from the 1981 census indicate that 19 per cent of all married persons from the minority religious communities were in mixed marriages in that year, and within these marriages 86 per cent of the children were Catholics. By 1991 the corresponding proportion of mixed marriages had risen to one quarter, but the related percentage of Catholic children had decreased to 78.

It is clear therefore that the incidence of mixed marriages has been rising, in fact the analysis contained in section 4 of this report indicate that the numbers of mixed marriages must have been increasing for some considerable time prior to 1981. These findings are consistent with those noted by Bowen (1983) who estimated that mixed marriages increased progressively in the post-war period, having been (in his view) of much less importance prior to that time. Mixed marriages have therefore, been a significant influence affecting the trend in the population of the minority religious communities especially when their cumulative and intergenerational affects are taken into account. One is indeed moved to conclude that the *measured* fall in fertility for the minority religious communities in recent decades is to a significant degree attributable to an increasing incidence of mixed marriages. This would have had a direct impact on the numbers of births and the birth rate for the minority communities, with consequential effects in accelerating the decline in their population numbers.

NUPTIALITY

While the fertility levels for the minority communities in Ireland may be lower than those for Catholics, the incidence of marriage within these communities has tended to be somewhat higher. However, the differences involved are not substantial and are not of a sufficient magnitude to offset (in terms of numbers of births) the relatively lower fertility associated with the minority group. If one takes marriage or nuptiality rates based on the numbers of married women in the fertile age band 15-44 years as a proportion of all women in this age group, the ratio for the minority communities is about 10 per cent higher than that for Catholics.

THE JEWISH COMMUNITY

The Jewish Community expanded rapidly in size in the late nineteenth century and the early part of this century, mainly because of inward migration from Eastern Europe. By 1946 the total population of the community had reached almost 4,000. Thereafter, however, it underwent a rapid decline due to emigration. The most recent census figures for 1991 put the total population of the Jewish community at just under 1,600.

OVERVIEW

To summarize briefly therefore, emigration in the 1920s and up to the period of the end of the second world war was the initial factor which precipitated the fall in the population of the minority communities. This had the effect of not only directly depleting their numbers, it also created a growing imbalance in the age structure of these communities as the majority of those who emigrated were young. This in turn gave rise to fewer births because of smaller numbers in the younger age groups and a rising death rate because of the growing preponderance of older persons within the group. In fact even as early as the 1926-36 period, deaths were exceeding births within the minority communities, i.e. the group was not sustaining itself in population terms, apart altogether from the effects of outward migration.

In the post war era the rate of emigration for the minority religious communities declined but the number of births continued to fall. Initially this would have been due to still declining numbers in the younger age groups (i.e. particularly those aged between 25 and 39 years). However, these numbers eventually stabilized and the continuation of low birth numbers is more likely to have been due to a rising incidence of mixed marriages and the associated loss of members for the minority communities which this entailed.

The intrinsically low fertility levels within the minority religious communities would not *of themselves* have precipitated a fall in the size of this group (even though they would, of course, be a constraint on potential growth). Other factors, such as emigration and mixed marriages were, at different periods, the main influences, even though the prior existence of relatively low fertility levels for the minority groups served to accentuate their effects.

The numbers in the minority communities stabilized in the 1970s and began to increase in the 1980s. This arose because of a substantial rise in the 'other stated religions category' which comprises a diversity of small, mainly Christian religious groupings. This increase can be attributed largely to transfers from other religious groups, mainly from the Catholic community. Throughout this more recent period numbers in the larger traditional Protestant Churches, such as the Church of Ireland, Methodists and Presbyterians, continued to decline, albeit at a diminished pace.

It is difficult to predict what the future may hold because of uncertainty about future Irish emigration rates generally and about the composition of the smaller Christian categories. It is likely that in the short term the numbers in the traditional Protestant denominations will continue to decline. However, decreased deaths due to falling numbers in the older age groups should slow this decline. In addition the rising rate of intermarriage may be offset by the falling proportion of Catholic children in such families and this would contribute to lower levels of attrition and, possibly, eventual stabilization of the numbers.

NOTE

1   If the mother is from the minority religious communities and her children are Catholic (which is the most likely outcome), then she is counted in the denominator of the fertility ratio for the minority communities but her children are not included in the numerator. This clearly serves to reduce the value of the index for the minority communities, the extent of this reduction depending on the incidence of mixed marriages and the distribution by religion of the children.

1
INTRODUCTION

THIS STUDY, WHICH WAS COMMISSIONED by the Forum for Peace and Reconciliation, contains an analysis of the demographic situation of the minority religious communities in the area which now constitutes the Republic of Ireland over the period from 1881 to 1991. Apart from providing basic demographic information, an important objective of the study was to identify the causative factors underlying the decline in the minority religious communities, especially the Protestant and Jewish communities, in the context of the changes which occurred in the general population.

The study draws heavily on statistical material relating to religious affiliation contained in past censuses of population. It also has regard to earlier studies on this subject, particularly those of Walsh (1970 and 1975), Kennedy (1973) and Bowen (1983).

The structure of the remainder of this report is as follows. Section 2 describes data sources and the types of classifications used in categorizing different religious groups. Section 3 sets out general trends relating to the numbers in different religious groups over the period from 1881 to 1991, including trends in a geographical context and relating to age profiles. In section 4 certain special factors are analysed which were considered to influence the trend in the numbers in the minority religious communities; these relate to fertility, nuptiality and mixed marriages. This is followed by section 5 which analyses birth and death rates for the minority communities and the associated aspect of natural increase. Section 6 deals with external migration while section 7 is concerned specifically with analysing demographic trends related to the Jewish community.

2

DATA SOURCES: CLASSIFICATIONS

SOURCES

Virtually all of the statistical information used in this study has been derived from past censuses of population which included questions on religious affiliation.[1] While this provides a valuable data source, its limitations must be borne in mind. The replies to all questions on census questionnaires are primarily based on the responses of householders. In the case of the questions on religion, while these yield reasonably clear and precise information in the great majority of cases, there are instances where the responses tend to be somewhat vague, thus giving rise to classification problems in the processing of the census results. An example of this is the growing number of persons who tend to describe themselves in general terms as 'Christian' without any indication of which denomination they belong to (if indeed this is the case). Another problem is the growing number of persons who refuse to provide any answers to the census question on religion, thus rendering it more difficult to analyse trends over time.[2]

Another feature to note is that Irish censuses are conducted on a *de facto* basis, i.e. within each household or institution only those who are present on census night are enumerated. While this has little effect on the overall aggregate census results, it can create some distortions in relation to analysing aspects such as family composition, since family members who are not present in a household on census night are not enumerated in that household. This is of some relevance in the identification in the census of 'mixed marriage' families (i.e. where the spouses are of different religions) as the absence of one spouse means that the family cannot be categorized in this way. In addition, as the census records current religious affiliation only, no account can be taken of conversions. There are aspects which need to be borne in mind in interpreting the analyses of mixed marriages contained in section 4.

It should also be borne in mind that there are limits to the extent that census based data can provide insights of a qualitative or sociological nature, which can be important in analysing phenomena related to religious affiliation. For example, regarding categorizations of children according to religious denomination, what is basically reported in the censuses is the parents' description of the child's religion. The meaning of this reply may be different for children whose parents are of different religious denominations. A child of such parents may have been baptized in a Catholic[3] church and described as such on the census form, but may attend a Protestant school and a Protestant church on occasions. Thus, while the child may not be counted in numerical terms as being a member of the Protestant community, he or she could still be part of that community in many ways.

There are also limitations arising from the data available from past censuses. A subdivision by both religion and age (simultaneously) is not available for censuses prior to 1926; classifications by marital status and age for different religious groups are not available prior to the 1946 census.

CLASSIFICATIONS

Many of the tables included in this report involve a dichotomous classification involving on the one hand 'Catholics' and on the other hand a group which is termed the 'minority religious communities' or the 'minority communities'. The latter includes all of the main Protestant denominations (i.e. the Church of Ireland, Presbyterians, Methodists etc.) as well as the Jewish community and those classified in censuses as belonging to 'other stated religions'. When viewed in aggregate statistical terms, this second category is, therefore, almost exclusively Christian; in fact it is also predominantly Protestant, to the extent of almost 80 per cent in terms of its membership. Where it has been possible to do so, separate figures have been given for as many denominations as possible, but there were obvious limitations to the extent that this could be achieved, for reasons of complexity and due to the fact that many past census tabulations do not contain detailed denominational classifications.

In categorizing persons by religious affiliation the census classifications also identify those who are recorded as having 'no religion' and those who refuse to respond to the census questionnaire on religion. In the results of earlier censuses (i.e. prior to 1961) these categories were generally included with the minority communities group. However, the numbers involved in those periods were extremely small, and their inclusion in this group thus had little effect on the relevant statistical aggregates, or their interpretation. During the 1960s, however, these groups began to assume greater significance and after 1971 they increased substantially in size. Between 1961 and 1991 the numbers who were recorded as having 'no religion' in the census increased from just over 1,000 to more than 66,000, while those who refused to supply information increased from 5,600 to over 83,000.

It is clear that if these groups continued to be amalgamated with the minority communities it would be impossible to derive any meaningful interpretation from the census data for recent decades regarding these communities. Thus for the period from 1961 on the 'no information' group has been included with Catholics and the 'no religion group' is either shown separately, or also, grouped with Catholics. In a statistical sense this is based primarily on practical considerations in order to facilitate interpretation. In the case of those who refused information, it was clear that they were predominantly Catholic: to assume otherwise would have implied a massive reduction in the minority communities population in recent decades — an eventuality which did not, in fact, occur. It should also be noted that the age profile from this group is markedly similar to that for Catholics and does not, for example, involve disproportionally larger numbers in the older age groups which is characteristic of the minority communities group as a whole. Similar considerations apply to the 'no religion' group, especially in regard to the very large increase in numbers in this group between 1971 and 1991 (nearly 65,000). It will be demonstrated in section 6 of this report that this increase must have consisted primarily of transfers from other religious groups, mainly from the Catholic community. It should be borne in mind, in any case, that the predominant size of the Catholic community is such that grouping the 'no religion' category with Catholics means that any derived statistics or indicators still reflect the salient characteristics of the Catholic community. It is only in the case of net migration data, which are estimated as residuals, that it is necessary (in section 6) to present a more complex analysis for recent decades involving a wide range of religious categories, including the 'no religion' group.

A further (and perhaps the most important) reason for adopting this revised grouping *was that the main focus of the study centred on the minority religious communities*. It was appropriate, therefore, for analytical reasons to devise a categorization procedure which preserved their distinctiveness (at least when viewed in aggregate) and which allowed us to meaningfully analyse trends over an extended period.

3
GENERAL TRENDS

NATIONAL TRENDS

The overall position regarding trends in the numbers of persons with different religious groups for the area which now constitutes the Republic of Ireland over the period from 1881 to 1991 is set out in Tables 1(A) and 1(B). Let us first consider the earliest period in our analysis, extending over the thirty years from 1881 to 1911, during which time the population of the area referred to declined by nearly 20 per cent, from 3.87 million to 3.14 million. The figures do not indicate any material trend difference for various religious groups, apart from the Jewish community which increased very rapidly, from less than 400 to nearly 4,000.[4] The Catholic population fell by over 650,000 during this time (nearly 0.7 per cent on an annual average basis) while the total for the minority religious communities as a whole fell by some 78,000, which reflects a similar rate of relative decrease. Broadly speaking, the rate of decrease during this period was much the same for the various Protestant denominations distinguished in the Tables.

The next period involved, from 1911 to 1926, was clearly one of special interest as it covered events of great political significance, notably the Great War of 1914-18 and, more importantly in a national context, the achievement of independence from the United Kingdom in 1921 of the area which now constitutes the Republic of Ireland. The latter event was attended by a considerable degree of political and social upheaval, including the armed conflict with the British security forces between 1919 and 1921 and internal civil war in 1922-23.

The figures indicate significant differences in the trends in the numbers for different religious groups during this period. While the Catholic population recorded a modest decline (0.2 per cent on an annual average basis), the decrease for the minority religious groups was much more rapid. This was over 2.5 per cent on an annual average basis, or more than three times the annual average rate of decline which prevailed for this group in the earlier period between 1881 and 1911. In absolute terms this involved a decline of over 106,000 in the population of the minority communities between 1911 and 1926 (from 327,000 to 221,000). The evidence suggests that this decrease was on a similar scale for individual Protestant denominations. The causation underlying this decrease is clearly a matter of considerable significance and is discussed in more detail later in this report. We will but comment briefly at this stage to the effect that outward migration among the indigenous minority community was an important factor, apart from the withdrawal of British security and administrative personnel who obviously left the country in large numbers during the period of political transition in 1922.

Over the succeeding twenty years, from 1926 to 1946, there was a slight rise in the Catholic population but the numbers in the minority communities continued to show a decline.

This was on a lower scale than that which occurred between 1911 and 1926 but it was still of significant proportions (1.3 per cent per annum), resulting in a fall in the minority communities population of nearly 52,000. In fact this decline more than offset the small increase in the Catholic population (35,000) and was thus the primary reason behind the overall fall in the total Irish population between 1926 and 1946.

The decrease in the size of the minority communities continued at much the same pace in the immediate post World War II period. However, the Catholic population also declined during this time, albeit at a slower pace. At this point, however, the decreases must be viewed primarily in the context of the economic circumstances which then prevailed. The 1950s was a period of deep recession and net emigration reached extremely high levels, especially in the latter half of the decade. The extent of the economic difficulties during this period is signalled by the fact that the national population reached its lowest ever level, 2,818,000, in 1961.

The position began to change after 1960 with the advent of more rapid economic growth and, as a consequence, significant increases in the total Irish population. While this overall growth inevitably gave rise to an expansion in the majority Catholic population, changes began to occur for other denominations as well. The rate of decline for the latter groups slowed noticeably in the 1960s; in the following decade this de-cline was completely arrested (i.e. the minority communities population stabilized between 1971 and 1981). In the 1980s the numbers in these religious groups actually showed a marked increase. This most recent trend (which involved a 15 per cent rise, or nearly 20,000 persons between 1981 and 1991) represents a faster rate of increase than for Catholics, the numbers of which rose by less than 1 per cent (some 24,000) during this period.

TABLE 1(A)

PERSONS OF DIFFERENT RELIGIOUS DENOMINATIONS AT EACH CENSUS: 1881–1946, 1961, 1971 AND 1981

Year	Religious denomination						Total Minority Community	No Religion	Not Stated	Total Persons
	Catholic	Church of Ireland	Presbyterian	Methodist	Jewish	Other stated Religions				
1881	3 465 332	317 576	56 498	17 660	394	12 560	404 688			3 870 020
1891	3 099 003	286 804	51 469	18 513	1 506	11 399	369 691			3 468 694
1901	2 878 271	264 264	46 714	17 872	3 006	11 696	343 552			3 221 823
1911	2 812 509	249 535	45 486	16 440	3 805	11 913	327 179			3 139 688
1926	2 751 269	164 215	32 429	10 663	3 686	9 730	220 723			2 971 992
1936	2 773 920	145 030	28 067	9 649	3 749	8 005	194 500			2 968 420
1946	2 786 033	124 829	23 870	8 355	3 907	8 113	169 074			2 955 107
1961	2 673 473	104 016	18 953	6 676	3 255	5 236	138 136	1 107	5 625	2 818 341
1971	2 795 666	97 739	16 052	5 646	2 633	6 248	128 318	7 616	46 648	2 978 248
1981	3 204 476	95 366	14 255	5 790	2 127	10 843	128 381	39 572	70 976	3 443 405
1991	3 228 327	89 187	13 199	5 037	1 581	38 743	147 747	66 270	83 375	3 525 719

TABLE 1(B)

ANNUAL AVERAGE CHANGES IN POPULATION FOR DIFFERENT RELIGIOUS DENOMINATIONS

IN SUBPERIODS BETWEEN 1881 AND 1991

Year	Religious denomination						Total Minority Community	No Religion	Not Stated	Total Persons
	Catholic	Church of Ireland	Presbyterian	Methodist	Jewish	Other stated Religions				
1881–1911	-0.69	-0.80	-0.72	-0.24	7.85	-0.18	-0.71			-0.69
1911–1926	-0.15	-2.75	-2.23	-2.84	-0.21	-1.34	-2.59			-0.37
1926–1946	0.06	-1.36	-1.52	-1.21	0.29	-0.90	-1.32			-0.03
1946–1961	-0.27	-1.21	-1.53	-1.48	-1.21	-2.88	-1.34			-0.32
1961–1971	0.45	-0.62	-1.65	-1.66	-2.10	1.78	-0.73	21.27	23.56	0.55
1971–1981	1.37	-0.25	-1.18	0.25	-2.11	5.67	0.00	17.91	4.29	1.46
1981–1991	0.07	-0.67	-0.77	-1.38	-2.92	13.58	1.41	5.29	1.62	0.24

Note: Prior to 1961 persons with 'no religion' and persons who refused to provide information on religious affiliation are included with 'other stated religions'.

Within the minority communities group, however, some diverse trends were evident. The increases in the 1980s applied exclusively to those classified in the census as 'other stated religions', amongst whom a diversity of smaller Christian denominations formed a significant part.[5] In fact the Church of Ireland, Presbyterian and Methodist communities continued to decrease in numbers in the 1980s. As this was a period of substantial net migratory outflows, it is implausible to suggest that this increase can be attributed to inward population movements. Consequently it must have occurred at the expense of other denominations. This inevitably raises the question as to which religious groups were primarily affected in terms of loss of members, an issue which will be considered later in this report.[6]

In recent decades there has also been a rapid rise in the numbers of persons who profess to have no religion. The numbers so recorded was only just over 1,000 at the 1961 census, but it had risen to over 66,000 by 1991.[7] The number who refuse to provide information on their religious beliefs in the census has also being growing. This total was only some 5,500 in 1961 but increased to over 83,000 at the 1991 census. This latter phenomenon, in view of its increasing scale, creates problems in interpreting the census data as it is not clear whether those who refuse to provide this information derive proportionately from the different religious denominations. However, the current size of the group, and the scale of the increases, indicate that the great majority are Catholics. If this were not the case, there would have had to be an extremely large parallel decline in the minority communities population.

GEOGRAPHICAL ASPECTS

Basic data relating to geographical distribution for different religious denominations are given in Appendix Table A2 which shows absolute population numbers by province for the census years from 1881 to 1991. These are transformed into relative changes (annual averages) for selected periods in Table 2 following.

Turning first to the earliest period analysed (1881–1911), Table 2 shows that the broadly comparable rates of relative decline applied to both Catholics and the minority communities in provincial areas. There were, however, very modest increases in Dublin for both groups. The rates of decline for the minority communities were somewhat more rapid in Connacht and Ulster, a feature which may have been connected with the land distribution provisions which came into force during this time.

The data show that the sharp decline in the minority communities population between 1911 and 1926 did not apply evenly throughout the country. The largest relative decreases occurred in Munster, Leinster (excluding Dublin), and Connacht, while those in Dublin, and in particular in the three counties of Ulster, were below the national average decline. The relatively large decrease in the minority communities in Leinster was to some degree associated with very substantial falls in some counties which contained large British army garrisons, particularly Kildare and Westmeath.[8] One can only speculate as to the reasons for the more rapid population decline for this group in Munster and Connacht. In these areas these communities were small and thinly spread and it may well be that, in the context of the times, a greater sense of apprehension prevailed which precipitated a greater outflow. It is noticeable in this regard that in the three Ulster counties, where the minority population was more numerous, the relative decline in their numbers was well below the national average. It does not follow, however, that all of those who moved from areas such as Munster and Connacht during this period migrated out of the country. Some may have moved to other areas and, indeed, this may serve to explain the relatively low annual average fall in the minority communities population in Dublin during this time. One would have expected the decrease in the Dublin area to be, if anything, significantly above the national average in view of the large numbers of British security and administrative personnel who were present there prior to 1921, the great majority of whom left when the national administration changed.

Between 1926 and 1946, even though the overall scale of the decline for the minority communities was less, higher than average relative decreases again occurred in Munster and Connacht and also, on this occasion, in the three Ulster counties. The annual average rate of decline for each of these provincial areas was somewhat less than 2 per cent while that for Leinster (excluding Dublin) was about 1 per cent and that for Dublin about 0.75 per cent. Between 1945 and 1961 the

TABLE 2

ANNUAL AVERAGE PERCENTAGE CHANGES IN POPULATION FOR
DIFFERENT RELIGIOUS DENOMINATIONS IN SUBPERIODS
BETWEEN 1881 AND 1991, BY PROVINCE

Period	Catholic	Other Denominations	No Religion	No Information	Total Persons
State			%		
1881–1911	−0.69	−0.70			−0.69
1911–1926	−0.15	−2.59			−0.37
1926–1946	0.06	−1.32			−0.03
1946–1961	−0.27	−1.34			−0.32
1961–1971	0.45	−0.73	21.27	23.56	0.55
1971–1981	1.37	0.00	17.91	4.29	1.46
1981–1991	0.07	1.41	5.29	1.62	0.24
Leinster (Excl. Dublin)					
1881–1911	−0.77	−0.65			−0.76
1911–1926	−0.17	−3.00			−0.41
1926–1946	0.10	−1.30			0.01
1946–1961	−0.30	−1.08			−0.33
1961–1971	0.44	−0.42	23.08	20.66	0.51
1971–1981	1.89	0.85	18.84	7.88	2.00
1981–1991	0.51	1.47	5.28	0.76	0.60
Dublin					
1881–1911	0.53	0.10			0.44
1911–1926	0.97	−2.30			0.39
1926–1946	1.41	−0.75			1.15
1946–1961	0.96	−1.14			0.81
1961–1971	1.60	−0.91	22.69	25.43	1.72
1971–1981	1.58	−0.58	15.46	2.45	1.64
1981–1991	0.02	1.51	4.97	0.14	0.22
Munster					
1881–1911	−0.83	−0.93			−0.83
1911–1926	−0.27	−3.67			−0.44
1926–1946	−0.23	−1.83			−0.28
1946–1961	−0.51	−1.00			−0.51
1961–1971	0.27	0.04	15.84	22.49	0.38
1971–1981	1.13	0.68	21.37	5.24	1.25
1981–1991	−0.09	2.28	5.96	3.47	0.11

TABLE 2 – CONTINUED

ANNUAL AVERAGE PERCENTAGE CHANGES IN POPULATION FOR
DIFFERENT RELIGIOUS DENOMINATIONS IN SUBPERIODS
BETWEEN 1881 AND 1991, BY PROVINCE

Period	Catholic	Other Denominations	No Religion	No Information	Total Persons
			%		
Connacht					
1881–1911	−0.95	−1.71			−0.98
1911–1926	−0.59	−2.97			−0.66
1926–1946	−0.54	−1.95			−0.57
1946–1961	−1.06	−1.78			−1.07
1961–1971	−0.82	−0.80	19.79	24.22	−0.70
1971–1981	0.72	0.62	29.91	3.59	0.83
1981–1991	−0.22	2.73	6.34	3.32	−0.03
Ulster (pt)					
1881–1911	−0.86	−1.17			−0.93
1911–1926	−0.40	−1.69			−0.65
1926–1946	−0.43	−1.69			−0.64
1946–1961	−1.17	−2.04			−1.28
1961–1971	−0.47	−1.34	27.10	20.53	−0.48
1971–1981	1.17	−0.68	22.11	5.12	1.06
1981–1991	0.06	−0.27	2.99	2.66	0.09

relative rates of decrease for the minority communities were again relatively more rapid in Connacht and Ulster (approaching 2 per cent on an annual average basis) whereas for other regions the rates of decline were about half this level.

An interesting feature of the trends for the 1960s is the relatively sharp decrease indicated for the minority religious groups in Dublin (about 1 per cent annual average as against a national figure of about 0.7 per cent). In the preceding period the rate of decline of the minority communities in Dublin had been noticeably less than in provincial areas. Interestingly this pattern continued into the 1970s. Between 1971 and 1981 these communities in Dublin decreased by 0.6 per cent on an annual average basis, while in Munster, Connacht and in Leinster (excluding Dublin) the group actually experienced an increase in numbers.

During the 1980s when the minority communities as a whole increased significantly in numbers, this rise applied to varying degrees in all regions except in the Ulster counties where the numbers in this group continued to fall. In fact a noticeable feature of the trend for the minority religious group in these three counties is that, even though they experienced a much smaller decrease during the eventful 1911–1926 period, since that time they have consistently recorded a more rapid rate of decline than that which applied nationally. To some degree this can be attributed to the fact that the minority religious groups outside of the main Protestant denominations did not record an increase in the three Ulster counties as they did elsewhere.

AGE STRUCTURES

We will conclude this general overview by considering the age structures for different religious groupings. The basic population data, taken from past censuses from 1926 on are given in Appendix Table A3, while in Table 3 following these are expressed in the form of percentage distributions.

The most significant feature to emerge from these data is the markedly older age profile of the minority communities population. Table 3 shows that nearly 16 per cent of this group were aged 65 years or over in 1991, compared with 11.5 per cent for Catholics. The former proportion is quite high, even by international standards, especially when one bears in mind that it was much higher in the recent past (it was nearly 18 per cent in 1971). The 1995 European Union Annual Demographic Statistics Report indicates a corresponding proportion of 15.1 per cent for the EU (15 States), a figure of 13.0 per cent for the wider grouping of States which it terms 'the more developed countries', and 12.7 per cent for the US.

At the other end of the age spectrum it will be noted that the population proportion aged less than 5 years within the minority community has been consistently less than that for Catholics. In 1991 the relevant proportions were 6.3 per cent and 7.8 per cent respectively, and 7.1 per cent and 10.3 per cent in 1981. There appears, therefore, to have been some convergence with regard to the shares for the youngest age group in the 1980s. This was a period when the total number of births fell very rapidly, a feature which seems to have applied more particularly to the Catholic population.

The differences in age structure between the Catholic and the minority religious communities were not as marked in earlier periods. This applied particularly to the proportions in the older age groups which did not differ to a very significant degree in the 1920s, for example. However, these differences became noticeably more pronounced as time progressed. We will defer for the present any detailed comment on the causation underlying these changes except to mention that high emigration among the minority community in the 1920s and in succeeding decades was an important factor. This issue is discussed in some detail in section 6.

It is relevant to refer to one further aspect in regard to age distributions. This concerns that part of the minority religious group related to those in the 'other stated religions' category. As already indicated this group underwent very rapid growth over the past twenty years. The age distribution for this group (which is not given in the accompanying tables) is very different from that of the minority communities as a whole. Relatively few persons are in the older age categories (only some 5 per cent are aged over 65 years) and there is a very heavy concentration in the 25-44 year age band which contains nearly 40 per cent of the total as against only 29 per cent for the minority population as a whole. This feature is consistent with the previously stated contention that the expansion of this group has been due mainly to transfers from other religious categories.

TABLE 3
DISTRIBUTION OF THE POPULATION FOR DIFFERENT
RELIGIOUS GROUPS CLASSIFIED BY AGE, 1926–1991

Religion, Age	1926	1936	1946	1961	1971	1981	1991
				%			
Catholics							
0–2 years	5.8	5.6	6.3	6.6		6.3	4.5
3–4	4.1	3.7	3.8	4.3	10.8	4.0	3.3
5–14	19.8	18.9	18.2	20.8	21.0	20.4	19.3
15–24	17.8	17.8	16.6	14.0	16.3	17.6	17.2
25–34	13.4	13.4	14.0	10.6	10.8	13.5	13.8
35–44	11.5	11.9	12.0	12.0	10.1	10.3	12.8
45–64	18.5	19.3	18.8	20.9	20.2	17.2	17.6
65+	9.0	9.4	10.3	10.9	10.8	10.6	11.4
Total	100.0	100.0	100.0	100.0	100.0	100.0	100.0
Other Denominations							
0–2 years	4.0	3.3	4.5	4.0		4.3	3.7
3–4	2.9	2.4	2.7	2.6	7.0	2.8	2.6
5–14	15.8	13.8	12.6	14.4	14.2	14.6	14.6
15–24	16.1	15.6	12.6	12.5	13.7	14.0	13.8
25–34	13.3	14.3	13.0	10.1	11.3	14.4	14.3
35–44	12.9	13.0	14.1	12.0	10.5	12.0	14.8
45–64	23.6	24.7	24.8	27.5	25.9	20.5	20.3
65+	11.4	12.9	15.7	17.0	17.5	17.4	15.7
Total	100.0	100.0	100.0	100.0	100.0	100.0	100.0
No Religion							
0–2 years						6.5	4.1
3–4					9.2	3.3	2.5
5–14					9.9	9.7	9.3
15–24					21.1	19.1	17.8
25–34					25.8	33.0	25.5
35–44					12.8	14.2	23.0
45–64					15.6	10.2	14.4
65+					5.7	4.0	3.5
Total					100.0	100.0	100.0

TABLE 3 — CONTINUED

DISTRIBUTION OF THE POPULATION FOR DIFFERENT

RELIGIOUS GROUPS CLASSIFIED BY AGE, 1926–1991

Religion, Age	1926	1936	1946	1961	1971	1981	1991
			%				
No Information							
0–2 years						7.9	6.4
3–4					11.7	4.3	3.9
5–14					20.7	19.8	19.3
15–24					16.5	17.2	15.6
25–34					11.2	17.4	13.9
35–44					10.3	11.3	13.5
45–64					18.6	14.6	16.9
65+					11.1	7.4	10.5
Total					100.0	100.0	100.0
All Persons							
0–2 years	5.7	5.4	6.2	6.5		6.3	4.5
3–4	4.0	3.6	3.8	4.2	10.6	4.0	3.3
5–14	19.5	18.6	17.9	20.5	20.7	20.1	18.9
15–24	17.7	17.6	16.3	13.9	16.2	17.5	17.1
25–34	13.4	13.5	14.0	10.6	10.9	13.9	14.1
35–44	11.6	12.0	12.1	12.0	10.1	10.4	13.1
45–64	18.9	19.6	19.1	21.3	20.4	17.1	17.6
65+	9.1	9.7	10.6	11.2	11.1	10.7	11.4
Total	100.0	100.0	100.0	100.0	100.0	100.0	100.0

4

FACTORS AFFECTING THE TREND
IN THE NUMBERS
IN THE MINORITY RELIGIOUS COMMUNITIES

The significant changes which have affected the minority religious communities in Ireland illustrated in the preceding section immediately prompt questions as to *why* these changes occurred. This section of the report is concerned primarily with a number of such causative issues. It is important to bear in mind however, that causations and outcomes can be interactive in the particular context involved here, especially over time. It is clear, for example, that various influences (e.g. migration) must have played a role in bringing about the changes in the age structure of the minority religious communities. However, these changes can, in turn, exert further causation. Changing age structures can, for example, exert an influence through their effects on birth and mortality levels and, as a consequence, on the rate of natural increase in a population (or subpopulation). However, the primary causative factors which we will discuss in this section relate to fertility, nuptiality, and the related question of mixed marriages. Each of these three influences will now be considered in turn. Migration is clearly a further candidate for consideration in this regard, but we will defer discussion of this aspect until section 6, as it fits more logically into the sequence of our analysis at that point.

FERTILITY

The usual method employed to analyse fertility within a population is to relate numbers of births in a given period (usually a year) to the female population in the fertile age groups (i.e. between 15 and 44 years). However this cannot be readily done in the context of comparing religious denominations as the official birth statistics do not involve a classification by religion. One can, however, by using census data classified by religious group, estimate relevant rates by relating the numbers of very young children enumerated (e.g. aged less than 1 year, less than 2 years, etc.) to the number of women in the above-mentioned fertile age band. Such estimations would not, of course, yield the same results as those based on birth registration data (it would, for example, exclude children who died soon after birth) but they would not differ significantly and they should be sufficient to show up any relative differences between religious groups, especially if these are substantial. Such calculations are given in Table 4 for marital births only in the form of estimated annual average births per 1,000 married women aged 15 to 44 years. The analysis is restricted to births within marriage as those still form the great majority of all births and there is still a much greater propensity for married women to have children, even though the proportion of extra-marital births in the overall total has been increasing significantly in recent years.[9] This approach is basically the same as that followed by Walsh (1970), in fact the figures represent a continuation of his data which related to 1946 and 1961.[10] In addition to the actual indicators as described, Table 4 also contains ratios (in column 4) which show the relationship between the fertility rates for Catholics and the minority communities.

TABLE 4

ESTIMATED ANNUAL AVERAGE LIVE MARITAL BIRTHS PER 1,000
MARRIED WOMEN AGED 15 TO 44 YEARS,
BY RELIGIOUS DENOMINATION

Year	Catholic	Other Denominations	Ratio of Catholic/OD Fertility (2)/(3)
(1)	(2)	(3)	(4)
1946	275.4	179.2	1.54
1961	254.6	151.3	1.68
1971	228.0	146.4	1.56
1981	185.5	119.2	1.56
1991	118.5	91.4	1.30

Sources: (1) Walsh, B.M., *Religion and Demographic Behaviour in Ireland*, ESRI, 1970. General Research Series, Paper No 55.
(2) Censuses of population 1971, 1981, 1991.

Notes: (1) The annual average number of births in each year was calculated by taking the population aged 0 to 2 and dividing by 3. The number of marital births for each religious group was then estimated by applying the national proportion of such births.
(2) For the years 1946 and 1961 the category 'other denominations' includes those who indicated that they had 'no religion' and those who did not provide information in the censuses on religious affiliation. For these years, however, the numbers involved for these two groups were extremely small. For later years (1971, 1981, 1991) the 'other denominations' category consists of the main Protestant religions and 'other stated religions', but excludes those with no religion and persons who declined to provide information on their religion in censuses. It is considered that this procedure ensures that the fertility indicator for the 'other denominations' group is reasonably consistent over the entire period in question.

The figures show that Catholic fertility levels have been consistently higher than those for the minority communities. Between 1946 and 1981 the relative excess was, broadly speaking, more than 55 per cent. During the 1980s, however, it is clear that Catholic fertility fell much more rapidly with the result that by 1991 the relevant indicator for this group was some 30 per cent higher than that for the minority group (the actual figures being 118.5 and 91.4). In demographic terms this (1991) relative excess, though less than for earlier periods, is still of significant proportions.

The relative differences in fertility levels between Catholics and the minority community as indicated by this analysis are not unexpected. As has long been acknowledged, and demonstrated, there are significant differences in fertility levels between the Catholic and minority communities population.[11] However, a somewhat surprising feature of the results is the extent of the fall in fertility for the minority communities over the period concerned, which was not a great deal less than that for the Catholic community. Between 1946 and 1991 Catholic fertility as measured by the indicators in Table 4 declined by over 55 per cent while that for the minority religious communities group decreased by almost 50 per cent. The decrease in fertility for the latter was particularly rapid during the 1970s when the decline equalled that for Catholics. One would, perhaps, have expected smaller decreases for the minority community, given the much lower actual fertility levels which initially prevailed.

There are possible reasons for this which are not necessarily related to fertility as such. One relates to the incidence of mixed marriages which, as we shall subsequently illustrate, can exert a significant influence on the indicators involved here. This is because of the likelihood of the relative displacement of mothers and children in a mixed marriage situation in regard to their inclusion (or exclusion) in the numerator and the denominator in the above mentioned index. If, for example, a mother from the minority communities has children who are Catholics (and this, as we shall later demonstrate, is the most likely outcome in a mixed marriage) she is included in the denominator of the relevant index for that community *but her children are not*. This has the effect of reducing the value of the index for the minority group, and increasing it for Catholics, even though the impact in the latter case is negligible due to the overall size of the Catholic population. This issue is discussed in more detail later in this section of the report.

There is an interesting corollary to this. If one accepts the proposition that mixed marriages were a significant factor in curtailing the number of births in the minority communities (and later evidence presented suggests that this was indeed the case) then it is likely that actual or real fertility levels within these communities may not have fallen all that much in the post war period; in fact they may have even increased slightly.

There are, of course, other factors which can exert an influence on the differences in the fertility levels indicated for the two groups in question. One such influence is social group structure which is significantly different for Catholics and the minority religious communities. This aspect is considered in some detail Appendix I. This, however, shows that variations in social structure between the two denominations would not, of themselves, give rise to the differences between the aggregate fertility levels set out in Table 4. Differences in the age distribution of married women in the fertile age band (15 to 44 years) for the two religious groups is another such possible influence. However, an inspection of these distributions for the two denominational categories for 1946 and 1991 reveals little difference between them, in either year. Furthermore, these structures have changed little over time, and to the extent that they have (e.g. relatively larger proportions in the younger age groups) they have applied equally to both groups. Thus, this factor is unlikely to have affected the fertility comparisons given in Table 4, either in cross-sectional terms for any one year, or over time.[12]

NUPTIALITY

Let us now consider the question of marriage rates or the degree of nuptiality in the population as a whole for different religious groups. This is still an important aspect to consider, even when viewed against the background of increasing numbers of extra-marital births, as married women are still much more likely to bear children than single women. Births within marriage still account for over 80 per cent of all births. It is, of course, even more important in analysing trends for past periods when the proportion of extra-marital births was very much smaller.

TABLE 5

NUPTIALITY RATES BY RELIGION FOR WOMEN AGED 15 TO 44 YEARS

Year	Catholic	Other Denominations	Ratio of Catholic/OD Nuptiality
(1)	(2)	(3)	(2)/(3)
1946	38.9	44.8	0.87
1961	46.2	51.2	0.91
1971	49.9	55.9	0.89
1981	56.9	61.0	0.93
1991	50.2	55.7	0.90

Sources: (1)   Walsh, B.M., (1970), *Religion and Demographic Behaviour in Ireland*, ESRI, General Research Series, Paper No 55.

(2)   Censuses of population.

Notes: (1)   The nuptiality rates are the numbers of married women aged 15 to 44 years expressed as a proportion of all women in this age group.

As in the case with the fertility related data, this analysis has to be confined to census years in which questions on religious affiliations were asked. In this (census) context the indicator used is a simple one, namely the number of married women in the fertile age group, 15 – 44 years, taken as a percentage of all women in this age band. The relevant figures are given in Table 5 covering census years from 1946 to 1991.[13]

This indicator shows that Catholic nuptiality has been consistently lower than that for the minority communities, broadly speaking by about 10 per cent. The evidence indicates that the divergence was somewhat greater in earlier periods (e.g. in the 1940s). The nuptiality rates increased for both communities between 1946 and 1981; both rates then declined markedly in the 1980s, even though the relationship between the two indicators remained largely unchanged.

Walsh (1970) noted that nuptiality for the minority communities in the Republic, while higher than that for Catholics, was lower than that for the Protestant community in Northern Ireland. He suggested that this may have been due to the small size of the minority religious groups in the Republic, combined with a desire to avoid intermarriage.

The nuptiality differentials as indicated serve to increase the number of births in the other denominations population relative to those for Catholics. However, it is clear that the scale of the divergence is not substantial and is not sufficient to offset the effects of the relatively lower fertility associated with the minority religious group.

MIXED MARRIAGES

While the somewhat higher incidence of marriage for the minority communities population contributes to increasing the numbers of births for that group relative to the Catholic population, there is another marriage related feature which tends to offset this. This concerns the question of inter-Church or mixed marriages, i.e. where parents are of different religious affiliations. In this context most interest centres on situations where one of the parents is Catholic in view of the application by the Catholic Church of the Ne Temere decree, particularly its provisions regarding the upbringing of children.[14] The following analysis, therefore, relates exclusively to circumstances where one parent is Catholic and the other is of another specific denomination, without any attempt being made to further subdivide the latter category. We have already commented, in the earlier section on fertility, how mixed marriages can influence the indicators of relative fertility as between the denominational groups in question

In order to provide some information on the exact circumstances which prevail in regard to mixed marriages special tabulations were extracted from the 1981 and 1991 censuses which identified families living in private households in which parents were of different religions and which provided counts of the children (of any age) in these families, also classified by religion.[15] The results are summarized in Table 6. This shows that in 1981 there were 6,570 such families enumerated with 14,813 children, of which 12,670 (over 86 per cent) were Catholic. There is some evidence that the Catholic proportion of children tended to be somewhat lower for mothers in the younger age groups. In the 1991 census the number of mixed marriage families had increased to 9,110 and the number of children to 20,420; on this occasion the number of Catholic children, though still substantial at 15,886, constituted a somewhat smaller proportion of the total, nearly 78 per cent.[16]

The data (not shown in the table) also distinguished the religion of the parents and from these there is some evidence that the Catholic proportion of children in a mixed marriage tends to be somewhat higher when the mother is Catholic. The relevant proportions of Catholic children born to Catholic and minority group mothers in 1991 were 81 and 73 per cent respectively.

TABLE 6

NUMBERS OF CHILDREN IN FAMILIES IN PRIVATE HOUSEHOLDS WITH
PARENTS OF DIFFERENT RELIGIONS, 1981 AND 1991

| Age of Mother | No of families | Children | | | Proportion Children Catholic (%) |
		Catholic	Other Denominations	Total	
1981					
15-24	463	508	123	631	80.5
25-34	3 014	5 246	1 073	6 319	83.0
35-44	2 024	4 872	661	5 533	88.1
45-54	717	1 593	161	1 754	90.8
55-64	287	470	30	500	94.0
65+	65	71	5	76	93.4
Total	6 570	12 760	2 053	14 813	86.1
1991					
15-24	248	271	74	345	78.6
25-34	2 792	3 902	1 523	5 425	71.9
35-44	3 828	7 722	2 229	9 951	77.6
45-54	1 682	3 275	575	3 850	85.1
55-64	454	606	113	719	84.3
65+	106	110	20	130	84.6
Total	9 110	15 886	4 534	20 420	77.8

Sources: Special tabulations from the 1981 and 1991 censuses.

Notes: (1)   Couples without children are not included.
             (2)   The children included in this table are of any age.

TABLE 7

NUMBERS OF CHILDREN (OF ANY AGE) IN HOMOGAMOUS AND MIXED
MARRIAGE FAMILIES IN 1981 AND 1991

| Religion of Parents | No of Families | Children | | |
		Catholic	Other Denominations	Total
1981				
Both Catholic	442,868	1,287,469	194	1,287,663
Both Other Denom.	14,298	114	32,679	32,793
Mixed	6,570	12,750	2,053	14,813
1991				
Both Catholic	451,994	1,188,049	520	1,188,569
Both Other Denom.	14,508	337	32,048	32,385
Mixed	9,110	15,886	4,534	20,420

Source: Special tabulations from the 1981 and 1991 censuses.

While these figures (not previously compiled) are of great interest, their real significance emerges when they are compared with comparable data for homogamous Catholic or minority communities families (i.e. in which both parents are either Catholic or of another religious group). This further information is given in Table 7 and shows that in 1991 the number of mixed marriage families (some 9,100) was quite large when viewed in the context of the number of homogamous minority communities families (14,500); the corresponding numbers of children were 20,400 in mixed marriages and 32,400 in homogamous minority communities families.

There are other ways of viewing this aspect, for example by considering rates based on the numbers of married persons from the minority communities who were in mixed marriages taken as a proportion of all married persons from the same religious group. This calculation yields the following results for 1981 and 1991.

MIXED MARRIAGE RATES (%) FOR THE MINORITY COMMUNITIES IN
1981 AND 1991

	Males	Females	Persons
1981	20.4	16.8	18.7
1991	26.4	21.2	23.9

These figures show that in 1991 nearly one quarter of all married persons from the minority religious communities were in mixed marriages. The proportion for males, over 26 per cent, was noticeably higher than for females, 21 per cent. This proportion has been increasing in recent decades; the corresponding overall percentage for 1981 was significantly lower, less than 19 per cent. In fact these data can be used to indicate that the numbers of mixed marriages had been increasing for some considerable time prior to 1981. This can be inferred from the very much higher corresponding proportions among younger married persons in 1981, as illustrated in Appendix Table A4. This table shows that nearly 30 per cent of married persons aged between 15 and 34 years from the minority communities were in mixed marriages at that time. These proportions are broadly comparable with those estimated by Walsh in his 1970 study. The inferences regarding trends are consistent with those observed by Bowen (1983) who estimated that mixed marriages increased progressively in the post war period, having been (in his view) of much less importance prior to that time.[17]

Mixed marriages are therefore very relevant to numerical loss in so far as the minority religious communities are concerned as the children of these marriages are disproportionately brought up as Catholics. These losses assume even greater significance if cumulative or intergenerational effects are taken into account. The evidence suggests therefore, that mixed marriages were a significant factor in contributing to the decline in the minority religious communities in the periods since the second world war. The impact of mixed marriages on the Catholic community (or, more precisely, on the number of Catholic children, which tends to be augmented) is minimal in relative terms, given that the number of homogamous Catholic families in 1991 was over 450,000 with an associated child population of nearly 1,190,000.

It is not clear, however, as to what *alternative* situation regarding the religion of children one might envisage in mixed marriage circumstances. One could consider, for example, a 50:50 subdivision of children in mixed marriages as reflecting a greater degree of equity in a religious context. In effect this practice existed to some degree in Ireland up to the early part of this century prior to the introduction of the Ne Temere decree. The custom sometimes prevailed whereby boys were brought up in the religion of the father and girls in that of the mother. If this criterion were applied to the 1991 data it would have the effect of raising the number of children affiliated to minority religions in mixed marriages from 4,000 to about 10,000, thus increasing the total number of such children from 37,000 to about 43,000.

Much of the emphasis in this section has been on the effect of mixed marriages on the recorded denominational affiliation of children and, in particular the numerical loss to the minority religious communities. It should be borne in mind that mixed marriages are now both an indicator of improved intergroup relations and a positive force for ecumenism, and can promote an enhancement of the religious life of many families. The issue of mixed marriages is deserving of more consideration than can be given here. Further research on this topic, using survey data, is currently being conducted by one of the authors of this report.

5

BIRTH AND DEATH RATES
FOR DIFFERENT RELIGIOUS GROUPS:
RATES OF NATURAL INCREASE

Having dealt with some of the principal factors which influence trends in the numbers in different religious communities, we are now in a somewhat better position to present and interpret a number of standard demographic indicators, i.e. birth and death rates and rates of natural increase.

BIRTH RATES

Turning first to birth rates (which consist simply of total births per thousand of the overall population in question), the relevant data are given in columns 2 to 4 of Table 8 which shows rates for Catholics and the minority communities for intercensal periods between 1926 and 1991. The absolute figures relating to actual births and aggregate population data on which these ratios are based are given in Appendix Table A.5. In a statistical sense the main technical difficulty here centred on categorizing total births according to religious groups for each intercensal period. Basically, the approach adopted was similar to that used in calculating the fertility indicators already discussed. For each census year in which questions on religious affiliation were asked the Catholic and minority communities proportions for the population aged 0 to 2 years was calculated and taken to represent the proportion which would relate to total births in these years. These proportions were then interpolated for the years between censuses and applied to total births in these years in order to give an annual series of births classified by religious group for the entire period from 1926 to 1991. The actual rates given in Table 8 are annual averages for each intercensal period, the relevant population denominators in each case being the average of the total population for each religious group at the beginning and end of the period.

The most noticeable feature is the low rates for the minority communities population when compared with the Catholics over the entire period in question. For the forty five years from 1926 to 1971, the Catholic birth rate exceeded that for minority communities by at least 50 per cent. The relative excess diminished slightly in the 1970s and there was a noticeable decrease in the 1981-1991 period when the relative difference declined to 36 per cent.

This outcome is hardly surprising in view of the results of the preceding analyses. The principal underlying factors derive from the relative fertility differences combined with the effect of mixed marriages. The higher rate of nuptiality among the minority population would have had an offsetting effect, but this was not large enough to have a significant impact.

One might have expected the birth rate for the minority communities to fall over the period in question in view of the decreases recorded in the fertility index as previously mentioned. The answer to this lies partly in the nature of crude birth rates. While the number of births in these communities did, of course, fall throughout this period (especially prior to 1961) the total population was also declining due to the combined effects of high numbers of deaths and outward migration. This served, in statistical terms, to maintain a stable birth rate, but at a very low level. For the Catholic population the sheer weight of the increases in the female population aged 15 to 44 years (especially after 1961) offset the decreases in fertility with the result that the birth rate for this community also remained constant (at a high level) for most of the period in question.

Apart altogether from their values relative to that for the Catholic population, the birth rates for the minority communities are extremely low by any standards, especially in the earlier periods under discussion. This feature was also noted by Walsh in his 1970 study. International data for twenty one countries on birth rates covering the period from 1926 to 1951 contained in the 1954 Report of the Commission on Emigration[18] do not reveal any countries with birth rates as low as those indicated for the minority communities in Ireland during this period. The lowest rate indicated in this source (14.7) was that for Belgium in the 1936-1945 period; most of the rates quoted were significantly higher than this. For later periods, the birth rates for minority communities are broadly similar to those prevailing in other countries. In the European Union (15 countries), for example, in the 1980s the overall birth rate was between 12 and 13 — a very similar figure to that indicated for the minority religious category in 1981-1991 given in Table 8.

TABLE 8

ANNUAL AVERAGE RATES PER 1,000 OF THE AVERAGE POPULATION FOR BIRTHS, DEATHS, NATURAL INCREASE AND NET MIGRATION FOR PAST INTERCENSAL PERIODS, BY RELIGION

Period	Birth Rates			Death Rates			Rates of Natural Increase		
	Catholic	Other Denom.	Total	Catholic	Other Denom.	Total	Catholic	Other Denom.	Total
				Annual average rates per 1,000 of the average population					
(1)	(2)	(3)	(4)	(5)	(6)	(7)	(8)	(9)	(10)
1926-36	20.1	13.0	19.6	14.0	16.6	14.2	6.2	-3.6	5.5
1936-46	20.8	13.5	20.3	14.2	17.9	14.5	6.5	-4.3	5.9
1946-61	22.1	14.7	21.7	12.4	16.2	12.6	9.6	-1.5	9.0
1961-71	21.9	14.1	21.6	11.1	17.1	11.4	10.8	-3.0	10.2
1971-81	21.9	14.7	21.6	10.1	16.1	10.4	11.8	-1.5	11.3
1981-91	17.7	13.0	17.5	9.1	12.5	9.3	8.6	0.4	8.3

Source: See Appendix Table A5.

Notes: (1)   For the period from 1926 to 1961 persons recorded as having 'no religion' and those who did not provide information on their religion are included with the 'other denominations' category. During this period the numbers involved were very small. For the period from 1961 to 1991 these two categories are included with Catholics. See text for an explanation of these groupings.

DEATH RATES

The intrinsically low birth rates evident for the minority communities immediately raises questions as to whether these rates exceed the corresponding death rates. A relevant factor here is that the older age profile for the minority communities would suggest a relatively high death rate. This in turn, focuses attention on the natural increase (births minus deaths) for these communities. This is discussed in the next section.

Death rates for the two religious groupings in question are given in columns 5 to 7 of Table 8.[19] The actual rates do, indeed, show that the mortality for the minority communities is significantly greater than that for Catholics, and that the relative differential has widened substantially over the years. In the 1926-1936 period the rate for the minority religious group, at 16.6 per 1,000 of the average population, was nearly 20 per cent higher than the corresponding rate for Catholics, which was 14 per cent. By the 1970s this differential had widened to over 50 per cent, even though it declined thereafter. The fact that such a differential existed as early as the 1920s would derive from the fact that even at this stage the minority communities were beginning to exhibit a growing distortion in their age profile, involving a preponderance of older persons. This was principally due to the heavy emigration which occurred within these communities between 1911 and 1926. Over succeeding decades the death rate for the entire Irish population (and by implication for the Catholic community) declined, mainly as a result of advances in medical and health care, the number reaching a level of 9.3 by 1991, compared with 14.2 between 1926 and 1936. These influences also applied, of course, to the minority communities, but the increasing proportion of older persons within this group exerted an offsetting influence and the death rate remained more or less constant until 1981. During the 1980s the death rate for this group fell noticeably to 12.5. In so far as one can determine, this was mainly due to a marked decline in the numbers in the 45 to 64 year age band between 1971 and 1981, a group that would have aged further in 1981-1991 and thus contributed to relatively fewer deaths. In other words the decline can be attributed to the onward movement in age of progressively smaller cohorts within the minority communities which had been depleted by emigration in earlier periods.

RATES OF NATURAL INCREASE

The death rates for the minority communities population exceeded the corresponding birth rates for all of the period covered except between 1981 and 1991. This gave rise to negative rates of natural increase i.e. apart altogether from any net gains or losses due to migration, these communities were not sustaining themselves in numerical terms (see columns 8 to 10 of Table 8). Throughout the entire period covered, the rate of natural increase for the Catholic population has been strongly positive, even though the total Catholic population declined on many occasions during this time span, or exhibited only moderate growth, because of heavy emigration. The negative aspect of the natural increase for the minority communities was particularly marked between 1926 and 1946. After 1971, however, the situation began to change and in the most recent decade between 1981 and 1991 the rate of natural increase for this religious group was positive, even if only very slightly so. This was mainly due to the fall in the minority communities death rate in this decade, as already discussed.

6

MIGRATION

SOME METHODOLOGICAL ASPECTS

Finally, let us consider the influence of external migration in so far as it has affected the numbers in different religious communities. Before any net migration trends are analysed it is necessary to comment briefly on the nature of migration estimates. The most reliable net migration estimates are those obtained for intercensal periods by linking changes in successive population stocks with the numbers of births and deaths occurring in these periods. This involves deriving aggregate net migration by subtracting the natural increase (births minus deaths) from the net change in population. This method cannot be directly used for deriving migration estimates for religious groups as the required vital statistics data are not disaggregated by religion. Another approach, the 'cohort survivorship technique', is to apply mortality or survivorship factors to the population of different ages at the beginning of an intercensal period in order to estimate the number of survivors at the end of the period.[20] The difference between the number of these 'survivors' and the actual population figures in the corresponding age group *in the next census* can then be taken to represent net migration in relation to the age cohort in question. This approach can also be applied to births in the intercensal period in question and the aggregation of the net migration figures for all cohorts and categories yields a total figure. It will be noted that with both these approaches the final net migration total is estimated as a residual and thus bears the brunt of any errors and misclassifications associated with the process.

It is possible to derive net migration estimates by religion using the latter cohort survivorship technique as described. This can be done by applying the mortality factors to the age differentiated totals for different religious groups in the intercensal period base year and then comparing these with the corresponding age cohorts for different religious categories from the next census. One can apply the same procedure to births in the intercensal period as it is possible to compile reasonably accurate estimates for numbers of births according to religion (see section 5). This method does not, however, take account of differential mortality patterns between religious groups, as the same common factors are applied to each group. It is not considered, however, that this significantly distorts the final estimates.

An important feature to bear in mind in relation to these estimates is that their validity can be significantly affected by flows or changes of state other than migratory movements. The method can be deemed to yield satisfactory estimates of net migration as long as the religious groups in question remain reasonably self-contained, and there are not many transfers between these groups. However, if the scale of such transfers increases, then the situation becomes much more complex and more difficult to interpret. In these circumstances the residual estimates reflect not only migratory movements, but also transfers between religious groups and it is not always possible to disentangle two influences. Broadly speaking, with Irish census data the issue of such transfers did not present a serious problem until the 1970s and, therefore, the above mentioned estimation method can be assumed to provide reasonable estimates of net migration for different religious groups between 1926 and 1971. The relevant data categorized according to religious denominations, are given in absolute terms in Appendix Table A5. Relative net migration data, expressed as annual average rates per 1,000 population, are given in Table 9.

After 1971 the situation became much more complex, mainly because of significantly increasing numbers in the category 'other stated religions' (which mainly involved a variety of smaller Christian groupings) as well as those who indicated that they had 'no religion' and those who refused to provide information on their religious affiliation in censuses. For these recent periods the formal methodology has still been applied, but interpretation of the results (set out at the end of this section) is difficult and is, of necessity, partly judgemental.

MIGRATION TRENDS 1911–1971

Let us first consider the period from 1911 to 1926 which, as already indicated in section 3, is especially important in view of the very significant events which it covered. Our earlier analyses indicated that the minority communities declined very rapidly during this time, from 327,000 to 221,000, down by 106,000, or 32 per cent. The corresponding relative decline for Catholics was very much lower at just over 2 per cent.

It is not possible to use the cohort survival method as described to estimate migration in the 1911-1926 period as simultaneous classifications of the total population according to religion and age are not available from censuses prior to 1926. This is unfortunate, especially in relation to a period when the minority communities population underwent a very substantial decline. This is not to suggest that certain features of the pattern of migration for different religious groups cannot reasonably be inferred from the available population trends, but it would have enhanced our analysis if more soundly based net migration estimates by religion for this period were possible.

It is of interest, nevertheless to try and estimate the decomposition of this large decrease into its constituent 'natural increase' and 'net migration' components. On the basis of the rates of the natural increase which applied to the minority communities in 1926-36 and in 1936-46 it can be broadly inferred that the natural increase associated with this group between 1911 and 1926 would have been about 10,000 (negative), bearing in mind that the period in question was of fifteen years duration. However, this figure would have been augmented (again in a negative sense) through deaths from the minority communities in the first world war. On the basis of data given in the 1926 census reports, these can be roughly estimated at about 5,000[21] implying a total 'adjusted' natural increase of about -15,000. This would suggest therefore that actual net emigration for the minority communities from what is now the Republic of Ireland between 1911 and 1926 was at least 90,000.[22] A significant proportion of this outflow would, of course, have been due to the withdrawal of British security forces and their dependants in early 1922. Relying again on estimates based on figures quoted in the 1926 census reports one can estimate that the size of this outflow (i.e. that part of it which related to the minority religious groups) was about 30,000.[23] This would thus imply a net outflow of about 60,000 from the 'indigenous' minority communities between 1911 and 1926. This is equivalent to a rate of between 14 and 15 per 1,000 of the average population, a much higher figure than that which applied to Catholics during this period, which was between 7 and 8. This rate is also higher than those for the minority communities in the following decades, which were between 9 and 10 (see below).

TABLE 9

ANNUAL AVERAGE NET MIGRATION RATES PER 1,000 OF THE AVERAGE

POPULATION FOR PAST INTERCENSAL PERIODS, BY RELIGION

Period	Rates of Net Migration		
	Catholic	Other Denom.	Total
(1)	(2)	(3)	(4)
1926-36	-5.4	-9.0	-5.6
1936-46	-6.1	-9.7	-6.3
1946-61	-12.4	-8.8	-12.2
1961-71	-4.7	-4.4	-4.6

Source: See Appendix Table A5.

Note: For the period from 1926 to 1961 persons recorded as having 'no religion' and
         those who did not provide this information are included with the 'other
         denominations' category. During this period the numbers involved were very
         small.
         For the period from 1961 to 1971 these two categories are included with
         Catholics. See section 2 for an explanation of these groupings.

As this estimate may even understate the net outflow in question, there would appear to be little doubt therefore that this transitional period witnessed a very considerable exodus of persons from the minority religious communities in Ireland. One must reasonably assume that the main causation underlying this exodus was a sense of apprehension in certain sections of these communities associated with the transition to national independence in 1922 and the upheavals which attended that event. Others may have concluded that their future prospects were not as advantageous as they were previously. This proposition appears to be borne out by the continuing high emigration for this group in the period after independence (as indicated in Table 9) and the fact that, while most of the emigrants involved were young, they also included significant numbers in the older age groups. Furthermore, the parallel occurrence of relatively substantial emigration in age groups covering those aged less than 15 years, and of persons aged between 25 and 44 years (see Table A6) suggests that the outflow involved many family groups. Support for these views can be found in a number of the other studies of the religious minorities in Ireland, especially those of Bowen (1983) and Kennedy (1973).

In the period up to the end of the second world war a still significant, if reduced, degree of emigration continued to apply to the minority religious communities. The relevant migration rates reached as high as 10 per 1,000 population, again markedly higher than the Catholic rates which were between 5 and 6 over this period (see Table 9). Bowen (1983) expressed the view that the more advantageous social profile of the religious minority communities, and their significant involvement in the commercial and business life of the country, should have led to less rather than relatively more emigration *vis à vis* Catholics during this time. While these continuing high outflows may be partly explained by some residual effects attributable to the political transition of the early 1920s, new legal measures introduced in the immediate post-independence period are also likely to have played a role. Throughout the 1920s, the new Irish Government introduced a series of laws which, in the view of the minority communities, would have reflected a strong Catholic or nationalist ethos. Most notable were measures prohibiting divorce, banning the sale of contraceptives, censorship of publications and films and the introduction of compulsory Irish tests in school examinations and in entry to public sector employment. While some of these measures must be considered as obvious and predictable consequences of the political transition (e.g. the promotion of the Irish language), the whole range of changes is likely to have been viewed at the time by the minority communities as moving towards a form of society in which they would not be completely at ease. The evidence suggests that in these circumstances many in the minority community opted to emigrate. A more detailed discussion of such issues in so far as they relate to this period is contained in Kennedy (1973, p. 12).

The situation changed in the post World War II period. The incidence of emigration for the minority communities decreased somewhat and Catholic emigration rose greatly, to a much higher level (12.4 per 1,000 population) than that which existed for the minority community. In this period, especially in the 1950s which involved periods of deep recession, the evidence suggests that economic considerations, which applied to all sections of the population, were the main influences which gave rise to very large migratory outflows. In the 1960s, with the advent of increased economic growth, overall emigration diminished. To the degree that it did exist, our analysis suggests that it applied equally to the Catholic and minority religious communities. Table 9 shows that between 1961 and 1971 virtually identical rates of net emigration prevailed for both communities, at about 4.5 per 1,000 of the average population.

ESTIMATING MORE RECENT TRENDS 1971-1991

The estimation of migration trends for different religious groups for recent decades is much more difficult. The emergence during the 1970s and 1980s of a growing tendency to change religious affiliation, or to withdraw from membership or adherence to any form of religious worship (i.e. no religion) means that the residual 'net migration' estimates derived from the above mentioned methods in effect represent a combination of migratory movements and transfers between religious groups (including, of course the 'no religion' category). The position is further complicated by the increasing propensity for persons not to reply to the census questions on religion.

Notwithstanding these difficulties, it is still of interest to apply the net migration estimation procedure to the data for recent decades and to attempt to interpret the outcomes. There is, to some degree, an identifiable pattern to the nature of the flows and transfers involved. The results are shown in Table 10 for the 1971–81 and 1981–91 intercensal periods. In these analyses, in order to provide better insights, the religious groupings have been extended somewhat compared with earlier tables. The three main Protestant denominations (Church of Ireland, Presbyterians and Methodists) have been distinguished as a separate group, with the remaining religious groups (other than Catholics) classified under the 'other stated religions' category. Those who were recorded as having 'no religion' are also separately distinguished, but persons who did not supply information on their religion in censuses are included with Catholics.[24] The residual 'net migration/transfers' estimates relate only to the population in the base years, 1971 and 1981, i.e. no account is therefore taken of flows or transfers relating to those who were born within each of these periods. The relevant data are given in absolute terms and as rates per 1,000 population for each intercensal period.

Looking first at the estimates for 1971–81 (which, it will be recalled, was a period which involved a substantial overall net migratory inflow) these show that the relative indicator for the Catholic community, at 1.9, is significantly less than the national rate of 2.9, while that for the main Protestant denominations is actually negative (-1.4). These figures suggest a loss for each community to the other religious groupings (including no religion). While the *relative* losses for the main Protestant denominations would appear to be greater (in view of the negative rate in an overall period of net inward migration), the actual losses for Catholics in numeric or absolute terms would have been larger in view of the predominant size of this group. The estimation procedures indicate very large relative transfers to the 'other stated religions' and 'no religion groups', especially the latter. If one excludes the possibility of actual migration, the estimates suggest that some 30,000 persons recorded in the 'no religion' category in 1981 were included as members of specific religious groups in 1971.

Between 1981 and 1991, a period characterized by heavy net outward migration, the rate of net loss for the Catholic group, -7.0, is greater (in a negative sense) than the national rate of -5.5, while that for the main Protestant denominations is somewhat lower at -3.6. One can tentatively interpret these figures as suggesting that the Catholic community lost members both through emigration and transfers to other groups, while the losses for the main Protestant denominations may have been mainly through outward migration (if one assumes that the pattern of migration applying to this group was broadly the same as that which existed for the population as a whole). As in the 1970s, it is clear from the very large rates of migration/transfer that the 'other stated religions' and 'no religion' categories were again augmented by significant movements from other religious groups. The evidence suggests that in this decade these inflows must have consisted predominantly of Catholics. A notable difference in this period (*vis à vis* the 1970s) was the large influx into the 'other stated religions' category.

TABLE 10

ESTIMATED NET MIGRATION/TRANSFERS FOR DIFFERENT RELIGIOUS GROUPS IN 1971-1981 AND 1981-1991

Period	Catholics (Including 'No Statement')	Main Protestant Denominations	Other Stated Religions	No Religion	Total
1971-81					
Population 1971	2,842,300	119,400	8,900	7,600	2,978,300
Migration/Transfers	+54,300	-1,700	+3,300	+29,300	+85,200
Annual Rate per 1,000 Population	+1.9	-1.4	+37.1	+385.5	+2.9
1981-91					
Population 1981	3,275,500	115,400	13,000	39,600	3,443,400
Migration/Transfers	-227,900	-4,100	+22,200	+20,500	-189,800
Annual Rate per 1,000 Population	-7.0	-3.6	+133.8	+63.9	-5.5

Notes: (1) While the 'migration/transfers' estimates for different religious groups relate both to migratory movements and transfers between religions, the estimates for the total population relate only to net migration.

(2) The estimates in this table relate only to the base year population (i.e. for 1971 and 1981) and take no account of net flows relating to those born in each period.

(3) The rates per 1,000 population are calculated on the basis of the base year populations for 1971 and 1981.

(4) The main Protestant denominations category includes the Church of Ireland, Methodists and Presbyterians.

7

THE JEWISH COMMUNITY

GENERAL TRENDS

The tiny Jewish community in Ireland in 1881 of 394 persons (twenty six counties), grew significantly with the arrival of Jewish immigrants from Russia in the late nineteenth century. It had increased to 1,506 by 1891, to 3,006 by 1901 and 3,805 by 1911 (see Table 11). The total growth in this period was on average almost 8 per cent per year.

An historical feature of the Jewish population has been its concentration in Dublin (about 90 per cent) except in the period 1891–1911 when about a quarter of the Jewish population lived outside the capital. This had fallen to about 15 per cent by 1926 and was most likely due to internal migration within Ireland as the total Jewish population showed only a very small fall in that period. Between 1926 and 1946 the Jewish population increased slightly, by on average 0.3 per cent per annum, in contrast to the fall in population experienced by the population as a whole.

Since 1946 the size of the Jewish community has shown a sharp and continuous decline, falling in absolute terms by over 2,300 persons in the period up to 1991, by which time the population stood at less than 1,600. The annual average rate of decline was 1.2 per cent in the period from 1946 to 1961, rising to nearly 3 per cent in the most recent intercensal 1981-91 period.

AGE STRUCTURE

An age by religion description is available from the censuses from 1926 and is given in Table 12. The most significant feature is the dramatic ageing of the Jewish population. In 1926 only 3 per cent of the population was over 65 years, compared with a quarter by 1991 — a major shift even allowing for improved mortality levels. Some 9 per cent of the Jewish population were aged under five years in 1926 compared with 4.5 per cent in 1991.

The age profile of the Jewish community can be contrasted to that for the Catholic and minority communities (see Table 3). In 1926 the age distribution of the Jewish community was more like that of the Catholic

TABLE 11

THE NUMBER OF JEWISH PERSONS RECORDED

IN THE CENSUSES FROM 1881 TO 1991

Year	Number	Annual Average Change in Population in Intercensal Period (%)	% in Dublin
1881	394		89.3
1891	1,506	+14.3	70.2
1901	3,006	+7.2	72.2
1911	3,805	+2.4	77.9
1926	3,686	-0.2	85.5
1936	3,749	+0.2	89.9
1946	3,907	+0.4	89.9
1961	3,255	-1.2	94.1
1971	2,633	-2.1	93.1
1981	2,127	-2.1	91.7
1991	1,581	-2.9	87.6

Sources: Censuses of population.

TABLE 12

AGE PROFILE OF THE JEWISH POPULATION

IN CENSUSES 1926–1991

Age Group	1926	1936	1946	1961	1981	1991
			%			
0- 4 years	8.7	7.6	7.4	7.1	5.2	4.5
5-14	20.7	15.4	13.5	14.6	12.2	11.0
15-24	23.4	20.1	14.5	12.5	14.2	11.6
25-34	16.2	19.7	16.7	9.7	13.4	11.5
35-44	11.9	14.8	17.9	14.1	11.3	13.9
45-54	10.4	10.1	14.3	17.8	9.5	12.3
55-64	5.4	7.8	9.0	13.6	12.8	10.2
65 +	3.3	4.5	6.7	10.6	21.4	25.0
Total	100.0	100.0	100.0	100.0	100.0	100.0

Source: Censuses of population.

Note: An age subdivision for the Jewish Community is not available from the 1971 census.

community than that of the minority communities as a whole, although at that point the Jewish population did have a higher percentage in the 15 – 64 years age group and fewer in the over 65 years group than did the Catholic population. By 1961 the Jewish profile had become more like that of the minority population except that it still had fewer persons aged 65 years or more. By 1981 the Jewish population had a noticeably older age profile than the minority population.

RATES OF NATURAL INCREASE

Fertility levels cannot be calculated prior to 1946 as classifications involving marital status by age by religion are not available from the census data. After 1946 the calculations for the Jewish community become increasingly unreliable because of the small absolute number of births. Therefore, 1946 may be the most reliable point in time for the calculation of fertility and birth estimates as the Jewish population was then at its highest. For 1946 we have calculated an estimate of the number of live marital births per 1,000 married Jewish women aged 15-44 years. The number, 129.9, is significantly lower than that for the minority and Catholic communities which were 179.2 and 275.4 respectively. We will subsequently show this (Jewish rate) is unlikely to have been seriously deflated by mixed marriages. Despite the apparently low fertility rate, at least at this time, the number of births in the period 1926–1946 appears to have been relatively high judging by the proportion of the population aged 2 years or less in that period. This is credible in the light of the following factors: (i) a relatively high nuptiality rate (51.9 in 1946 compared with 38.9 for Catholics and 44.8 for the minority religious group as a whole) and (ii) the relatively high proportion of the Jewish population in the fertile age groups.

An estimation of the natural increase in the intercensal period 1936-46 indicates that estimated Jewish births were 584 and exceeded deaths (421), giving a positive natural increase of 163. These figures translate into annual average rates of 15.3, 11.0 and 4.3 per 1,000 of the average Jewish population respectively in that intercensal period. This means that in that period the Jewish community had a lower annual average birth rate than the Catholic population but a higher rate than the minority population generally (see Table 8). It also had a lower death rate than the other two groups. The positive rate of natural increase for the Jewish community contrasted with that of the minority population generally.

While the estimation of births outside this period is less reliable, it would appear that births were greater than deaths in the 1946-1961 period, i.e. there was a natural increase. This view is supported by the age profile of the Jewish community. That profile also supports the view, however, that there has been a natural *decrease* in the community since the 1970s. However, the numerical decline of the community between 1946 and 1981, while aggravated by an ageing community, would appear to be primarily due to outward net migration as described in Table 13.

TABLE 13

THE JEWISH COMMUNITY: ESTIMATED NUMBER OF DEATHS
AND NET MIGRATION IN INTERCENSAL PERIODS
AND RELATED ANNUAL AVERAGE RATES OF DEATHS
PER 1,000 POPULATION

Period	Estimated deaths (of age cohorts at the start of the intercensal period)	Annual average rate of deaths per 1,000 of the average population	Estimated migration (of age cohorts at the start of the intercensal period)	Annual average rate of migration per 1,000 of the average population
1926-36	332	8.9	-156	-4.2
1936-46	362	9.5	-13	
1946-61	767	14.3	-590	-11.0
1961-81	873	16.2	-782	-14.5
1981-91	354	19.1	-340	-18.3

MIGRATION

Prior to 1946 Jewish migration was low in both absolute terms and relative to the rest of the population. Since 1946 it has been much higher in a negative sense than for the other religious groups. The negative rates indicated for the post war intercensal periods are very high by any standard, bearing in mind particularly that they relate only to the cohorts alive at the beginning of each intercensal period and do not include the outward migration of children born within these periods. They are, therefore, indicative of a very substantial population loss to the community as a result of migratory outflows. In the most recent intercensal period (1981-91) the migration figure may include some transfers to the 'no religion' group in line with the experience of the other religions.

MIXED MARRIAGES

Because of the small size of the Jewish community only a general comment about mixed marriages can be made. The conclusions to be drawn from the special tabulations from the census must be qualified by an awareness that they refer only to current denomination and therefore do not take conversions into account. Only details of mixed marriages where the mother is Jewish have been obtained. Bearing in mind these limitations, the effect of intermarriage on numerical loss would seem to be low.

TABLE 14

NUMBER OF JEWISH AND NON-JEWISH CHILDREN
BY RELIGION OF MOTHER
AND CATEGORY OF MARRIAGE, ALL AGES 1981

Marriage Type	Families	Jewish Children	Non-Jewish Children
All Marriages Mother Jewish	268	527	19
Mixed Marriages Mother Jewish - Father not Jewish	17	14	17

While the picture is incomplete it is clear that mixed marriages are only a small proportion (6 per cent) of all marriages involving a Jewish mother. Within these marriages, while the numbers are small, approximately one half of the children are brought up in the Jewish faith.

NOTES

1   In the period covered all censuses carried out between 1881 and 1946 included questions on religion. Thereafter such questions were included in the censuses of 1961, 1971, 1981 and 1991.

2   It should be noted that even though Irish censuses have always been conducted on a statutory basis which places a legal obligation on householders to complete the census form, replies to the question on religion affiliation have in practice not been insisted on.

3   Throughout this report we adopt the common usage of Catholic for Roman Catholic.

4   This was mainly as a result of sizeable migratory inflows following social upheavals in Eastern Europe in the early part of this century. A further analysis of population trends for the Jewish community is given in section 7.

5   Even though the 'other stated religions' category contains the Jewish and Muslim communities, within this group Christian categories predominate. This is clear from Appendix Table A1 (taken from the 1991 census) which shows the numbers for the principal religious groups involved. However, the largest sub-category in this group were those who described themselves as 'Christian' (some 16,300 out of the total 38,700 for the group as a whole). We can only speculate as to what the origins of these persons are. They are likely to include persons attached to Christian 'house churches' and other forms of non-institutionalized worship, non church attending Catholics and Protestants who still identify themselves as Christian, and possibly, some children of mixed marriages whose parents prefer not to label them, or themselves, as either Catholic or Protestant. This group also included over 3,700 persons who were classified as 'lapsed Roman Catholics'.

6   See section 6, in particular the subsection on 'Estimating More Recent Trends, 1971 to 1991'.

7   There is other evidence which tends to reaffirm that significant increases have occurred in recent decades in the numbers both of persons without any religious affiliation and those who are members of smaller religious groups. Data on the number of marriages by form of ceremony, for example, indicate a large rise in the number of purely civil ceremonies (as distinct from those performed according to the rites of the main Christian denominations) from less than 40 in 1961 to almost 650 in 1991 (see Appendix Table A7).

8   In County Kildare for example, the minority communities population fell by 70 per cent, from 11,750 to 3,500, between 1911 and 1926.

9   In 1971 extramarital births comprised only 2.7 per cent of all births, but by 1991 this percentage had risen to 16.6.

10   Calculations relating to marital fertility are not possible for the censuses prior to 1946 as tabulations involving classifications by religion and marital status were not given in the census results.

11   See Appendix I for further information on this issue.

12   Simulations with these age structures (using constant age specific fertility rates for all women for 1991) would suggest that the slight differences which exist in the age distributions between the two religious groups would have the effect of raising the Catholic fertility level by some 4 per cent when compared with that for other denominations.

13   Similar calculations are not possible for earlier years as tabulations involving
      marital status and religion were not compiled for censuses prior to 1946.

14   Prior to the Papal decree of Ne Temere in 1908 the Catholic Church recognized
      mixed marriages as valid even if they were not celebrated before a Catholic priest.
      While it is believed that some Catholic priests demanded a promise of the partners
      that any children would be baptized and educated as Catholics before they would
      solemnize a marriage, it was not always insisted upon.

      With Ne Temere mixed marriages were treated like marriages involving two
      Catholics in that to be valid in the eyes of the Catholic Church they had to be
      contracted before a Catholic priest. Before a Catholic priest would solemnize a
      marriage between a Catholic and a person of another faith a dispensation had to
      be obtained from the Church from the impediment of it being a mixed marriage.
      Catholic Bishops would not grant a dispensation from the impediment until both
      partners promised to baptize and educate the children as Catholics. In this way
      the promises became necessary for validity.

      The Vatican's apostolic letter of 1970, Motu Proprio, represented a significant
      relaxation of the conditions of Ne Temere. It declared that as a condition of a
      dispensation being granted from the impediment of a mixed marriage only the
      Catholic partner need promise that she/he do all in her/his power to have all the
      children baptized and brought up in the Catholic Church.

15   See section 2 of this report regarding the coverage of household members in
      censuses.

16   Since the minority communities (especially in recent years) included significant
      numbers in the 'other stated religions' category (see Table 1(A)) there is a possibility
      that the number of Catholic children in mixed marriages could be overstated. This
      could arise, for example, if one spouse in a family was recorded in the census as a
      'lapsed Catholic' and the other as 'Catholic', as such a marriage would have been
      classified as 'mixed'. It is likely that all the children in such a family would have
      been returned as Catholics. The position of those who recorded themselves as
      'Christian' might also be unclear in these circumstances. The numbers involved,
      however, are relatively small and unlikely to affect the pattern of the results as given.

      This can be reaffirmed by considering only mixed marriages involving Catholics
      and Church of Ireland members (the largest of the minority religious groups). In
      such marriages the proportion of Catholic children in 1991 was 73 per cent, almost
      as high as the proportion for all mixed marriages given in Table 6. Compton and
      Coward (1989) using a small sample (n = 108) of mixed marriages in Northern
      Ireland also found that the majority of children within these marriages were
      recorded as Catholic (56 per cent, as against 37 per cent for other denominations).

17   There is some evidence which raises a query regarding this proposition. Maguire
      (1993) in analysing the situation of working class Protestants in three districts in
      Dublin city in the early 1900s found that some 15 per cent of Protestant males in
      this class were in mixed marriages with Catholics. It is possible, of course, that the
      incidence of mixed marriages may have declined after the early 1920s, given that
      this was a period of greater intercommunal tension. An interesting feature of
      Maguire's results is that the proportion of Catholic children in these earlier mixed
      marriages was remarkably similar to the figures revealed by the present study, just
      under 80 per cent.

18   Commission on Emigration and other Population Problems, Reports, 1954, Table 67, p. 90.

19   The derivation of these rates, which involved a great deal of background computation, is explained in Appendix II.

20   This is basically the same method as that adopted in estimating the number of deaths by religious group as explained in Appendix II.

21   The reference in this case is the general report on the 1926 census of population (Volume X), page 12. Quoting Registrar Generals' data this source indicates that the number of Irish warrant officers, non-commissioned officers and men who died outside of Great Britain and Ireland from 1914 to 1918 was 27,400. The number of Irish officers killed is not recorded. If one assumes that about one half of the above total were from the counties of the Republic and that, in turn, one third of these were from the minority religious communities, this suggests a war deaths figure of about 5,000.

22   This is probably a minimum figure as the estimated natural increase in this period may not have been as large (in a negative sense) as -15,000. It is likely that the net migration associated with the minority communities prior to 1911 would not have been uncharacteristically large in relative sense and would not, therefore, have contributed to serious imbalances in population structure (with regard to age, for example) which would, in turn, have led to undue reductions in the natural increase.

23   See the general report of the 1926 census (Volume X), p. 47. This source indicates that, according to the 1911 census, the number of British army, navy and police personnel in Ireland in 1911 who were members of minority religious groups was 21,400. If one assumes that there were 37 dependants for every 100 such personnel (the known proportion for the British army in Dublin) this would suggest a larger group of about 30,000, the great majority of whom would have left the country in 1922.

24   The reasons for this are set out in section 2.

REFERENCES

Bowen, K. *Protestants in a Catholic state; Ireland's Privileged Minority*, Dublin: Gill and Macmillan, 1983.

CENSUS OF POPULATION, 1926, Volume III, Part I, Religions, Stationery Office, Dublin.

CENSUS OF POPULATION, 1926, Volume X, General Report, Stationery Office, Dublin.

CENSUS OF POPULATION, 1936, Volume III, Part I, Religions, Stationery Office, Dublin.

CENSUS OF POPULATION, 1946, Volume III, Part I, Religions, Stationery Office, Dublin.

CENSUS OF POPULATION, 1961, Volume VII, Part I, Religions, Stationery Office, Dublin.

CENSUS OF POPULATION, 1971, Volume IX, Religion, Stationery Office, Dublin.

CENSUS OF POPULATION, 1981, Volume V, Religion, Stationery Office, Dublin.

CENSUS OF POPULATION, 1991, Volume V, Religion, Stationery Office, Dublin.

Compton, P. and Coward J., *Fertility and Family Planning in Northern Ireland*, Aldershot: Avebury, 1989.

COMMISSION ON EMIGRATION AND OTHER POPULATION PROBLEMS — REPORTS (1954). Stationery Office, Dublin.

Kennedy R.E., *The Irish: Emigration, Marriage and Fertility*, Berkeley: University of California Press, 1973.

Maguire, M. 'A Socio-economic analysis of the Dublin Protestant Working Class 1870-1926', *Irish Economic and Social History*, XX, Dublin, 1993, 35-61

White, J., *Minority Report*, Dublin: Gill and Macmillan, 1975.

Walsh, B.M., *Religion and Demographic Behaviour in Ireland*, Dublin: Economic and Social Research Institute, 1970, General Research Series, Report No 55

Walsh, B.M. 'Trends in the Religious Composition of the Population in the Republic of Ireland', *Economic and Social Review*, Vol. 6, No 4 July 1975.

TABLE A1

POPULATION CLASSIFIED BY RELIGION AND SEX IN 1991

Denomination	Persons	Males	Females
Roman Catholic	3,228,327	1,595,688	1,632,639
Church of Ireland	89,187	43,718	45,469
Presbyterian	13,199	6,686	6,513
Methodist	5,037	2,412	2,625
Jewish	1,581	782	799
Baptist	1,156	542	614
Quaker	749	349	400
Lutheran	1,010	421	589
Other Stated Religions	35,828	18,636	17,192
of which			
Christian (unspecified)	16,329	8,097	8,232
Muslim (Islamic)	3,875	2,407	1,468
Lapsed Roman Catholic	3,749	1,969	1,780
Jehovah's Witness	3,393	1,538	1,855
Buddhist	986	562	424
Hindu	953	572	381
Mormon	853	405	448
Agnostic	823	501	322
Evangelical	819	384	435
Bahai	430	217	213
Greek Orthodox	358	226	132
Atheist	320	230	90
Apostolic or Pentecostal	285	132	153
Brethren	256	113	143
Pantheist	202	122	80
Other stated denominations	2,197	1,161	1,036
No religion	66,270	40,205	26,065
Not stated	83,375	43,979	39,396
Total	3,525,719	1,753,418	1,772,301

Source: 1991 Census of population

TABLE A2

NUMBER OF PERSONS IN EACH PROVINCE

CLASSIFIED BY RELIGION 1881–1991

Province Year	Catholic	Other Denominations	No Religion	No Information	Total Persons
Total					
1881	3 465 332	404 294			3 869 626
1891	3 099 003	369 691			3 468 694
1901	2 878 271	343 552			3 221 823
1911	2 812 509	327 179			3 139 688
1926	2 751 269	220 723			2 971 992
1936	2 773 920	194 500			2 968 420
1946	2 786 033	169 074			2 955 107
1961	2 673 473	138 136	1 107	5 625	2 818 341
1971	2 795 666	128 318	7 616	46 648	2 978 248
1981	3 204 476	128 381	39 572	70 976	3 443 405
1991	3 228 327	147 747	66 270	83 375	3 525 719
Leinster (Excl. Dublin)					
1881	774 310	85 769			860 079
1891	689 185	79 359			768 544
1901	633 244	71 379			704 623
1911	614 303	70 545			684 848
1926	598 776	44 662			643 438
1936	593 990	39 496			633 486
1946	610 513	34 411			644 924
1961	583 395	29 225	141	1 056	613 817
1971	609 873	28 017	1 125	6 906	645 921
1981	735 804	30 490	6 320	14 743	787 357
1991	773 880	35 294	10 574	15 897	835 645
Dublin					
1881	320 515	98 395			418 910
1891	322 822	96 394			419 216
1901	348 524	99 682			448 206
1911	375 742	101 454			477 196
1926	434 059	71 595			505 654
1936	519 341	67 584			586 925
1946	574 593	61 600			636 193
1961	663 509	51 889	630	2 304	718 332
1971	777 771	47 371	4 869	22 208	852 219
1981	909 685	44 690	20 492	28 297	1 003 164
1991	911 454	51 891	33 269	28 690	1 025 304

TABLE A2 – CONTINUED

NUMBER OF PERSONS IN EACH PROVINCE CLASSIFIED BY RELIGION

1881–1991

Province Year	Catholic	Other Denominations	No Religion	No Information	Total Persons
Total					
Munster					
1881	1 249 384	81 731			1 331 115
1891	1 098 072	74 330			1 172 402
1901	1 007 876	68 312			1 076 188
1911	973 805	61 690			1 035 495
1926	934 703	35 199			969 902
1936	913 216	29 056			942 272
1946	892 971	24 335			917 306
1961	826 618	20 938	286	1 361	849 203
1971	849 382	21 024	1 244	10 352	882 002
1981	949 938	22 489	8 629	17 259	998 315
1991	941 675	28 179	15 402	24 277	1 009 533
Connacht					
1881	783 116	38 541			821 657
1891	692 369	32 405			724 774
1901	619 815	27 117			646 932
1911	588 004	22 980			610 984
1926	538 277	14 630			552 907
1936	513 232	12 236			525 468
1946	482 938	9 859			492 797
1961	411 312	7 532	35	586	419 465
1971	378 613	6 951	213	5 125	390 902
1981	406 811	7 395	2 915	7 289	424 410
1991	397 848	9 685	5 392	10 106	423 031
Ulster (pt)					
1881	338 007	100 252			438 259
1891	296 555	87 203			383 758
1901	268 812	77 062			345 874
1911	260 655	70 510			331 165
1926	245 454	54 637			300 091
1936	234 141	46 128			280 269
1946	225 018	38 869			263 887
1961	188 639	28 552	15	318	217 524
1971	180 027	24 955	165	2 057	207 204
1981	202 238	23 317	1 216	3 388	230 159
1991	203 470	22 698	1 633	4 405	232 206

Source: Censuses of population

Note: Prior to 1961 persons classified as having 'no religion' or who did not provide information on religious affiliation are included with 'other denominations'.

TABLE A3
POPULATION FOR DIFFERENT RELIGIOUS GROUPS CLASSIFIED BY AGE, 1926–1991

RELIGION, AGE	1926	1936	1946	1961	1971	1981	1991
Catholics							
0–2 years	160 857	154 998	175 830	176 788	300 541	203 206	145 208
3–4	111 795	102 174	106 827	114 567		128 180	106 212
5–14	545 238	525 280	506 914	555 584	586 898	654 078	623 193
15–24	490 933	492 552	461 446	373 711	456 131	564 827	556 142
25–34	369 352	372 205	390 949	283 540	302 677	434 118	445 238
35–44	316 390	330 026	333 613	319 701	282 604	330 746	414 777
45–64	510 289	535 138	522 702	559 082	565 093	549 589	568 379
65+	246 423	261 547	287 752	290 500	301 722	339 732	369 178
Total	2 751 277	2 773 920	2 786 033	2 673 473	2 795 666	3 204 476	3 228 327
Other Denominations							
0–2 years	8 733	6 497	7 620	5 735	8 958	5 536	5 286
3–4	6 468	4 597	4 488	3 700		3 564	3 742
5–14	34 912	26 848	21 328	20 885	18 192	18 775	20 882
15–24	35 505	30 287	21 331	18 128	17 536	17 932	19 766
25–34	29 289	27 864	21 935	14 624	14 499	18 441	20 427
35–44	28 454	25 299	23 866	17 385	13 459	15 383	21 196
45–64	52 145	47 971	41 936	39 848	33 184	26 378	29 005
65+	25 105	25 137	26 570	24 563	22 490	22 372	22 489
Total	220 611	194 500	169 074	144 868	128 318	128 381	142 793
No Religion							
0–2 years					699	2 576	2 910
3–4						1 287	1 794
5–14					755	3 827	6 658
15–24					1 604	7 572	12 680
25–34					1 964	13 071	18 139
35–44					972	5 628	16 356
45–64					1 187	4 041	10 223
65+					435	1 570	2 464
Total					7 616	39 572	71 224

TABLE A3 – CONTINUED

POPULATION FOR DIFFERENT RELIGIOUS GROUPS CLASSIFIED BY AGE, 1926–1991

RELIGION, AGE	1926	1936	1946	1961	1971	1981	1991
No Information							
0–2 years						5 620	5 309
3–4					5 457	3 035	3 282
5–14					9 652	14 045	16 098
15–24					7 707	12 225	13 010
25–34					5 204	12 381	11 588
35–44					4 801	7 996	11 243
45–64					8 655	10 394	14 076
65+					5 172	5 280	8 769
Total					46 648	70 976	83 375
All Persons							
0–2 years	169 590	161 495	183 450	182 523		216 938	158 713
3–4	118 263	106 771	111 315	118 267	315 655	136 066	115 030
5–14	580 150	552 128	528 242	576 469	615 497	690 725	666 831
15–24	526 438	522 839	482 777	391 839	482 978	602 556	601 598
25–34	398 641	400 069	412 884	298 164	324 344	478 011	495 392
35–44	344 844	355 325	357 479	337 086	301 836	359 753	463 572
45–64	562 434	583 109	564 638	598 930	608 119	590 402	621 683
65+	271 528	286 684	314 322	315 063	329 819	368 954	402 900
Total	2 971 888	2 968 420	2 955 107	2 818 341	2 978 248	3 443 405	3 525 719

Source:　Censuses of population

Note:　See Table A2

TABLE A4

MIXED MARRIAGE RATES

FOR THE MINORITY RELIGIOUS COMMUNITIES IN 1981, BY AGE

Age of Participant in 1981	Males	Females	Total
15-34	30.0	27.1	28.6
35-44	21.3	16.6	18.5
45 +	11.0	6.6	8.9
Total	20.4	16.8	18.7

Source: Special tabulations from the 1981 census.

Notes: (1)   The 'mixed marriage rate' for males is the number of males from the minority communities in the appropriate age group who were in mixed marriages taken as a percentage of *all* married males from these communities in the same age groups. The rates for females and persons are similarly defined.

(2)   As in the other Tables in this report, the minority communities category includes the main Protestant denominations and 'other stated religions', but excludes 'no religion' and those who refused to provide information on religious affiliation in the census.

TABLE A5
ESTIMATED TOTALS FOR BIRTHS, DEATHS, NATURAL INCREASE AND
MIGRATION BY RELIGIOUS GROUP FOR INTERCENSAL PERIODS
BETWEEN 1926 AND 1991

	Catholic	Other Denominations	Total
		(000)	
1926–36			
Population 1926	2 751.3	220.6	2 971.9
Births	556.5	27.0	583.5
Deaths	385.9	34.4	420.3
Natural Increase	170.5	−7.4	163.2
Net Migration	−147.9	−18.7	−166.6
1936–46			
Population 1936	2 773.9	194.5	2 968.4
Births	577.5	24.6	602.1
Deaths	395.7	32.5	428.1
Natural Increase	181.8	−7.9	174.0
Net Migration	−169.7	−17.6	−187.3
1946–61			
Population 1946	2 786.0	169.1	2 955.1
Births	903.0	34.6	937.7
Deaths	507.9	38.2	546.1
Natural Increase	395.1	−3.5	391.6
Net Migration	−507.7	−20.7	−528.3
1961–71			
Population 1961	2 680.2	138.1	2 818.3
Births	606.7	18.8	625.5
Deaths	308.3	22.8	331.1
Natural Increase	298.4	−4.0	294.4
Net Migration	−128.7	−5.8	−134.5
1971–81			
Population 1971	2 849.9	128.3	2 978.2
Births	675.8	18.8	694.6
Deaths	312.7	20.7	333.4
Natural Increase	363.1	−1.9	361.2
Net Migration			103.9

TABLE A5 — CONTINUED
ESTIMATED TOTAL FOR BIRTHS, DEATHS, NATURAL INCREASE AND
MIGRATION BY RELIGIOUS GROUP FOR INTERCENSAL PERIODS
BETWEEN 1926 AND 1991

	Catholic	Other Denominations	Total
		(000)	
1981–91			
Population 1981	3 315.0	128.4	3 443.4
Births	593.4	17.6	611.0
Deaths	305.6	17.0	322.6
Natural Increase	287.7	0.6	288.3
Net Migration			−206.0
Population 1991	3 382.9	142.8	3 525.7

Note: The methods used in compiling these figures are described in the main text.

TABLE A6

ANNUAL AVERAGE RATES OF NET MIGRATION PER 1,000 POPULATION IN
1926–1936 FOR SELECTED AGE GROUPS, BY RELIGIOUS GROUP

Age in 1926	Catholic	Other Denominations
0– 4	+2.3	-1.8
5–14	-6.9	-10.5
15–24	-19.4	-16.7
25–34	-4.6	-7.5
35–44	-1.5	-5.0
45–54	-1.8	-4.9

Source: Censuses of population and authors' estimates

Notes: (1)   These rates are based on the age specific populations at the beginning of the period (i.e. in 1926).

(2)   Note that in this table the 'Other Denominations' category includes those recorded in censuses as having 'no religion' and those who refused to provide information on religious affiliation. However, in the period concerned the numbers in the latter categories were very small.

TABLE A7

NUMBER OF MARRIAGES 1961–1991, BY FORM OF CEREMONY

Year	Catholic	Church of Ireland	Presbyterian	Other Denominations	Civil	Total
1961	14,772	375	92	51	39	15,329
1971	21,118	566	111	49	170	22,014
1981	19,647	392	63	56	454	20,612
1991	16,293	392	52	55	649	17,441

Source: Annual Reports on Vital Statistics of the Department of Health.

APPENDIX I

CENSUS DATA ON FERTILITY OF MARRIAGE

Analyses relating to fertility of marriage for different religious groups were included in census of population publications up to 1981. These, however, involved a different approach to that set out in section 4. They were based on questions which sought information on 'the number of previous children born to present marriage'. Clearly, such an indicator, which involves a strong retrospective element since it covers all previous births, will yield quite different results from those as set out in Table 4 in section 4. It is also a much more complex indicator to interpret, as it clearly depends on the duration of the marriage and on the age of the wife at marriage.

Nevertheless these data yield results which in many respects are broadly comparable with those given in this report. Table (i), given at the end of this Appendix, contains census data for 1981 showing numbers of children born per 100 married women classified according to religious group and socio-economic group, for marriages of between five and ten years duration and of all durations. Observing first the total figures for both duration categories it will be noted that Catholic fertility significantly exceeds that for the minority religious communities. The relevant indicators for all durations of marriage are 326 for Catholics and 239 for the minority communities, indicating a Catholics' 'excess' of 36 per cent. The corresponding indicators for marriages of between five and ten years duration are 234 and 197, respectively, indicating a difference of 19 per cent.

The facility with these data to introduce a classification according to socio-economic group is important, as it can be argued that variations in social class could account for a significant part of fertility differences between Catholics and the minority communities. Fertility levels are generally lower for those in the more affluent social categories and somewhat higher for those from more disadvantaged backgrounds. In this regard there are marked differences between Catholics and the minority communities in Ireland in terms of social profile, involving a greater concentration among the higher social classes for the latter group. This is a feature which has been revealed in successive censuses, even though it may not be as pronounced now as it was in earlier periods.

It can be demonstrated, however, as indicated in the following analysis, that social structure does not have a very significant impact on differences in *overall* fertility levels. In fact previous census results have consistently shown Catholic fertility levels to be significantly higher than those for the minority community across all social categories and for all durations of marriage and ages of mother. The data given in Table (i) clearly reaffirm this pattern.

It is of interest to try and determine the extent of the differences in overall fertility levels that can be attributed to social class. Tables (ii) and (iii) of this Appendix contain a simulation which attempts to provide such an estimate. It is based on the fertility data for all marriage durations as previously mentioned. It is clear that in the context of computing the fertility indices involved here, the *overall average* for the number of children born per married women (326 for Catholics, 239 for other denominations) can be represented as a weighted average of the individual fertility levels for different social classes, with the weights being the proportion of married women within each class. If one focuses on the rate for the minority community, it is possible to recalculate this using the corresponding weights for the Catholic population of married women, while retaining the specific social group fertility levels for the minority community. This, in effect, would purport to show what the overall level of fertility for the minority community would be if the Catholic social structure prevailed. The difference between the result of this calculation and the original overall fertility level should reflect the effect of variations in social structures.

The relevant comparison is given in the last row of Table (iii) and does not, in fact, indicate any difference between the two outcomes. It is true that the use of the weights for Catholics results in a greater contribution to total fertility from the social groups relating to unskilled activities, but this is offset by a much smaller contribution from other social classes associated with high fertility, particularly the farmers category which, interestingly, accounts for a markedly higher proportion of married women in the minority community group (22 per cent as against 14 per cent for Catholics). In summary, therefore, the evidence suggests that social class differences have little effect on variations in *overall* fertility levels between the religious groups in question.

TABLE (I)

AVERAGE NUMBER OF CHILDREN BORN PER 100 MARRIED WOMEN
IN 1981 CLASSIFIED ACCORDING TO RELIGION AND SOCIAL GROUP

Social Group	Duration of Marriage between 5 and 10 Years		All Durations of Marriage	
	Catholic	Other Denominations	Catholic	Other Denominations
Farmers, etc.	268	237	398	303
Other Agricultural Occupations	255	243	372	268
Higher Professional	232	186	299	217
Lower Professional	215	161	257	188
Employers, Managers	232	189	323	231
Salaried Employees	229	185	313	221
Intermediate Non-Manual Workers	197	145	246	177
Other Non-Manual	228	188	333	239
Skilled Manual	243	213	329	243
Semi-Skilled Manual	223	217	323	243
Unskilled Manual	260	245	381	304
Unknown	245	197	337	228
Total	234	197	326	239

Source: Census of population 1981 Vol. XI.

TABLE (II)
NUMBERS OF MARRIED WOMEN AND AVERAGE NUMBER OF CHILDREN PER 100 MARRIED MARRIED WOMEN RELIGION AND SOCIAL GROUP, FOR ALL DURATIONS OF MARRIAGE, 1981

Social Group	Catholic			Other Denominations		
	Married Women		Av. no children/100 marr. women	Married Women		Av. no children/100 marr. women
	No	%		No	%	
(1)	(2)	(3)	(4)	(5)	(6)	(7)
Farmers etc.	79 394	13.9	398	5 976	22.1	303
Other Agric. Occupations	16 565	2.9	372	573	2.1	268
Higher Professional	16 836	2.9	299	2 451	9.1	217
Lower Professional	38 348	6.7	257	1 915	7.1	188
Employers, Managers	41 324	7.2	323	4 217	15.6	231
Salaried Employees	12 958	2.3	313	1 207	4.5	221
Intermediate Non Manual	76 799	13.4	246	3 460	12.8	177
Other Non Manual	70 038	12.2	333	1 657	6.1	239
Skilled Manual	114 832	20.1	329	2 975	11.0	243
Semi-Skilled Manual	37 463	6.5	323	644	2.4	243
Unskilled Manual	40 840	7.1	381	539	2.0	304
Unknown	26 933	4.7	337	1 463	5.4	228
Total	572 330	100.0	326	27 077	100.0	239

Source: Census of population 1981 Volume XI.

TABLE (III)

SIMULATION OF OTHER DENOMINATIONS FERTILITY RATIO

ON THE BASIS OF THE CATHOLIC SOCIAL GROUP PROFILE

(USING 1981 CENSUS DATA)

Social Group	Original weights	Simulated weights
Farmers etc.	66.9	42.0
Other Agric. Occupations	5.7	7.8
Higher Professional	19.6	6.4
Lower Professional	13.3	12.6
Employers, Managers	36.0	16.7
Salaried Employees	9.9	5.0
Intermediate Non Manual	22.6	23.8
Other Non Manual	14.6	29.2
Skilled Manual	26.7	48.8
Semi–Skilled Manual	5.8	15.9
Unskilled Manual	6.1	21.7
Unknown	12.3	10.7
Total	239.4	240.5

APPENDIX II

THE COMPILATION OF DEATH RATES
FOR DIFFERENT RELIGIOUS GROUPS

The derivation of the death rates shown in Table 8 in section 5 involved a great deal of background computation. Basically, the approach adopted for each intercensal period (which is similar to that used by Walsh in his 1970 study) was to apply age differentiated survivorship ratios taken from appropriate life tables to the age group totals for each religious group in the base year population in order to estimate the number of those still alive at the end of the period. The number of deaths for each religious group was then calculated by deducting the numbers of survivors from the original numbers in the age cohorts in question. This does not, however, give a complete picture as it covers only those who were alive at the commencement of the period. One must also consider deaths of those born within the period, a sizeable number in view of the fact that infant mortality is still of significant proportions, and was very much higher in earlier periods. This involved a similar estimation process to that described above, with appropriate survivorship ratios being applied in this instance to the number of births for each religious group in each intercensal period instead of to population age totals.

It should be noted that the same survivorship ratios were applied across all religious groups, as the official life tables do not involve a distinction by religion. This means that the method does not take account of inherent mortality differences between religious groups (as distinct from those deriving from variations in age structures), but it is not considered that this significantly affects the estimation of the rates in question.

The following provides an example (for the 1936-1946 period) of the actual computations involved.

		Catholic	Other Denomination
(1)	Alive in 1936	2,773,920	194,500
(2)	Expected Survivors to 1946	1,420,542	163,390
(3)	Estimated Deaths from 1936 population, (1)-(2)	353,378	31,110
(4)	Estimated Births 1936-1946	579,742	24,700
(5)	Estimated Survivors to 1946 from (4)	525,985	22,409
(6)	Estimated Deaths in 1936-1946 from (4), i.e. (4)-(5)	53,757	2,291
(7)	Estimated Total Deaths	407,136	33,401
(8)	Total estimated deaths corrected to agree with total of all registered deaths, i.e. (7) x 0.9718	395,655	32,459
(9)	Estimated Death Rates per 1,000 of the average Population, 1936-1946	14.2	17.9

Note: The actual number of registered deaths in 1936-1946 was 428,132. This compares with a figure of 440,537 as estimated by the above method. The relevant ratio between these two totals is 0.9718, as used at stage (8) to adjust the original estimates derived.

NOTES ON CONTRIBUTORS

AUGHEY Arthur

Dr Arthur Aughey is Senior Lecturer in Politics at the University of Ulster at Jordanstown. He is a member of the Community Relations Council and of the Cultural Traditions Group. He is also a member of the Northern Committee of the Irish Association and a founder member of the Cadogan Group. He has written extensively on Northern Irish politics, in particular on Ulster unionism, and has also contributed to studies of British Conservatism. Amongst his publications are: *Conservatives and Conservatism* (with Philip Norton) 1981 and *Under Siege: Ulster Unionism and the Anglo-Irish Agreement* (1989).

BROWN Terence

Terence Brown is Professor of Anglo-Irish Literature in Trinity College Dublin. He has published and lectured widely on many aspects of Irish literature and cultural history. He is a Fellow of Trinity College Dublin, a member of the Royal Irish Academy and chairman of the Cultures of Ireland Group. Among his publications are a study of the poet Louis MacNeice and a study of poets from the North of Ireland. He is the author of *Ireland: A Social and Cultural History* and *Ireland's Literature: Selected Essays* and is currently at work on a critical biography of W. B. Yeats.

DICKSON Brice

Brice Dickson was born in Belfast in 1953 and educated at Oxford. He was called to the Bar in Northern Ireland in 1976. He is a Professor of

Law at the University of Ulster since 1991 where he teaches constitutional law, human rights and commercial law. Professor Dickson is a Deputy Chair of the Equal Opportunities Commission for Northern Ireland and was a Churchill Fellow to South Africa in 1994. He is the author of *The Legal System of Northern Ireland*, editor of *Civil Liberties in Northern Ireland*, *The Committee on the Administration of Justice Handbook*, and co-editor of *The Digest of Northern Ireland Law*.

KEOGH Dermot

Dr Dermot Keogh is Professor of History, University College Cork, and Senior Fellow at the Institute for Irish Studies, Queen's University, Belfast. He studied at University College Dublin and later at the European University Institute, Florence, where he received his doctorate in 1980. Professor Keogh is a specialist in Church-State relations and has written on the subject of Church and politics in Europe, Australia and Latin America. Among his recent publications are *The Vatican in Ireland 1922-1960*, *Twentieth Century Ireland* and *Ireland and Europe 1919-1989*. He has co-edited *Northern Ireland and the Politics of Reconciliation*.

O'LEARY Richard

Richard O'Leary is a graduate student in Sociology at Nuffield, Oxford where he is writing his D.Phil. thesis on religious intermarriage. He was previously a Research Assistant in the Economic and Social Research Institute, Dublin where he worked on the effects of co-education on girls' achievement.

SEXTON J.J.

J.J. Sexton is a Research Professor in the Economic and Social Research Institute, Dublin. His areas of expertise include demography and the labour market, especially migration, occupational employment forecasting, the evaluation of manpower programmes and manpower policies generally. He previously worked as a Senior Statistician in the Central Statistics Office.